ASPIRATIONS FOR EXCELLENCE

Portrait of Alexander Jackson Davis, ca. 1845, by Mary Freeman Goldbeck.

Drawings and Archives, Avery Architectural and Fine Arts Library, Columbia University in the City of New York (1940.00.00740).

Aspirations for Excellence

Alexander Jackson Davis and the First Campus Plan for the University of Michigan, 1838

JULIA M. TRUETTNER

ANN ARBOR
THE UNIVERSITY OF MICHIGAN PRESS

Published in the United States of America by
The University of Michigan Press
Manufactured in Canada
∞ Printed on acid-free paper
2006 2005 2004 2003 4 3 2 1

Book design by Wesley B. Tanner/Passim Editions, Ann Arbor

A CIP catalog record for this book is available from the British Library.

LIBRARY OF CONGRESS CATALOGING-IN-PUBLICATION DATA

Truettner, Julia M.
Aspirations for Excellence: Alexander Jackson Davis and the first campus plan for the University of Michigan, 1838 / Julia M. Truettner.
p. cm.
Includes bibliographical references and index.
ISBN 0-472-11277-5 (Cloth : alk. paper)
1. University of Michigan — Buildings — History — 19th century. 2. Campus planning — Michigan — Ann Arbor — History — 19th century. 3. Davis, Alexander Jackson, 1803–1892 — Criticism and interpretation.
I. Title.
LD3281.T78 2002
727'.3'0977435—dc21 2001008276

Foreword

THE STUDY OF THE PAST OFTEN BEGINS with a curiosity about a particular event, place, person, or thing. Often ignored in this direct approach is any consideration of what might have been. That is often a vexing postscript to history. It is hard to sustain an analysis of what did not happen, because existing archives overwhelmingly favor events that indeed took place. Occasionally though, amid the records of the past are documents that shed light on a past that might have been but, in the end, never was. Julie Truettner has found such a group of documents and, in this fine study, essentially tells the story of an architectural conception for the campus of the University of Michigan that for many reasons never materialized. The archive that sparked this study is a group of nine watercolor presentation drawings made by Alexander Jackson Davis as a proposal for a campus for the newly constituted University of Michigan in Ann Arbor. Prepared in 1838 in his now famous Gothic Revival style, these drawings provide a visual record of how one of the leading architects of the time envisioned the campus.

The nine drawings, the source for this inquiry, have been stored among the Davis papers at the Metropolitan Museum of Art in New York. Rarely seen, with only a few ever reproduced, these renderings are a chapter in the history of the university that has been all but forgotten. Their clarity, precision, and beauty pose the question of what might have been. Basing her study on solid research, Julie Truettner, building historian for the University of Michigan, tells the story of the Davis commission and why what might have been in the end was not to be. We are grateful to her for this effort.

This publication represents one of a number of projects of the University Committee on History and Traditions. The committee, which reports to the president of the university, is charged with making better known the achievements of the university and its constituent communities over nearly two centuries. The committee is grateful to Ms. Truettner for her work in this project, and to Lee C. Bollinger, president of the University of Michigan (1997–2001), for his support of the work of the committee and his commitment to furthering a better awareness and understanding of the distinguished history of our university.

Francis X. Blouin, Jr.
Chair
University Committee on History and Traditions

Preface and Acknowledgments

STARTING FROM A DEEP INTEREST in the history of the University of Michigan's Ann Arbor campus and its buildings, I had several objectives in mind when undertaking this work. One was to celebrate the glorious designs produced by the noted architect Alexander Jackson Davis for the university, by bringing them to the public's attention. Few of the drawings executed by Davis for Michigan have ever been published, and only one of those in color. Since none remain in Michigan, I wanted to bring awareness of these renderings to those interested in the university's history, and to make known where they are archived. Eight of the nine drawings by Davis for Michigan that survive are artistic watercolors. All are in the Davis collection at the Metropolitan Museum of Art in New York City and are reproduced in this book in the color plates. In addition, black-and-white prints of these drawings are located throughout the text, where discussions of them occur. In bringing these images together, I wish those with ties to the University of Michigan, as well as historians and Davis aficionados, to experience artistic works that they might otherwise never have a chance to see.

A second major goal in preparing this work was to delve into the mystery of Michigan's earliest campus plans and building designs to discover what influence of Davis's may have been articulated in the structures that were actually built by the university in the 1840s. The fractured evidence that survives in relation to these early plans and designs, and the presence of Alexander Jackson Davis in Ann Arbor, fashion an intriguing mystery, the solution for which became an irresistible quest. It was not the goal or intention here to simply lay out the existing facts and the general conclusions that can be drawn from that limited resource. It was rather to painstakingly collect, dissect, ponder upon, and extrapolate from the many bits of information that survive in a multitude of forms the identifiable facts in order to tell the most thorough story possible of the birth of the physical campus in Ann Arbor. That it takes the form of unraveling a long-unsolved mystery will add, I hope, to the interest of the work. I also wished to discover what other persons influenced the physical development of the campus, to determine who they were, how they came to be involved, and what their part in the campus planning effort may have been.

As a part of that goal, I wished to seek out and bring together in one place all the various documents (letters, minutes, newspaper articles, etc.) and drawings, maps, and photos that could be located to create as complete as possible a picture of the University of Michigan's physical growth in the mid–nineteenth century from its birth in 1817 and its reformation in Ann Arbor in 1837. If the evidence that I have so far uncovered is insufficient to the tale I tell and the mystery I attempt to unravel, then I wish also to point those interested in further study to where this multifarious documentation can be found, through the extensive notes and bibliography.

Finally, I wished to bring about an appreciation for all those who were involved in the early planning and building efforts, from the first board of regents, to the architects A. J. Davis and Ammi Young, to the builders Isaac Thomson and Harpin Lum. In exploring the backgrounds of Davis and Young, I endeavored to paint a picture of the personalities involved, for those who may be unfamiliar with them, and also the other architects and artists involved. While studying Davis and his development as an artistic architect, I saw that the persons whom he consorted with in the arena of the design arts were important influences upon his work, although Davis had the innate talent and view for originality needed to transform the ideals of the early-nineteenth-century art world into creative new designs for the collegiate venue. I wanted the reader to be able to get a feel for how the presence of talented artists and architects, such as Ithiel Town, Martin Thompson, John Trumbull, Samuel Morse, and Thomas Cole, might have impacted Davis and his artistic development in architecture. As for Thomson and Lum, the goal was to give a glimpse into the lives of these lesser-known persons and to expose the important roles they played. Last, there was a desire to celebrate the early ambitions of the regents in seeking designs from such well-known architects as Davis and Young, for their remote little college, and how in this, as in all aspects of the creation and growth of the university, the regents aspired for excellence, permanence, and continuity.

Grateful acknowledgment is made to the following organizations and institutions for providing photographs, illustrations, and documents used in this book: Metropolitan Museum of Art, Avery Architectural and Fine Arts Library at Columbia University, New York Public Library, New-York Historical Society, Dartmouth College Library, Vermont Historical Society, Bostonian Society, Burton Historical Collection at the Detroit Public Library, New Haven Colony Historical Society, Library of Congress (Historic American Buildings Survey), Louisiana's Old State Capitol, Kenyon College Archives, Yale University Libraries, University of North Carolina–Chapel Hill, New York University, and the University of Michigan (Bentley Historical Library, University Planner's Office, Media Union Rare Book Room, and Hatcher Graduate Library Map Library).

No effort undertaken to study any aspect of Alexander Jackson Davis's career is possible without the body of valuable work that was done over many years by Jane B. Davies. Not only was Ms. Davies indispensable to this writer through her published works on Davis, but also through her personal recommendations on where to search in New York for information on Davis's designs for the University of Michigan. Her death in February 2000 deprived the world of architectural historians of a passionate practitioner, and Davis of a noted fan and advocate.

The enthusiastic support of Francis X. Blouin, chair of the History and Traditions Committee, and Frederick W. Mayer, University Planner, has been of the greatest inspiration, as has been the interest in this project shown by all the other members of the committee, Howard Markel, Carol S. Hollenshead, Nicholas H. Steneck, Robert M. Warner, and Thomas A. Roach. Grateful acknowledgment is also made to University of Michigan president Lee C. Bollinger (1997–2001), who appointed the History and Traditions Committee and supported this endeavor. Ann Arbor historian and preservationist Mary M. Culver also provided valuable assistance to this project, in particular in preparation for research conducted in New York, through her contact with Jane Davies.

Contents

Illustrations

Abbreviations

Avery
: Drawings and Archives Department, Avery Architectural and Fine Arts Library, Columbia University

Bentley
: Bentley Historical Library, University of Michigan, Ann Arbor

Met
: Prints and Drawings Department, Metropolitan Museum of Art, New York City

New Haven Colony
: Whitney Library, New Haven Colony Historical Society Archives

NYPL
: Manuscripts and Archives Division, New York Public Library, Astor, Lenox and Tilden Foundations

RP
: *Regents' Proceedings,* University of Michigan (Ann Arbor: University of Michigan, 1915). References are to vol. 1837–64 unless otherwise indicated.

ASPIRATIONS FOR EXCELLENCE

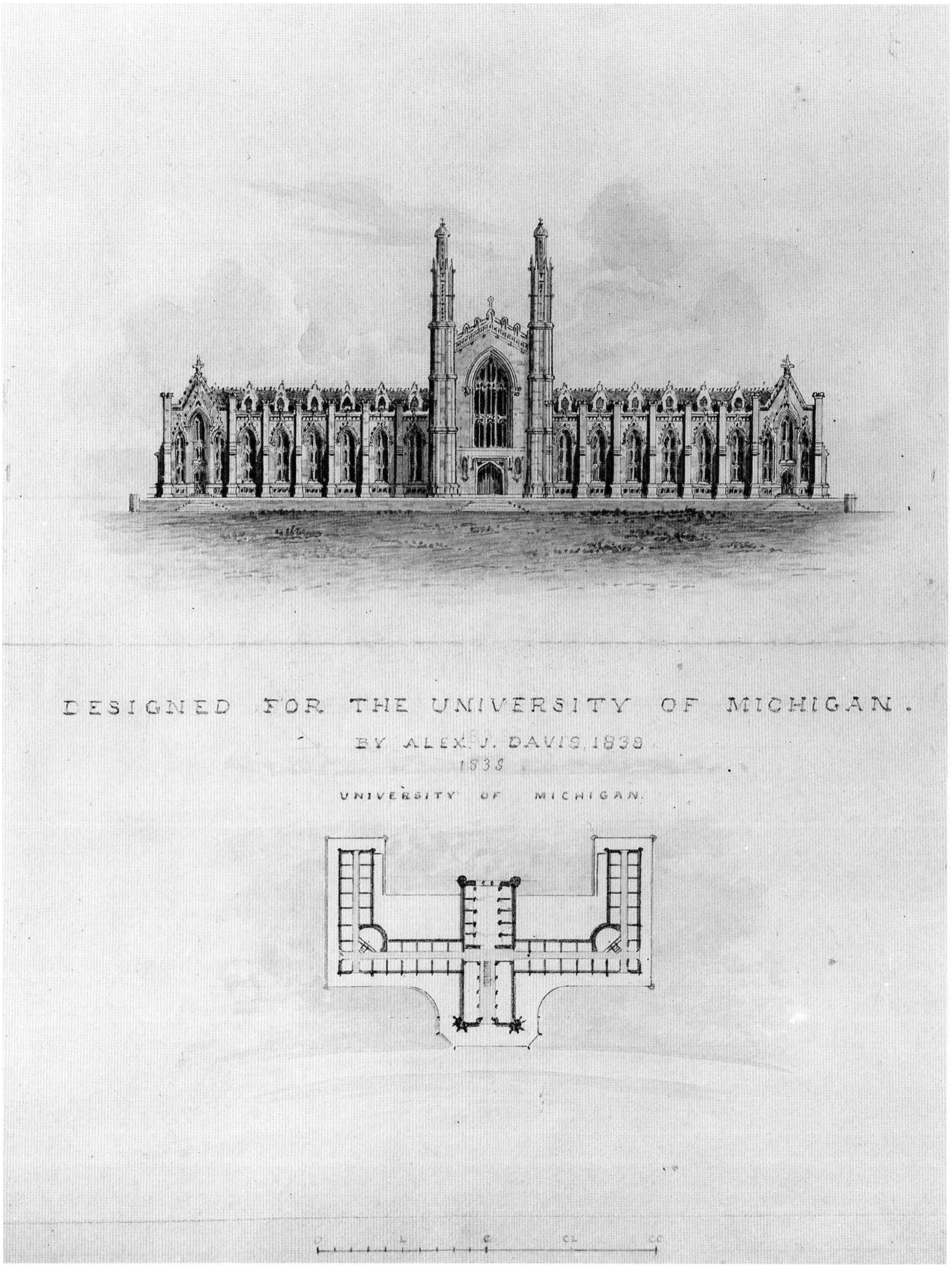

Fig. 1. University of Michigan, Ann Arbor, 1838. Design by Alexander Jackson Davis. Not executed.

Metropolitan Museum of Art, Harris Brisbane Dick Fund, 1924 (24.66.1405 [118]; diary VI, folio R, p. 143).

Introduction

In 1838, the distinguished New York architect Alexander Jackson Davis was approached by members of the Board of Regents of the University of Michigan to provide designs for what would be the first buildings on the new Ann Arbor campus. The designs that Davis produced for Michigan have been well known and often considered as among the finest collegiate plans ever devised in America in the Gothic Revival style. Davis biographer Roger Hale Newton does not hesitate to say that of Davis's institutional designs "by far the noblest scheme" was the one developed for the University of Michigan (fig. 1). Indeed, of these designs Newton believed that there had "been no finer or more glorious conception of the collegiate gothic manner produced during the 19th century in America, and possibly so far in the 20th."[1] Those familiar with the University of Michigan's Law Quad, built 1924 to 1933 in a twentieth-century revival of the nineteenth-century Gothic Revival (fig. 2), might wonder at such a statement made by Newton in 1942. The Law Quad admirably stands up to Davis's standards, as do other notable Gothic college buildings constructed in the previous century, including that for New York University.

To be sure, the Gothic designs by Davis were magnificent and would have set a superlative example for campus development in Ann Arbor had they been executed. However, they were not. Instead, the University of Michigan built four professors' houses in 1840 and a classroom-dormitory building in 1841 (see figs. 37 and 48). These were executed in a rather simple, but many felt elegant, classical style. The architect of these buildings has remained unknown, although often speculated upon.

Did the University of Michigan's flirtation with a certain glory begin and end with Davis's Gothic designs of 1838? Perhaps not. The glory implied here is the association of one or more Michigan buildings, or campus plan, with the renowned Alexander Jackson Davis. Tantalizing evidence suggests that Davis may have had a hand in the designs of the classical buildings that were actually built. In addition, the placement of the earliest buildings, through 1880, may have been based on one of the campus plans drawn by Davis for the University of Michigan.

1. Roger Hale Newton, *Town and Davis, Architects: Pioneers in American Revivalist Architecture, 1812–1870* (New York: Columbia University Press, 1942), 236.

Fig. 2. William W. Cook Law Quadrangle, University of Michigan, Ann Arbor, photo 1932 by Melvin Ivory. Designed by Edward Palmer York and Philip Sawyer. Built 1924–33, extant.
Bentley Historical Library, University of Michigan (Ivory Photo Collection, box 18, no. 18-242).

The leap from Davis's known and unexecuted Gothic designs to the classical buildings that were realized is not so very great a leap as it may seem. At least since Newton's book on Ithiel Town and Davis was published in 1942, it has generally been believed that Davis prepared for the University of Michigan an alternate design in the classical, or Greek Revival, style. Newton explained this by saying that the Midwesterners were "definitely and solely committed to the Greek Revival just then" and not ready to partake of the romantic revival styles, primarily the Gothic, then sweeping through the East.[2] "Davis," Newton wrote, "therefore, evidently prepared alternate plans," and Newton further indicated that the nature of the classical designs was unknown "except for portions appearing upon the magnificent gothic drawings."[3] (See plate 10.) Newton's remark that the university's Gothic designs were not built because the Midwest was still too wedded to Greek Revival was a bit unfair. In truth, the regents approved of and intended to build Davis's Gothic designs, but the state of finances forced them to reluctantly abandon those plans.

Later writers, when touching upon the subject of Davis's Michigan designs, also indicated that

2. Ibid., 236.

3. Ibid., 237. Although Newton's book is an invaluable source of information on the careers of Ithiel Town and Alexander Jackson Davis, it can be frustrating to use due to the lack of adequate annotations and references, as Newton does not indicate the sources of much of his information.

Davis provided designs in both Gothic and classical styles.[4] There appears to be no explanation as to Newton's source for this claim of an alternate classical design. Could his avowal be based solely on one surviving drawing? Did later writers unknowingly perpetuate a bit of misinformation? Other writers, in referring to possible classical designs for Michigan, have indicated that such designs are extant and to be found at the Metropolitan Museum of Art in New York.[5] Classical and Gothic designs for New York University do survive, as do intriguing alternate designs for Bristol College, Pennsylvania.[6] However, no drawings in the classical style by Davis have been located that can be attributed to Michigan. The mystery seems to have perpetuated itself.

Regardless of the style of designs produced, the relationship between Davis and the Regents of the University of Michigan has itself generated a cloud of confusion, which has roiled on these past 160 years. Perpetuated by a dearth of available and reliable documentation, the confusion has led histories of the university and its buildings to variously refer to the original university architect as being from New York, New Haven, or Vermont. Relying almost solely on the sketchy minutes of early regents' meetings, historians identified the New York architect as Alexander Jackson Davis, and the Vermonter as Ammi Burnham Young.[7] The New Haven architect remained unidentified.

An unsung scholar of University of Michigan building history, Wells Ira Bennett, made an admirable attempt in 1937 to clarify the muddled history of Davis's relation to the university.[8] As with previous historians, Bennett relied almost solely on sources available in Ann Arbor. He was aware, however, that some drawings by Davis related to Michigan survived at the Metropolitan Museum of Art. He also knew of Edna Donnell's 1936 treatise on Davis, probably the first scholarly work based on the collection of Davis's papers and drawings that had been acquired by the Metropolitan.[9] Although Bennett wrote an informative article based on a painstaking review of the *Regents' Proceedings* and other locally known sources, his ability to close the book on this issue was hampered in two ways. First, he was unaware of the existence of primary Davis material related to Michigan that sheds important light on the mystery at hand. This material includes two critical documents, one of which is the actual contract executed between Davis and the Regents of the University of Michigan in 1838. There is also a letter written by the Vermont architect Ammi

4. Paul Venable Turner, *Campus: An American Planning Tradition* (Cambridge: MIT Press, 1984), 124; and Francis R. Kowsky, "Simplicity and Dignity: The Public and Institutional Buildings of Alexander Jackson Davis," in *Alexander Jackson Davis–American Architect, 1803–1892,* ed. Amelia Peck (New York: Rizzoli International, 1992), 50.

5. Turner, *Campus,* 317. It is possible that the source of Newton's deduction was Davis's own daughter, Flora Foster Davis, who was still living when Newton wrote his book and helped him with it. This is, however, more speculation, since the extent of Ms. Davis's knowledge of her father's works can never be known, although she likely aided him in sorting and organizing his papers and drawings in his later years.

6. See figures 21, 58, 59 and 60, and related discussion.

7. References to *Regents' Proceedings,* vol. 1837–64, will hereinafter be cited in the text.

8. Wells Bennett, "Alexander J. Davis, Architect," *Michigan Alumnus Quarterly Review* 43, no. 11 (winter 1937): 414–20. Bennett (1888–1966) was a professor of architecture at the University of Michigan from 1912 to 1958, and dean of the College of Architecture from 1938 to 1958. An unpublished manuscript written by Bennett describing the history of the University of Michigan's buildings survives, entitled "Building the University of Michigan" (1965). Bennett was preparing it for the sesquicentennial celebration of 1967 but died before it was completed. The text itself is fairly complete, but the illustrations had not been added, nor references, index, etc. (Wells Ira Bennett Collection, box 3, Bentley).

9. Edna Donnell, "A. J. Davis and the Gothic Revival," *Metropolitan Museum Studies* 5, part 2 (September 1936): 183–233.

Young to Davis explaining how he came to be involved in building designs for Michigan. In this letter Young quotes an important letter he received from Lieutenant-Governor Edward Mundy (see appendix).[10] It is not until now that these and other previously "undiscovered" resources have been brought into the Davis-Michigan discussion.

Wells Bennett was hampered in his quest in a second way, his reliance on a widely used map known to contain inaccuracies. This is a map of Ann Arbor in 1854 by Darwin A. Pettibone, which incorrectly depicted the layout of the Ann Arbor campus (see figs. 51 and 64). Bennett certainly knew the plan as shown represented a campus that never was, but may have inferred that it yet depicted a scheme that was planned at some time to be executed.[11] This map has long been the source of much uncertainty in written histories of the University of Michigan. Not only is the campus plan inaccurate, but an etching appearing in the margin of the map of the "west front" of the campus buildings, depicts as a fait accompli one building that was actually never built (see fig. 63). The source for this image adds to the fascinating history of the physical development of the campus. Bennett was also unaware that Davis had visited Ann Arbor and the campus site in the fall of 1838, a fact that he might have turned to great benefit. Although Bennett wrote a detailed account of the Davis connection, he was well aware that he posed as many questions as he answered, and that additional evidence would have to be uncovered if the mystery were to be more exhaustively exposed. With the exploration now of numerous previously uninvestigated documents and drawings, a more thorough explanation can be provided of what Alexander Jackson Davis did and did not do for the University of Michigan more than 160 years ago.

In this effort to unravel the mystery of the possible Davis design in the classical mode and the potential sources of the University of Michigan's early buildings and their placement on the forty-acre site, it is beneficial to begin with the birth of the Ann Arbor campus.

10. Contract between the Regents of the University of Michigan and Alexander J. Davis and Isaac Thomson, September 18, 1838, Alexander Jackson Davis Collection I, file N-6, item 40-9416, Avery; and letter Ammi B. Young to Alexander J. Davis, June 20, 1838, Letterbook 1821–90, pp. 392, 392a, 392b, Alexander Jackson Davis Papers, NYPL. See appendix for transcriptions of these documents.

11. An 1853 map of Ann Arbor by Henry Hart (see figure 50) shows the same incorrect configuration of campus, as does an 1856 Washtenaw County map, but neither includes the "West Front Michigan University" illustration.

Michigan's First University Is Launched

The state universities in Michigan owe their origin to the seeds sown by the famous ordinance of 1787, which delineated the manner in which the Northwest Territory was to be organized and governed, and which stated in part, "Religion, morality, and knowledge, being necessary to good government and the happiness of mankind, schools and the means of education shall forever be encouraged."[1] These lofty words appeared in large letters on the proscenium arch above the stage of old University Hall (built 1872, demolished 1950) and were later etched into the parapet of Angell Hall (built 1924). They serve to inspire us and are the university's way of paying homage to the moment of its inception.

It would be thirty years before the territorial government, which had been organized in 1805, moved to create an institution of higher learning. On August 26, 1817, the government passed "an act to establish the Catholepistemiad, or university, of Michigania."[2] This new institution was to be governed by a faculty committee. At the time there were only two faculty members, Reverend John Montieth and Father Gabriel Richard, who served as president and vice president, respectively.[3] On April 30, 1821, an act was passed to establish in Detroit an institution called the University of Michigan, to be governed by a board of trustees. This act simultaneously repealed the act that had created the Catholepistemiad and transferred its lands and funds to the new institution. This new university operated in Detroit until 1837. (It operated as a college in theory only. Although a building for the use of the university was opened in 1818 on Bates Street in Detroit, no collegiate level courses were taught. Instead, it housed a grammar school and a "Lancasterian" school, in which the older students took on some of the teaching duties related to the younger children.)[4]

When the Territory of Michigan was organized in 1805, some lands had been granted to be

1. William B. Cudlip, *The University of Michigan: Its Legal Profile* (Ann Arbor: University of Michigan, 1969), ix–x. The full title of the 1787 ordinance was "An Ordinance for the Government of the Territory of the United States Northwest of the River Ohio," and was adopted by Congress on July 13, 1787.

2. Andrew Ten Brook, *American State Universities, Their Origin and Progress, A History of Congressional University Land-Grants, A Particular Account of the Rise and Development of the University of Michigan, and hints toward the future of the American University System* (Cincinnati: Robert Clarke, 1875), 91.

3. Howard H. Peckham, *The Making of the University of Michigan, 1817–1967* (Ann Arbor: University of Michigan Press, 1967), 6–7.

4. The university's first building was built 1817–18 on the corner of Bates and Larned Streets in Detroit. "A building 24 x 50 feet was erected. In the upper story was a grammar school, in the lower a Lancasterian branch." Handwritten notes of an undated (probably ca. 1850–60) speech by Charles Trowbridge, former secretary to the 1821–37 board of trustees, and later a regent of the reorganized 1837 University of Michigan, Charles Trowbridge Papers, Bentley. The building on Bates was occupied by the Board of Education of the City of Detroit from 1844, until demolished in

used for educational purposes. With the creation of the Catholepistemiad in 1817, and by the unrelated but concurrent Treaty of Fort Meigs, three sections of land were granted by the Odawa (Ottawa), Ojibwa (Chippewa), and Bodewadimi (Potawatomi) peoples to support an institution of higher learning. The lands so provided were not given for the specific use as the physical site of a college, but rather were to be used as a source of income for the institution. The act of 1821, which repealed that of 1817, delineated that two townships within the territory of Michigan were to be set aside for the support of a territorial university.[5] Sales of these lands in subsequent years were to provide the primary source of finances for the university. Following statehood in 1837, the closure of numerous banks due to wildcatting in 1838–39, and the depression of 1839, the fledgling university was forced to dispose of its lands for far less than anticipated. The net result was that the Regents of the University of Michigan found it necessary to obtain a loan of one hundred thousand dollars from the state in 1838, in order to meet the institution's early operating expenses and to provide funds for buildings in Ann Arbor.[6]

On January 26, 1837, Michigan was admitted to the Union, and on March 18, 1837, under the state constitution, a law was passed for the reestablishment of the University of Michigan, to be administered by a newly created board of regents. Generally known as the "Organic Act" of the university, it was based on a scheme by John D. Pierce, state superintendent of public instruction. Two days after the Organic Act was passed, a law was enacted that identified Ann Arbor as the location of the university. There had been some discussion prior to this about locating the university outside of the city of Detroit. Several towns vied for the honor of being selected, but Ann Arbor was chosen when the Ann Arbor Land Company offered to donate forty acres for the site of the new institution.

The first board of regents, appointed in 1837 by Governor Stevens T. Mason and confirmed by the new state government, consisted of eighteen members, of which six were ex officio, with vote. This board of regents, as formed, owed its creation to Superintendent Pierce. During the constitutional convention of 1835, Representative Isaac E. Crary, formerly of Connecticut and shortly to be appointed to the first board of regents, served as chairman of the Committee on Education. Crary had studied the Prussian system of education and wrote a plan based on it. As a result, a provision was included in the constitution for a state superintendent of public instruction. It was through Crary's recommendation that John Davis Pierce was appointed to the position in July 1836. In December 1836, Pierce presented his report to the convention for the organization of a state university. This report became the basis for the Organic Act of 1837. Pierce's plan called for the creation of a board of regents to administer the University of Michigan, and Pierce went so far as to de-

1858. A plaque commemorating this building was placed on its former site in 1901 by the University of Michigan Association of Detroit (*Michigan Corrects Its Seal: A Reprint of the Briefs, Arguments, and Records whereby the Board of Regents of the University of Michigan officially recognized the University's Foundation Date, August 26, 1817, and Corrected Its Seal* [Detroit: Detroit Alumni of the University of Michigan Chapter, the Lambda of Beta Theta Pi, 1930], 1). A state historical marker, which pays tribute to the univerity's 1817 founding and its first building, was unveiled and dedicated at the site, in November 2001, as part of the city of Detroit's tricentennial celebration.

5. Cudlip, *The University of Michigan*, x.

6. Peckham, *Making of University of Michigan*, 19.

scribe who should be on the board and what their duties would be. Pierce was apparently the first, in Michigan, to use the term *regent* rather than *trustee*. During his studies of educational systems of the eastern United States, he had evidently encountered the term and adopted it.

In addition to Governor Mason, the ex officio members of the first board of regents were Lieutenant-Governor Edward Mundy, Chief Justice William Fletcher, State Chancellor Elon Farnsworth, and Justices George Morell and Epaphroditus Ransom. Justice Charles Whipple served as secretary, although he was not an appointed member of the board. The ex officio members were very important to the university, especially in the earliest years, and were among the most active and influential members of the board. Governor Mason served as president of the board and attended the majority of meetings. Among the appointed members, some of the most influential included Dr. Zina Pitcher, Judge Ross Wilkins, Representative Isaac Crary, U.S. Indian Agent Henry Schoolcraft, and Major Jonathan Kearsley. Appointed in March 1838, Kearsley was to play a crucial role in the physical development of the university. No president or other chief administrator was appointed at this time to preside over the university, nor had such been appointed when instruction began in 1841. The university was operated by a faculty committee until the state constitution of 1850 directed that a president was to be elected. Henry Philip Tappan subsequently became the first president of the University of Michigan in 1852.

The members of the early board of regents were men of experience and prominence who brought considerable knowledge and wisdom to the table. None of them, however, had a background in education, but rather were lawyers, judges, physicians, senators, and congressmen. Many had been members of the constitutional convention of 1835, and many had served in various capacities for the territorial and state governments. None of the original board members was a clergyman; the first regent to so be was Reverend George Duffield, appointed in July 1839. The majority of the regents originally were from New England, a fact that had direct relevance on the eventual hiring of an architect for the university, and indeed, a majority of settlers in Michigan had New England roots.

The first meeting of the first Board of Regents of the University of Michigan was held in Ann Arbor on June 5, 1837. Their principal tasks were to define the organization and government of the university, and to select which forty-acre parcel to accept from the Ann Arbor Land Company as the site for the new university. The two primary options were a hilly site on the north side of town overlooking the Huron River, or a level site south of this and east of the developing downtown. The regents opted for the flatter site, and the Ann Arbor campus was born. The original forty-acre parcel is the area of Central Campus now bounded by State Street, South and North University Avenues, and the East University walkway (formerly East University Avenue). This site had been part of a larger farm and in 1837 consisted primarily of open pasture, scattered trees, and an orchard.

Several committees were appointed by the president of the board of regents (Governor Mason) at this meeting, including a Committee on Buildings and Improvements to the University Lands, consisting of Samuel Denton, Ross Wilkins, and John Porter (*RP,* 3). However, little action pertaining to buildings, at least officially, was taken in the first several months of the university's existence, other than a resolution adopted in November 1837 to appoint Fletcher, Mundy, and Denton "a select Committee to take charge of the University Grounds, to have the same appropriately fenced in, and to make the necessary contracts for lumber and a suitable quantity of stone and brick" (*RP,* 16).

It was not until four months later that the issue of the physical development of the campus was firmly taken in hand. At their March 1838 meeting, the regents adopted a resolution to appoint a building committee, whose members would be Lieutenant-Governor Mundy, Chief Justice Fletcher, and Chancellor Farnsworth. Their duties were

> (1) to fix upon and recommend to this Board a plan for the University buildings; (2) to prepare accurate estimates of the stone, lime, brick, timber, iron, and other materials required, with their probable cost, delivered on the ground, and the periods at which the delivery is required to be made; (3) to contract under the direction of the Board for such materials, on printed proposals, designating the articles, dates of delivery, and sureties required, and stipulating to make the respective payments at such periods as the University funds may justify; and (4) the propriety of employing a suitable architect to superintend, under their directions, the erection of the buildings, and the arrangement of the grounds. (*RP,* 39)

The building of the university seemed at last to be off and running, although months would pass with little activity recorded in the regents' minutes. However, long before this Building Committee was appointed, the search for a university architect had unofficially begun on two fronts.

Davis versus Young

THE ISSUE OF AN ARCHITECT for the University of Michigan's new Ann Arbor campus first appears in the official records in September 1838. On the sixteenth of that month, the board of regents adopted "the plan offered by Alexander J. Davis, Architect of New York City," and further instructed that construction of part of the plan was to begin immediately. On the following day, September 17, 1838, the board approved a payment of six hundred dollars to Davis (*RP,* 55–56). The sudden appearance of the name of such a prominent architect in the official record, along with the payment of such a considerable fee, raises a number of questions. How did the regents come to obtain a building plan from Davis? Why is there no indication in the record of prior contact with the architect? Davis's being hired by the university certainly could have been as simple as someone close to the board knowing of Davis and his work and recommending him to the regents. This, indeed, is not far from the truth. But later reports filed by the Building Committee reveal that the selection of Davis as the university's architect was anything but a straightforward affair.[1]

Long before Alexander Jackson Davis's name first appears in the *Regents' Proceedings* in September 1838, members of the board of regents had already begun looking for an architect to serve the university. At least by the time the first regents' meeting was held in June 1837, and possibly earlier, two architects had been approached about providing designs for the University of Michigan. Beyond the *Regents' Proceedings,* surviving documentation that might shed light on this issue is sparse. However, two crucial letters, together with the aforementioned Building Committee reports, begin to reveal a riddle that has long plagued historians of University of Michigan building history. That is, how did the regents come to engage two different distinguished architects for the design of their buildings? Alone, the *Regents' Proceedings* do not provide the answers. But the two letters, previously unknown, help guide the way through the murky confusion (see appendix for transcriptions of these documents). What emerges from these documents is the story of different members of the board of regents, apparently unbeknownst to each other, contacting different architects.

Although it is tempting to assign nefarious or political purposes to regents seemingly going behind one another's backs, it was more likely a case of unintentional miscommunication, or a simple

1. *RP,* April 13, 1839, 82–83; and *RP,* March 6, 1840, 124–27, see appendix for transcriptions.

lack of adequate communication. It must be kept in mind that at this time the university had no corporeal existence and the regents lived in scattered cities, meeting at best quarterly. It is possible that prior to that first meeting in June 1837, recently appointed regents thought to help the progress of the physical development of the campus by beginning to contact potential architects. It is also possible that one or more board members was personally acquainted with the architects in question and felt it expedient to get that person on board.

In any case, it is certain that by June 1837 (the month of the first regents' meeting) a board member had contacted the architect Ammi Burnham Young of Vermont in relation to designs for the University of Michigan. By that fall, if not before, a different regent had also contacted architect Alexander Jackson Davis of New York for the very same purpose. Of course, it was common even then for more than one architect to compete for the same commission. However, in the case of Michigan, no competition for design of the university's buildings was ever announced to the public, much to the consternation of local builders.

Untangling the relations of the regents to Ammi B. Young and Alexander J. Davis poses the question of why the names of these two architects should have come to the fore in the issue of buildings for the university. The answer may be quite simply that Young and Davis were two of the more well known and highly regarded architects of public and institutional buildings of the time. But in fact what was equally important was that they both came from, and primarily worked in, New England. As noted before, the majority of the members of the board of regents of 1837–38 came to Michigan from New England. The logical conclusion is that Davis and Young were already known to one or more members of the board. They may have been personal acquaintances, or the board members may have known them through their reputations in their home states. Because of the diplomatic way in which Young and Edward Mundy, chairman of the Building Committee, described the nature of the relation of Young and Davis to the regents, it may never be known which regents precisely knew of and recommended these two architects to the board.

It is possible, however, to speculate. Surviving evidence shows that both Regent Farnsworth and Regent Fletcher had been in contact with Alexander J. Davis, and Regent Mundy with Ammi Young. This is not proof of prior acquaintanceship, as these three regents comprised the Building Committee appointed in March 1838, and they would have been acting on behalf of the board. That both Young and Davis had been contacted well before the appointment of this Building Committee raises interesting questions. A look at the backgrounds of the early regents provides some clues, if not clear-cut answers. Several board members could have known of Ammi Young through his noted works in the states the regents originally came from. It is also possible that one or more regents were personally acquainted with Young and maintained contact with him. Indeed, Young implies as much in one letter.[2] These may have included Regents William Fletcher,

2. Letter Young to Davis, June 20, 1838; see appendix.

Elon Farnsworth, Samuel Denton, Henry Schoolcraft, and Epaphroditus Ransom, among others, who had ties to Vermont, New Hampshire, and Massachusetts, where Young practiced.[3]

Similar connections can be made between Alexander Jackson Davis and members of the board of regents. At the time, however, Davis's reputation was far more widespread than Young's, as Davis, alone or with his one-time partner Ithiel Town, had produced designs for notable buildings across New England, into the South, and as far west as Illinois. Influential regents who may have known Davis through their ties in New York or New Haven included Zina Pitcher, Samuel Denton, Henry Schoolcraft, Isaac Crary, and William Fletcher.[4]

Clearly, their reputations alone may have been enough to put the names of Ammi Burnham Young and Alexander Jackson Davis before the eyes of the regents, many of whom were from New England, where Young's and Davis's works were so well known. The surviving evidence paints a somewhat different picture. Although reputation may have been the driving force by which Davis came to be considered by the regents, it appears that personal contacts were what brought Young to the forefront of the design endeavor.

As previously mentioned, both Ammi Young and A. J. Davis had been contacted by a regent before the Building Committee was appointed in March 1838. In fact, both architects had been approached many months prior to this, indeed as early as mid-1837. Ammi Young indicated, in a letter of explanation he wrote to Davis, that personal acquaintances brought to his attention the possibility of this work in Michigan. Young wrote, "I have friends in Michigan who have for some time been quite anxious for me to go to Michigan to reside, supposing it would be much to my advantage in a pecuniary point of view. They have frequently wrote me on the subject, in my answers to them [I] have universally discouraged the idea, unless I could be ensured of good business in my profession.—About a year and a half ago I received a letter from one of my friends there, stating that buildings would be required to be erected for the University of Michigan in a short time, and desired me to hold myself in readiness to engage as an Architect in the erection of them if wanted, as there could be but little doubt I should, as my friend there would make strong interest to have me appointed."[5] Young was then just completing the capitol at Montpelier, but said he would consider the Michigan job if he had the time. Young's letter to Davis is dated June 20, 1838, making the

3. The links between Ammi Young and these regents can be made in this manner. Regent and Building Committee member William Fletcher was a native of New Hampshire, as was Young, who had made a name for himself there as the designer of major buildings for Dartmouth College in 1828–29. Several regents may have known Young from Vermont, where Young had opened an office in 1830 and soon thereafter received the commission to design the new statehouse at Montpelier. Regents with ties to Vermont included Building Committee member Elon Farnsworth of Woodstock, Vermont; Lucius Lyon of Shelburne; Gideon Wittemore of St. Albans; and Samuel Denton and Henry Schoolcraft, both of whom attended college in Vermont. Regent Epaphroditus Ransom hailed from both Vermont and Massachusetts and may have known Young as associated with both states. At the time the university approached him for plans, Young had won the widely publicized competition for design of the Boston customhouse. Another influential board member who might have known Young due to his Massachusetts connections was George Morell, a native of Lenox, Massachusetts.

4. The possible links between Davis and some regents included that Zina Pitcher, an influential board member, came from Washington County, New York. Four other regents, previously mentioned as having possible ties to Young, may also have known of Davis through other connections in New York. These include Samuel Denton from Wallkill, and Henry Schoolcraft from Albany. In addition, both William Fletcher and George Morell had studied law in New York. A. J. Davis, through his association with Ithiel Town, also practiced extensively in New Haven. At least one regent may have known Davis through his work there, and that was Isaac Crary of Preston, Connecticut.

5. Letter Young to Davis, June 20, 1838; see appendix.

"year and a half" earlier that he'd heard from his friends sometime in early 1837. This would place it before the first regents' meeting (June 1837) and possibly before the re-creation of the university and appointment of the first board of regents in March 1837. This is probably an exaggeration on Young's part, as it is unlikely much thought was given to buildings prior to the assembling of the first board and the selection of the campus site.

Nevertheless, by late summer 1837, Ammi Young had certainly been contacted by his "friends" in Michigan. So, too, had Alexander Jackson Davis. In October 1837, Regent Farnsworth wrote to Davis informing him that the regents had already asked Young for building plans. Davis apparently did not receive this letter, and it does not survive. It is solely mentioned in an extant letter Farnsworth wrote to Davis in June 1838.[6] The October 1837 letter was apparently the second from Farnsworth to Davis, as Farnsworth wrote, "So long a time elapsed without reply to either my first or second letter," and later indicated the second letter was dated October 1837. This implies that the regents had contacted Davis concerning designs by fall of 1837. It is tempting to identify one of Ammi Young's "friends" in Michigan as Elon Farnsworth of Detroit. Farnsworth may have known of Young through his work in Vermont, Farnsworth's home state, and he could therefore be the friend Young describes as "residing at Detroit." In his correspondence to Davis, Farnsworth may have been clearing the way for his friend Young, to whom he had all but promised the job. Whether Farnsworth was the friend in Michigan trying to procure the work for Young will probably never be known. The "friends" Ammi Young so tactfully refers to could have been any one of several board members.

Inadequate evidence survives to shed light on the dealings of the board of regents with Young and Davis between fall 1837 and April 1838. The first real documentation concerning the hiring of an architect is dated from April 1838. In his letter to Davis, Young quoted in total a letter he received from Edward Mundy, chairman of the Building Committee, dated April 11, 1838. Mundy wrote, "The regents of the University of Michigan are taking measures preparatory to building. They have not yet adopted a plan nor determined upon the material believing it proper first to consult a suitable architect and give him an opportunity to examine the site and inspect the materials convenient to the place. The University is well endowed and we wish to put up a building that will combine convenience, durability and magnificence. You have been mentioned to us by your friend here, in whom we have every reliance and the Committee of building, have instructed me their chairman to invite you to pay us a visit, with a view to your employment as an Architect and superintendent of buildings."[7] The existence of this letter is substantiated by Mundy, who in a report of the Building Committee indicated that on April 11, 1838, "being strongly advised, by several gentlemen of high standing, of the merits and talents of an architect, of Ammi B. Young, of Vermont, they through their chairman [Mundy] addressed a letter to him inviting him to make

6. Letter E. Farnsworth to A. J. Davis, June 1, 1838, Letterbook 1821–90, pp. 120 and 120a, A. J. Davis Papers, NYPL; see appendix.

7. Letter Young to Davis, June 20, 1838; see appendix.

a visit to Michigan and proposing to employ him as the Architect of the University" (*RP*, 82–83; see appendix).

The extant record thus reveals that in April 1838 the regents were actively seeking to hire Ammi Young as their architect. Alexander J. Davis does not yet appear in the record. By that time Young had begun work on the Boston customhouse and could not come out to Ann Arbor, but indicated his willingness to draw some plans for Michigan if the regents wished it of him. On May 15, 1838, Mundy wrote to Young, sending him a map of Ann Arbor and other information, and requesting that he begin designs for Michigan.[8] Although no direct evidence survives, Davis was apparently at this time also beginning designs for Michigan. In his letter to Davis, Young wrote (after having received Mundy's letter of May 15, 1838), "you may judge of my surprise at learning from your letter you had previously been applied to for designs. For my part, do not see why it should be so, as the whole tenor of the letters I have received, do not hint at any thing of the kind in the remotest degree, if they had, should have considered myself released of any obligation to them."[9] Not only had the regents not given up Young in favor of Davis at the time of this letter (June 1838), they again wrote to Young through Mundy on July 18, 1838, sending Young more information on the campus site (*RP*, 83).

Young's letter to Davis is a remarkable document that at once enlightens the discussion while also posing more questions. One of the most notable things about the letter is its date—June 20, 1838. This predates any official contact between Davis and the regents, and yet Young is responding to a letter from Davis asking how Young came to be involved with the University of Michigan project. From this it can be deduced that Davis had been contacted by someone at Michigan and had begun work. Davis's query to Young may have been as a response to the letter Davis received from Regent Farnsworth dated June 1, 1838, in which Farnsworth indicated that the regents were expecting plans from "Mr. Young of Boston."[10] This is the same letter in which Farnsworth indicated that he had written two previous letters to Davis as early as fall 1837 that Davis apparently did not receive.

It is evident that by June 1838 both Young and Davis felt they had been engaged to provide designs for the University of Michigan. Both had clearly realized this would be an important and highly desirable commission, and Davis felt that both their positions relative to the regents needed to be clarified. In his letter to Davis, Young indicated his willingness to withdraw from the Michigan project providing the regents would pay him for the work he had done. Being heavily occupied with the Boston customhouse project, Young would not have been able to come to Ann Arbor to superintend the building construction, and therefore was willing to walk away.

With this knowledge of Young's position in hand, Davis awaited word from the board of regents. In his report, Regent Mundy indicated that shortly after he last wrote to Young, on July 18,

8. Both Ammi Young's letter to Davis of June 20, 1838, and the Building Committee's report of April 13, 1839, mention the letter from Mundy to Young dated May 15, 1838.

9. Letter Young to Davis, June 20, 1838; see appendix.

10. Letter Farnsworth to Davis, June 1, 1838; see appendix.

1838, concerning the project, he received a letter dated July 19, 1838, from Regent Fletcher "saying that the Board of Regents had the day before determined to proceed with all convenient dispatch with the university Buildings, and that he was requested to write to him desiring him to see Mr. Davis, the architect from whom the Regents expected a plan" (*RP,* 83). Mundy was then visiting family in New Jersey, and from there he went to see Davis in New York. In his office diary, Davis recorded that on August 7, 1838, "Hon. E. Mundy, Lieut. Gov. of Michigan called on University."[11]

Suddenly, in late summer 1838, Alexander Jackson Davis finally enters the surviving record. Mundy, with good reason, is surprised to have been told that the regents expected a plan from Davis—not a few days after Mundy had sent more information to Young concerning the designs. Mundy indicated that he informed Davis that Young had already been hired, and asked Davis how he came to be engaged by the regents. An excellent question that Davis responded to just as diplomatically as Young, by saying that "a correspondence had existed between himself and one of the members of the Board, to whom anterior to the appointment of this [Building] Committee had been given authority to procure a plan for the building" (*RP,* 83). The committee's having been appointed in March 1838 suggests that prior to that date Davis had intelligence from a board member of such a nature as to give Davis the understanding that he had the Michigan job sewn up. No wonder Davis was shocked by Farnsworth's letter of June 1, 1838, telling him that Young had already been hired; and no wonder Davis wrote to Young for an explanation. Which member of the board corresponded with Davis remains unknown.[12]

When Regent Mundy met with Davis on August 7, 1838, he learned from Davis that Young had expressed his willingness to withdraw from the project. This provided the regents with a way to settle the whole issue of an architect for Michigan, an affair that had gotten rather convoluted. Mundy must indeed have been close to the arrangements that resulted in the hiring of Ammi Young, because he sought in the end to deal fairly with the architect. He felt later that Young might have been poorly treated at the time the board waffled between the architects, and that the relationship between the regents and Young had not been properly concluded. Mundy wrote to Young and explained how Davis had been hired and how they understood that Young had been willing to withdraw from the project. Young responded by saying he had spent much time on the designs for Michigan and enclosed a bill for three hundred dollars. Mundy, speaking for the Building Committee, and indicating they felt Young was due this compensation for his work, proposed a resolution for the board that would pay Young. Unfortunately, this resolution was "laid on the table" (i.e., tabled) and never taken up again (*RP,* 83).[13] There is no record that Young was paid anything at this time for his work for Michigan. On April 8, 1840, Mundy again tried to obtain payment for Young. At that time the regents "*Resolved,* that the claim of Ammi B. Young, together with the correspon-

11. Diary 1827–53, p. 189, A. J. Davis Papers, NYPL.

12. It should be noted that although a large quantity of Davis's papers and drawings survive, much was also lost in a devastating fire that destroyed his house in 1884.

13. The phrase "laid on the table" is frequently encountered in early *Regents' Proceedings* and means that action on an item has been postponed, or "tabled," as is the expression used today.

dence and papers relating thereto, be referred to the Committee on Finances, and that the said Committee be authorized to settle the same with Mr. Young should they find anything due him" (*RP,* 129). This is the last time Young's name appears in the official university records. None of the papers pertaining to his claim survive, nor did the Committee on Finance submit a report to the regents describing how they settled the matter. No payments to Young are listed in the year-end report on expenditures, so it is doubtful he ever received any payment for his work for the University of Michigan.

As a result of these confusing actions of 1837 and 1838, Alexander Jackson Davis became the first architect for the University of Michigan and prepared to make a visit to the site of the new campus. Before continuing with that story, it is important to know something about the histories of Ammi B. Young and Alexander J. Davis that made them such desirable commodities to the fledgling university and its new board of regents.

Ammi Burnham Young

Born on June 19, 1798, in Lebanon, New Hampshire, Ammi Burnham Young was the son of a carpenter and builder, Captain Samuel Young. Ammi was apparently a self-taught engineer and architect, as there is no evidence of his obtaining a college education, although he would receive two honorary A.M. degrees, from the University of Vermont in 1838 and from Dartmouth College in 1841. Young probably obtained his technical knowledge from his father, and some of his design direction from the influential pattern books of the day, in particular those by Asher Benjamin.[14] Young also worked in the early 1820s in Boston with the noted architect Alexander Parris, who is best known for his design of the Quincy Market in Boston, 1824–26.[15] By the late 1820s, Young had begun designing buildings, and in 1828 an early noted design of his, for the Congregational Church, was built in his hometown of Lebanon.

Also in 1828, the first of Young's buildings for Dartmouth College, Wentworth Hall, was completed in Hanover, New Hampshire. This was followed by Thornton Hall in 1829. These two buildings by Young were placed on either side of the college's main structure, Dartmouth Hall (built 1791, architect unknown). Taken together the three buildings make up the core of Dartmouth's "Old Row" (fig. 3). Wentworth and Thornton Halls were extremely simple and clean in design, with their gable ends faced toward the open campus green, giving them a gentle, classical appearance, reflective of the revered Federal style.

To this Old Row was added Reed Hall, designed by Ammi Young and built 1839–40 by his brother Dyer H. Young. Similar in design to Ammi Young's two earlier Dartmouth buildings, Reed Hall nevertheless reflects a noticeable development of the classical vocabulary with the in-

14. Henry-Russell Hitchcock and William Seale, *Temples of Democracy: The State Capitols of the United States of America* (New York: Harcourt Brace Jovanovich, 1976), 104.

15. Talbot Hamlin, *Greek Revival Architecture in America* (1944; reprint, New York: Dover, 1964), 106; and Talbot Hamlin, "Ammi Young," in *Dictionary of American Biography,* ed. Harris E. Starr, vol. 11, supplement 1 (New York: Charles Scribner's Sons, 1944), 716.

Fig. 3. Dartmouth Row, Hanover, N.H., ca. 1835. Etching by Nathaniel Currier. From left: President's House (mistakenly shown at north end of row, rather than actual location at south end on current site of Reed Hall), Wentworth Hall by Ammi B. Young (1828), Dartmouth Hall (1791), Thornton Hall by Ammi B. Young (1829). All extant except President's House. Courtesy of Dartmouth College Library.

troduction of features such as corner pilasters, wide frieze board, and graduation of window sizes, from tallest on first floor to shortest on upper floors (see fig. 70). Young would later design a fourth building for Dartmouth, the Shattuck Observatory, completed in 1853. All four of Young's buildings for Dartmouth survive.[16]

With the success of his work at Dartmouth and other commissions in his native New Hampshire, Ammi Young was able to expand his practice by setting up an office in Burlington, Vermont, in 1830. As he had in Lebanon, Young advertised his availability and skill as an architect and civil engineer to execute plans and models.[17] Soon after his expansion into Vermont, Young received the commission in 1833 to design the new statehouse at Montpelier. Supervising the construction of the capitol was to be his primary occupation through 1838. Designed in the Greek Revival style, the Vermont Statehouse featured Doric porticoes and a low dome (fig. 4). It was not unlike the

16. Ammi Young's brother, Ira, a Dartmouth alumnus, was a professor of astronomy at Dartmouth, and it was through his efforts that Dartmouth obtained its observatory. Ira Young solicited another Dartmouth alum, George C. Shattuck, to provide funds for the building and to request that it be designed by his brother Ammi. Ira himself traveled to Europe to procure a suitable telescope, and the Shattuck Observatory was opened in 1853.

17. Lawrence Wodehouse, "Ammi Burnham Young, 1798–1874," *Journal of the Society of Architectural Historians* 25, no. 4 (1966): 269; and Hitchcock and Seale, *Temples of Democracy*, 104.

Fig. 4. Vermont Statehouse, Montpelier, 1833. Design by Ammi B. Young. Built 1833–38; severely damaged by fire 1857 and rebuilt with longer wings and taller dome with drum. Demolished.
Courtesy of Vermont Historical Society [VHS-363].

North Carolina Statehouse designed by Town and Davis, also in 1833, although Young's building was less elaborate and not in as clearly expressed a cruciform shape (see fig. 14).

As construction on the Vermont capitol was winding down, Ammi Young entered the widely publicized competition for design of the new customhouse in Boston. Winning the competition, Young moved to Boston in 1838 to supervise its construction. This project would consume much of his time, and not be completed until 1849. This building, too, was a Doric cruciform temple in design and carried a low dome (fig. 5). The use of granite and the classical vocabulary gave the customhouse a wonderful sense of monumentality and strength. Here, as at the Vermont Statehouse, the pedimented Greek Doric order was combined with a Roman dome. This combination gained widespread popularity due to well-publicized designs by such architects as Young, Davis, and Ithiel Town. What helped to give the Boston customhouse a unique and solid beauty was Young's use of engaged columns between the windows, rather than the antae that were more commonly employed. The customhouse was widely admired and achieved a certain national acclaim.

It was during this time, at Montpelier in 1837 and Boston in 1838, that Young was contacted about plans for the University of Michigan. However, nothing written about Young and his career

Fig. 5. Boston customhouse, photo ca. 1900. Designed by Ammi B. Young. Built 1838–49; dome replaced with multistory tower 1915; extant.
Courtesy of The Bostonian Society/Old State House [neg. 2293].

mentions the possibility of his work for Michigan. Other than the letter Young wrote to Davis in 1838, which is preserved among Davis's papers, no documentation appears to have survived that would reveal the extent of the designs Young may have produced for Michigan in 1838.

Young's success with the Boston customhouse brought him to the attention of the federal government and led him into the most important decade of his career. The antebellum decades of the nineteenth century were a time of great physical growth for the federal government, and the Department of Treasury was faced with the need to construct a large number of public buildings, including customhouses, courthouses, post offices, hospitals, and so on. In 1851, Treasury secretary Thomas Corwin appointed Young to look into a great fracas that had erupted over the design of the customhouse at New Orleans, and the deficits perceived in the design executed by Alexander T. Wood.[18] Prior to Young's involvement, Wood had been dismissed from the job and architect James H. Dakin put in charge. In the case of the New Orleans customhouse, Young settled the dispute, and the building as executed reflected the combined influence of Wood, Dakin, and Young.

18. Daniel Bluestone, "Civic and Aesthetic Reserve: Ammi Burnham Young's 1850s Federal Customhouse Designs," *Winterthur Portfolio* 25, nos. 2–3 (1990): 134–35; and Arthur Scully, Jr., *James Dakin, Architect: His Career in New York and the South* (Baton Rouge: Louisiana State University Press, 1973), 162–84. Scully provides an exhaustive look at the New Orleans customhouse contretemps.

Fig. 6. Detroit customhouse, photo 1875. Designed by Ammi B. Young. Built 1856–60; demolished 1964.
Courtesy of the Burton Historical Collection, Detroit Public Library.

As a result of his involvement in both the design of the Boston customhouse and the amelioration of the skirmish in New Orleans, in September 1852 Ammi Young was appointed supervising architect in the Office of Construction in the Treasury Department. He moved to Washington, D.C., and began a productive ten-year period during which he was to influence architecture across the nation. In taking on this post, Young followed in the footsteps of the noted architect Robert Mills (1781–1855), whose influence in the government had been on the decline.[19] Although calling himself "architect of public buildings,"[20] Mills, who was best known for his designs of the Treasury Building and the Washington Monument in 1836, did not at that time have an official government appointment. Young was therefore considered the first supervising architect for the federal government.

19. Hamlin, *Greek Revival Architecture*, 107.

20. Wodehouse, "Ammi Burnham Young," 275.

In this governmental position, Young embarked on a decade of prolific design and construction of federal buildings. Because of the need for alacrity in construction and economy in expense, Young developed standardized building types and pursued innovative construction techniques. Drawing from classical models, Young formulated an architectural vocabulary well suited for customhouse designs—the Italian Palazzo mode. This style proved quick to design, while also allowing some flexibility in its expression, so that Young's customhouses, although similar to one another, were each allowed a measure of individuality. An example executed in Michigan was the customhouse at Detroit, built 1856–60 (fig. 6). In the development of the palazzo form, Young sought a design that reflected permanence and utility, rather than extravagant classical monumentality that often placed public buildings in too formal a relationship to the people. Young's designs showed not only more economy in execution and better use of space and resources, they also allowed the buildings to better relate to the person on the street, making them appear more accessible than the many more monumental government buildings.

One of Ammi Young's most important innovations not only aided the dual need for speed and economy in the execution of federal buildings, but also addressed the critical issue of fireproofing the structures. This was through his widespread use of iron in building construction. The government highly valued Young's designs and construction techniques and widely published the plans and details of these buildings.[21] During his tenure as supervising architect for the federal government, Young designed over seventy buildings that were executed and many more that were not. With the coming of the Civil War, construction of federal buildings declined sharply and Young was dismissed from his position in July 1862. He retired to his home in Washington, where he died on March 13, 1874, at age seventy-five.

Alexander Jackson Davis

One of the greatest American romantic revivalist architects was born in New York City on July 24, 1803. With a long life that would span almost the entire nineteenth century, Alexander Jackson Davis came into the world possessing an innate sense of the beauties of the natural and built environments. His father Cornelius Davis (1760–1831) was a bookseller who also edited and published theological pamphlets, and his mother was Julia Jackson Davis (1777–1862) of Orange County, New York. Alex spent part of his childhood in and around central New York State, but as an adult his life was spent primarily in New York City. If he had any formal schooling it had ended by age sixteen, at which time he was sent to work in his half-brother Samuel's printing office in Alexandria, then in the District of Columbia.[22]

21. E.g., *Plans of Public Buildings in the course of construction, under the Direction of the Secretary of the Treasury, including the specifications thereof,* by Capt. A. J. Bowman, U.S. Corps of Engineers (Washington, D.C.: Treasury Department, 1855).

22. Even as a youth, A. J. Davis's artistic talents had been evident through paintings and drawings he executed, and while with his brother, he developed a strong interest in the theater, designing costumes and sets. For William Dunlap's history of the arts of design in America, Davis described his youthful interest in art and composition. Writing in third person, Davis said of himself that he was "Like another Franklin, strongly addicted to reading, he limited himself to the accomplishment of a fixed task, and being a quick compositor, he would soon complete it,

The eagerness to pursue his artistic bent, combined with a natural talent, could not be contained long, and at age twenty A. J. Davis returned to New York City to study art. In New York society, Davis had earlier made the acquaintance of Colonel John Trumbull, renowned American painter of patriotic subjects. Trumbull (1756–1843) had become famous as a painter of revolutionary war scenes, as well as depictions of historic moments such as the signing of the Declaration of Independence. Trumbull was also a sought-after portrait painter whose subjects included such notables as Washington and Jefferson, and in 1817 he was commissioned by Congress to produce four paintings of the Revolution for the Capitol Rotunda. Trumbull also dabbled in architecture in his native Connecticut, where he produced a plan for Yale College in 1792 (see figs. 52 and 53). This plan led to the birth of the famous Yale Old Brick Row, which was to influence campus development at numerous colleges. Later, in 1831, Trumbull would design an art gallery for Yale, to house a collection of his paintings that he donated to the college. Opened in 1832 and including fifty-five of his works, Trumbull Gallery was considered the first college museum in America.[23]

Colonel Trumbull, so titled from his service in the revolutionary war, took a liking to A. J. Davis, a young man whose talent he recognized and admired. Through Trumbull, Davis gained entry to the Antique School, where he was able to make drawings from plaster casts of classical antiquities. The Antique School had been founded in 1823 by Trumbull and Samuel Finley Breese Morse, another artist of prominence in New York City. Both artists were also active in the American Academy of Arts, which had been founded in 1802 as the New York Academy of Fine Arts. Through these connections, Davis was also able to study at the academy. Friends of his advised Davis to devote himself to architecture because, as Davis wrote (in third person), it was "a branch of art most likely to meet with encouragement, and one for which, by the particular bent of his mind, he appeared to be well fitted."[24] These friends were John Trumbull and fellow artist Rembrandt Peale.

While he was studying at the Antique School, Davis executed a series of drawings of New York buildings that were published by a well-known bookseller, A. T. Goodrich. These lithographs included a view of the new Merchants Exchange, a highly regarded building designed by locally prominent architect Martin E. Thompson. During 1826, Davis also drew, on stone, a selection of views of twelve public buildings in New York City that were printed by Anthony Imbert, the city's leading lithographer. Beginning in July 1827, a series of drawings by Davis of New York buildings, the first being a view of Trinity Church, was published in the *New York Mirror*.[25] At about the time

and fly to his books, but not like Franklin, to books of science and useful learning, but to works of imagination, poetry, and the drama; whence, however, he imbibed a portion of that high imaginative spirit so necessary to constitute an artist destined to practice in the field of invention. I have known him . . . pass hours in puzzling over the plan of some ancient castle of romance, arranging the trap doors, subterraneous passages, and drawbridges, as pictorial embellishment was the least of his care, invention all his aim." William Dunlap, *History of the Rise and Progress of the Arts of Design in the United States,* vol. 2 (New York: George P. Scott, 1843), 409.

23. Helen A. Cooper, *John Trumbull: The Hand and Spirit of a Painter* (New Haven: Yale University Art Gallery, 1982), 18.

24. Dunlap, *Arts of Design,* 409.

25. Especially notable are engravings appearing in the *New York Mirror* for October 20, 1827 (St. Paul's Church, see fig. 66); April 11, 1829 (St. John's Chapel from the Park); September 26, 1829 (six images of public buildings, including the Rotunda; the first Merchants Exchange, designed by Martin Thompson; and the U.S. Branch Bank, also by Thompson); March 20, 1830 (six views of churches); and May 15, 1830 (six more

he was executing these drawings in 1826, and possibly in 1825, Davis also obtained employment as a draftsman in the office of New York architect Josiah R. Brady (?1760–1832). With these experiences, especially the notice he gained from his views of the city, Davis was able to open his own office in the Merchants Exchange on Wall Street and offer his services as an "architectural composer," which was how he listed his profession in the city directory of 1827.[26]

In November 1825, A. J. Davis attended a meeting organized by Samuel F. B. Morse, where the topic of discussion was the possible formation of an association for the "Promotion of the Arts, and the Assistance of Students."[27] This action was taken due to many artists' dissatisfaction with the earlier founded American Academy. Although ostensibly a society for artists, most could not afford the cost of shares in the academy, which became an organization operated by merchants. John Trumbull, longtime president of the academy, was one of only a few artists who had the financial resources necessary. Students in particular felt they were poorly treated by the American Academy, which made access to its resources difficult.

As a result of the meeting of artists called by Morse, on January 14, 1826, the National Academy of the Arts of Design was formed.[28] The term *design* was used to signify painting, sculpture, architecture, and engraving, and to differentiate it from the fine arts, which included literature, poetry, music, and landscape design. Among the founding members representing painting were Morse, Asher B. Durand, William Dunlap, Henry Inman, Rembrandt Peale, and Thomas Cole, with John Frazee representing sculpture. Architecture was represented by two persons, Ithiel Town and Martin E. Thompson. The young A. J. Davis would have been considered a student at the time, but later became an associate member. The National Academy held its first exhibition in 1826, and at its second, in 1827, Davis exhibited a design of his own for the first time.

Davis's association with the National Academy lasted until only around 1829, and thereafter he was more closely involved with his mentor John Trumbull's American Academy. The importance of these academies—the National, American, and Antique School—to Davis and his career cannot be understated, for it was in studying and exhibiting at the academies that Davis became acquainted with other artists whose spheres of influence on the young man would be great. Not the least of these were the architects Town and Thompson, who would help shape Davis's early architectural career. Other notable and influential persons in this sphere of peers were the prominent artists already mentioned, S. F. B. Morse and Thomas Cole. Later the great landscape architect Andrew Jackson Downing would enter this circle.

The office Davis set up for himself in 1826 in the Merchants Exchange he shared for a brief time with James Eddy (1800–1889), a lithographer from Rhode Island. Lifelong friends, they collabo-

views of churches). Most of these images were engraved by A. J. Davis's friend James Eddy. Issues of the *New York Mirror,* from 1827 through 1833, were available on microfilm at the Hatcher Graduate Library, University of Michigan, Ann Arbor.

26. Carrie Rebora, "Alexander Jackson Davis and the Arts of Design," in Peck, *Alexander Jackson Davis,* 29.

27. Eliot Clark, *History of the National Academy of Design, 1825–1953* (New York: Columbia University Press, 1954), 10.

28. Ibid., 13–14.

rated on numerous illustrations, with Eddy engraving drawings done by Davis, including most of the series drawn by Davis for the *New York Mirror* (see fig. 66 for one example). To further expand his education, Davis made a visit to Boston in 1827. Davis took with him letters of introduction from John Trumbull and Ithiel Town, among others, and through an acquaintance gained admittance to the Boston Athenaeum, then considered the city's finest private library. Here Davis was able to study and copy models from classical antiquities and literature. While in Boston he also became acquainted with two of its most prominent architects, Alexander Parris (1780–1852) and Isaiah Rogers (1800–1869).

In 1828, Davis returned to New York City and the office he shared with James Eddy. Having yet to obtain his first architectural commission, Davis was already acquainted with the leading architects and artists of New York and Boston. The letter of introduction he had obtained from Ithiel Town revealed that they had been acquainted for some time,[29] and in fact during 1827–28 Davis had occasionally been commissioned by both Town and architect Martin Thompson to draw views of some of their buildings in New York and New Haven. At this time Town and Thompson, the two most prominent architects in New York City, were working in association with one another and maintained offices in the Merchants Exchange, a greatly admired building designed by Thompson. It was in these offices that Davis was able to study the vast resources available in Town's famous library of architecture and art. In his diary Davis recorded that on March 15, 1828, in Town's library, he made his first drawings from Stuart and Revett's *Antiquities of Athens*,[30] and that he dated this as the beginning of his professional career as an architect.[31] After a second trip to Boston in the fall of 1828, Davis returned to New York, where in early 1829 Ithiel Town proposed that they form a partnership for the practice of architecture. On February 1, 1829, the firm of Town and Davis, Architects, was born.

Davis's new partner, Ithiel Town, brought to their association a nationally ranked reputation, a large circle of friends and contacts in the design fields, a high place in society, and a wealth of experience and resources. Almost twenty years Davis's senior, Town was to have a strong and lasting influence on his young, talented partner. Born on October 3, 1784, in Thompson, Connecticut, Ithiel Town was the son of Martha Johnson Town and Archelaus Town, a farmer. In his youth Ithiel worked in the carpentry trade, and in 1804 he moved to Boston, where until 1810 he studied at a school of architecture conducted by Asher Benjamin. Although a noted architect in his own right, Benjamin (1773–1845) gained renown as the author of several widely used builder's pattern or handbooks.[32] Here Town, who also studied at the Boston Athenaeum, became acquainted with the famous and influential architect Charles Bulfinch. A mentor of Benjamin's, Bulfinch (1763–1844) was the first professional architect born in America. Prior to Bulfinch, the trade was practiced by "gen-

29. Newton, *Town and Davis*, 92.

30. James Stuart and Nicholas Revett, *The Antiquities of Athens and other Monuments of Greece*, 3 vols. (London: J. Haberkorn, 1762–87).

31. Jane B. Davies, introduction to Peck, *Alexander Jackson Davis*, 18.

32. Two of Asher Benjamin's earliest and most popular handbooks were *The Country Builder's Assistant* (Greenfield, Mass.: Thomas Dickman, 1797), and *The Architect, or Practical House Carpenter* (Boston: R. P. and C. Williams and Annin and Smith, 1830).

tlemen architects," such as Thomas Jefferson and William Thornton, whose actual professions lay elsewhere, or by builders who also served as architects. Studying with Asher Benjamin and Charles Bulfinch, Ithiel Town would have had access to the works of the most important architects in history, including Vitruvius, Palladio, Vignola, Inigo Jones, Christopher Wren, and James Gibbs. It was here that Town's passion for books on architecture and art was born, which would lead to the creation of his celebrated library.

In 1812, Town moved home to Connecticut and settled in New Haven, where he began his career as an architect. Although he would later set up a practice in New York City, he always maintained an office and home in New Haven and executed many commissions in both cities. Town soon designed numerous landmark buildings in New Haven, especially in the wildly popular Greek Revival style, of which Town became a noted proponent. The Greek Revival style, based not only on the study of surviving buildings from Greek antiquities, but also on the Roman, is generally credited as having been introduced to the United States by the distinguished architect Benjamin Henry Latrobe (1764–1820). In 1798, Latrobe designed the Bank of Pennsylvania, considered the first building in the Greek Revival style in America.[33] "Greek mania" caught on and spread like wildfire across the United States in the early nineteenth century, supplanting the previously esteemed Federal and Georgian styles.

One of the most important factors fueling the spread of the Greek Revival style was the growing prevalence at this time of the publication of builder's handbooks or pattern books, which at the turn of the nineteenth century were becoming widely available. These handbooks, especially those by Asher Benjamin, Minard Lafever, Peter Nicholson, Edward Shaw, and John Haviland, provided builders and architects with detailed descriptions of the classical orders both Greek and Roman, and instructions for executing them. It was the widespread availability of these books in the early 1800s that was one of the primary causes of the rapid dissemination of this architectural style across the country.

Americans took to the Greek Revival style with its massive yet delicate features because it was felt to embody the American ideals of strength, beauty, democracy, honesty, and permanence. But this was not a revival in the sense that classical antiquities were being copied exactly. It was rather a way for architects to take forms of strength and beauty and transform them into something truly original, truly American. Architects and builders intentionally experimented with the Greek and Roman in an attempt to create designs that were new and not simply imitative of the ancient forms. One of the most common stylistic changes seen was through the simplification of the classical orders. This was especially evident in the popular Doric style through the elimination of such "proper" features as mutules with guttae, triglyphs, and the decorative embellishments of the metopes in the frieze (fig. 7), the ideal of which was embodied in the Parthenon on the Acropolis in Athens. Greek precedents also became mixed with the later variations of the Roman styles. One of

33. Hamlin, *Greek Revival Architecture*, 65.

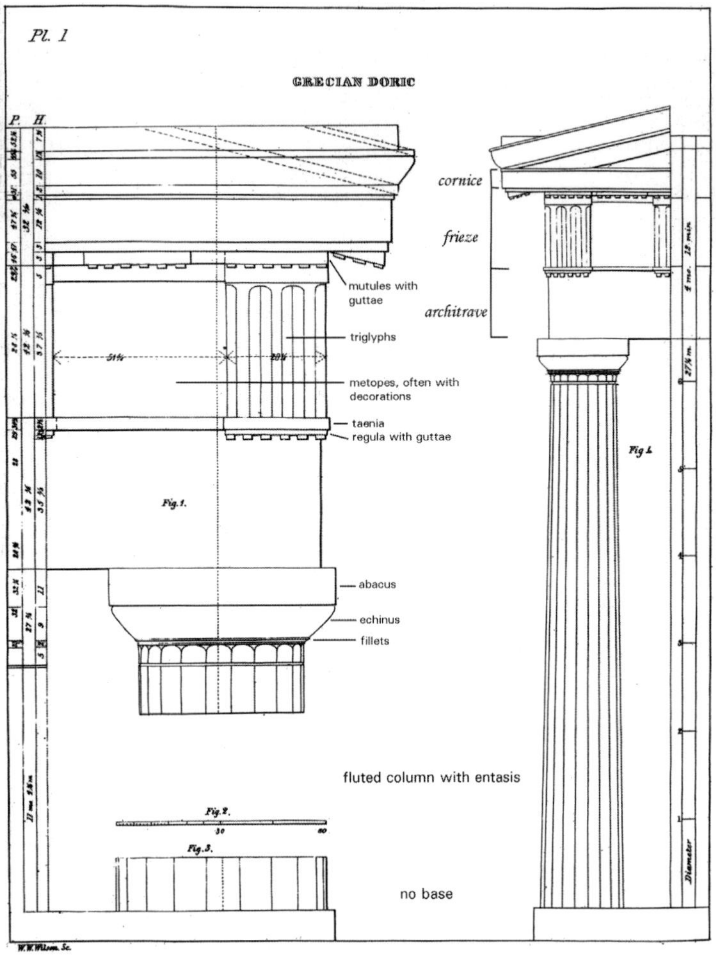

Fig. 7. Greek Doric order, adapted from illustration in Edward Shaw's book *The Modern Architect* (Boston, 1854), plate 1, with labels for features of the order inserted by J. M. Truettner.
Courtesy of Hatcher Graduate Library, University of Michigan.

the more unusual combinations that became extremely popular in the United States was the addition of a Roman dome to Greek temple structures. Countless state capitols and other governmental buildings followed this mode. Ithiel Town and his soon-to-be partner A. J. Davis were to develop their own unique and powerful variations on the classical ideals.

This was an extraordinary time for the practice of architecture in America, for not only did it experience the explosion of pattern books, but it also marked the emergence of the professional architect in the United States. One of the earliest practitioners to step into this role was Ithiel Town, who like his contemporaries, embraced the Greek Revival style. Beginning his professional career in the early nineteenth century, Town found himself designing almost exclusively in the classical revival style. Having just settled in New Haven he received the commission in 1812 to build the Center Church on the large public green, which on one side faced old Yale College. Although the

Fig. 8. Center Church, New Haven Green, photo ca. 1935. Designed by Asher Benjamin and Ithiel Town. Built 1812–14; extant.
Library of Congress, Prints and Photographs Division, Historic American Buildings Survey (HABS, CONN,5-NEWHA,1-4).

design of the church has generally been attributed to Town, evidence survives that indicates that the plan for the building was purchased from Town's old teacher Asher Benjamin.[34] The architectural style of the church was based on James Gibbs's landmark church, St. Martin-in-the-Fields, built 1721–27 in Westminster, London (see fig. 65). The importance of this highly publicized and widely copied style to the University of Michigan story will be discussed later.

In the execution of the Center Church (fig. 8), Town certainly made changes to Benjamin's de-

34. J. Frederick Kelly, *Early Connecticut Meetinghouses: Being an Account of the Church Edifices Built before 1830 Based Chiefly upon Town and Parish Records*, vol. 2 (New York: Columbia University Press, 1948), 12–13. Kelly quotes a report by the contractors for Center Church: "A plan for a meeting house was procured at considerable expense of Mr. Benjamin an eminent architect in Boston, which after a number of alterations was adopted as the model of the proposed building."

sign, so that with little surviving documentation it has been impossible to determine how much of the church was Town's design. Center Church was completed in 1814, at which time Town was also occupied with his second major commission in New Haven, which was Trinity Church. In a complete change of pace for Town, Trinity Church was designed in the newly emerging Gothic Revival style. Built a year after Center Church, Trinity stood nearby it on the New Haven Green. In 1815 a third church, North Church or the United Church, was completed on the Green as well.[35]

Ithiel Town's career took off from here, and in 1824 he designed the Eagle Bank at New Haven, which has been considered the first exact copy of an ancient Greek temple built in America.[36] Sporting an Ionic portico, the design was copied from Stuart and Revett's drawing of the Erechtheum on the Acropolis in Athens.[37] In 1827, Town would design the New Haven State Capitol, which was built 1827–31, in the style of a Doric temple between and behind his two churches on the Green (see fig. 9). Although enjoying a prolific practice in Connecticut, by the early 1820s Town was also becoming a noted architect in New York City. Not only had his New Haven designs become well known, Town also gained a large measure of renown for an invention and for a collection.

An engineer perhaps as much as an architect, Ithiel Town was interested in the field of scientific invention, especially as it pertained to the construction industry. In the 1810s he devised a new system of bridge construction based on a lattice truss. On January 28, 1820, he was granted a patent for the so-called Town Truss. Thereafter he traveled widely selling his truss system across the country. While on these sales trips, Town also sought architectural commissions and obtained some of the most highly coveted for his firm, such as for the state capitols of Indiana and North Carolina. The Town Truss became one of the most widely used systems for covered bridge construction, and the royalties that Town reaped from his patent provided him with the means to indulge another passion—the collection of books.

During the years he had studied with and known Asher Benjamin and Charles Bulfinch in Boston, Town had developed a fancy for books about art and architecture that was nurtured and encouraged by his mentors. Once on his own and making a good living, Town began to collect books and engravings on the design arts. He made at least one tour through Europe to acquire the best that were to be had, and those that were not yet available in America. By the mid-1830s Town's library was renowned across New England, for it contained over ten thousand volumes plus thousands of loose engravings, and other works of art.[38]

35. Elizabeth Mills Brown, *The United Church on the Green: An Architectural History, New Haven, Connecticut* (New Haven: United Church, 1965), 28–34; and Elizabeth Mills Brown, *New Haven: A Guide to Architecture and Urban Design* (New Haven: Yale University Press, 1976), 107. North Church was designed by Ebenezer Johnson and built by David Hoadley. Its design was based on those by well-known New York church architect John McComb Jr., which in turn were based on James Gibbs's St. Martin-in-the-Fields.

36. Newton, *Town and Davis*, 48.

37. Stuart and Revett, *Antiquities of Athens*, vol. 2, chap. 2, plate 4.

38. A widely read society columnist described a visit to Town's library at his home in New Haven: "In the second story, is a spacious apartment, forty-five feet in length, twenty-three in breadth, and twenty-two in height, with two sky-lights, six feet square. . . . There, and in the lobbies, and study, are arranged, in Egyptian, Grecian, and Gothic cases, of fine symmetry, between nine and ten thousand volumes. Many of these are rare, expensive, and valuable. More than three fourths are folios and quartos. A great proportion are adorned with engravings. It is not easy to compute the number of these embellishments—though the proprietor supposes them to exceed two hundred thousand. There are also some twenty or twenty-five thousand separate engravings—some of them the splendid executions of the best masters, both ancient and modern. In

Fig. 9. Connecticut State Capitol, New Haven Green, 1827. Design by Ithiel Town, as delineated by Alexander Jackson Davis. Built 1827–31; demolished 1887.

Metropolitan Museum of Art, Harris Brisbane Dick Fund, 1924 (24.66.1401 [leaf 28]). All rights reserved, Metropolitan Museum of Art.

Town originally housed the bulk of this remarkable collection's books and drawings on architecture in his office in the Merchants Exchange in New York City. A sketch by A. J. Davis of Town and Davis's offices in the second Merchants Exchange, shows two bays of fifteen feet by twenty-three feet each, made to accommodate Town's books.[39] Although astounding in its breadth and size, what made Town's library so famous was that he opened it to the public. He let it be known that anyone who wished was free to study his books. Inventories taken just before and after his death revealed that he owned the most important books on architecture. Countless architects, draftsmen, and builders benefited from Town's collection, not the least of whom was A. J. Davis. Shortly after entering into partnership with Davis in 1829, Town left for an extended tour of Europe with his friend, the artist Samuel F. B. Morse. During this trip Town collected a significant number of books and engravings, which he sent home to his partner in New York. This European tour with Morse was an especially important event in Town's life. In fact, biographer Roger Hale Newton wrote that it "cannot be overestimated. It influenced all [Town's] subsequent work, his associates, and, through his library, a wider circle of contemporaries than will ever be known. Indeed, it may well have been one of the most significant milestones along the road to modern architecture and the definitive factor in sponsoring it. We know that no one else on this side of the Atlantic had gathered such a famous library; that few occupied so universally respected a position in his field either here or in London; or wielded so strong an influence in the Fine Arts as Ithiel Town, the architectural mentor."[40] What also cannot be overestimated is the influence that Town's personality, connections, and library were to have on his young apprentice, A. J. Davis. Later, after he dissolved his partnership with Davis in 1835, Town retired to New Haven and moved his library into the large fireproof room in the house he designed in 1834 especially to receive it.

When Ithiel Town had branched out and begun to practice in New York City, he developed an association in late 1826 or early 1827 with Martin Euclid Thompson. The two gentlemen were previously acquainted and were the sole representatives of architecture among the founding members of the National Academy of Design in January 1826. Already an established architect in New York, the talented and artistic Thompson (1787–1875) had gained special notice for his design of the U.S. Branch Bank on Wall Street, built 1822–23, and whose facade is now preserved in the Metropolitan Museum of Art.[41] In 1827, the Merchants Exchange, designed by Thompson, was completed on Wall Street. The Exchange was widely admired, leading Greek Revival historian Talbot Hamlin to note, "In beauty and richness the building had no peers in the city. It was dignified, simple, and commodious"; compared with others of the day, it was "more original, more daring, more power-

these particulars, this library surpasses all others in our country. There are also one hundred and seventy oil paintings, besides mosaics, and other works of art, and objects of curiosity." Lydia H. Sigourney, "Residence of Ithiel Town, Esq.," *Ladies' Companion,* January 1839, 123.

39. R. W. Liscombe, "A 'New Era in My Life': Ithiel Town Abroad," *Journal of the Society of Architectural Historians* 50, no. 1 (1991): 13.

40. Newton, *Town and Davis,* 97.

41. When the bank was due to be demolished in 1913, a way to save the greatly admired classical facade was sought, and it was purchased by a private individual. The facade was then donated to the Metropolitan Museum of Art, where, in 1925, it was installed as the exterior facade of the new American Wing, today enclosed in an interior courtyard. Morrison H. Heckscher, "The Metropolitan Museum of Art: An Architectural History," *Metropolitan Museum of Art Bulletin* 53, no. 1 (1995): 54–55.

Fig. 10. St. Mark's-in-the-Bouwerie, New York City, photo 1895 by Edward Wenzel. Built 1795–99, architect unknown. Tower designed by Martin E. Thompson while with Town and Thompson, built 1828; portico added 1854; extant.

Collection of The New-York Historical Society (neg. 1094).

ful; the recessed [Ionic] portico was a new note, its cupola was unusually effective, and its large Exchange Room both delicate and monumental."[42] The new firm of Town and Thompson took offices in the Exchange, installed Town's library, and opened their "Architectural Rooms" to the public. During their two-year association Thompson designed several notable buildings, two of which will have direct bearing on the University of Michigan story. Beyond those, one of his most important commissions was for the U.S. Marine (later Naval) Hospital of New York, built 1830–38, a large granite structure in a subdued classical style that survives. A later yet prominent design reflected the growing interest in the Gothic Revival, which was especially influenced by the "Pio-

42. Talbot Hamlin, "Martin Thompson," in *Dictionary of American Biography,* ed. Dumas Malone, vol. 9 (New York: Charles Scribner's Sons, 1936), 467–68.

Fig. 11. Washington Square North town houses, New York City, photo ca. 1930. Design attributed to Martin E. Thompson, built 1827–33; most extant.
Courtesy of New York University Archives.

neers in American Revivalist Architecture" (Town and Davis).[43] This was Thompson's design for the Arsenal, built in Central Park in 1848–51. This great castellated structure with its crenellated towers now houses the New York City Department of Parks and Recreation.

Of the two Thompson designs to be taken note of, one is St. Mark's-in-the-Bouwerie, in New York City. The body of the church was built in the Georgian style from 1795 to 1799; the architect is unknown. In 1828, a steeple in the Gibbsian style was added (fig. 10). Although sometimes credited to Town and Thompson or just Town, the steeple is generally considered to be Martin Thompson's work. A few years later, Town and his new partner Davis would design a portico in the Ionic vocabulary that would have further completed the church's transformation from Georgian to Greek (see fig. 68). This design, however, was not executed, and St. Mark's remains today much as it did after it received its massive cast-iron portico in 1854.

Between 1827 and 1833 an elegant row of town houses was built along Washington Square North in New York City (fig. 11). One of the most striking elements of these dwellings was the use of classical entry porticoes, some of the Ionic order and some of Doric (see fig. 39). This was one of

43. Newton, *Town and Davis*, xviii.

the earliest uses of this type of classical entry on a house in New York City. Design of "The Row," as it was known, is attributed to Martin Thompson.[44] These house designs were strikingly similar to house facades designed by Thompson for a Murray Street site on Columbia College land in 1829.[45] The Washington Square row became extremely well known since, in addition to its handsome appearance, it was home to some of the most notable names in New York society, including Edith Wharton, Henry James, and the eminent late-nineteenth-century architect Richard Morris Hunt. The entry portico designs were picked up and widely copied, across New York and at least as far west as the young town of Ann Arbor, Michigan.

By early 1829, Town and Thompson had dissolved their association and Town had turned his interest to their young apprentice, Alexander J. Davis. In February 1829, the firm of Town and Davis, Architects, was created, with offices maintained in the Merchants Exchange. As noted, Town's personality, experience, reputation, connections, and library had a great influence on Davis, who was almost twenty years younger than Town. They began what has been considered the first partnership of its kind in America, a professional architectural firm that was in business for any appreciable length of time.[46] Prior to this, some architects had worked together, most notably Town and Thompson, but these were short-lived, loose associations in which the architects primarily shared offices, worked independently, while also pursuing some commissions in common. In fact, the exact nature of Town and Thompson's association remains unclear. With Town and Davis was born the professional firm, which was formally organized, in which commissions were sought and designs signed in concert, and in which the partners probably expected to remain until the day the elder Town should retire.

The fruitful partnership of Town and Davis, Architects, would last for six years, until May 1835, and be revived again in 1842 for one year. But even during the time when they were not in official partnership, Town and Davis worked together to produce some designs in common, in particular the New York University chapel's interior, and an entry for the Illinois State Capitol competition in 1837. The firm of Town and Davis was to be extremely productive and influential. It is not the purpose of this study to attempt a thorough exploration of the firm's history, as such biographies exist.[47] However, their major contributions and stylistic tendencies can be touched upon, especially as they influenced Davis's work for the University of Michigan. When the partnership began in February 1829, Ithiel Town was deeply committed to the Greek Revival style, although he also dabbled in the newly evolving Gothic Revival. Davis's earliest works with Town were therefore in the classical style. He helped with some of the later construction drawings for the New Haven Capitol, which had been designed by Town in the Doric temple mode (see fig. 9).

44. Hamlin, *Greek Revival Architecture,* 136, 344–45; Donald Martin Reynolds, *The Architecture of New York City: Histories and Views of Important Structures, Sites, and Symbols* (New York: Macmillan, 1984), 84; and Ada Louise Huxtable, *Classic New York: Georgian Gentility to Greek Elegance* (New York: Doubleday, 1964), 96.

45. Hamlin, *Greek Revival Architecture,* 136, and plate 29; and Hamlin, "Martin Thompson," 467.

46. Newton, *Town and Davis,* 17–18.

47. Newton, *Town and Davis;* and Peck, *Alexander Jackson Davis.*

Fig. 12. Indiana State Capitol, Indianapolis, 1831. Design by Ithiel Town and Alexander Jackson Davis. Built 1831–34; replaced by new capitol 1878.
Drawings and Archives, Avery Architectural and Fine Arts Library, Columbia University in the City of New York.

Fig. 13. Choragic Monument of Lysicrates (restored). Drawn by James Stuart and Nicholas Revett, in *The Antiquities of Athens and Other Monuments of Greece* (London, 1762), vol. 1, chap. 4, plate 3.
Courtesy of Rare Book Room, Media Union Library, University of Michigan.

In 1829, Davis received what is considered his first commission as an architect. This was for a house in New Haven for James A. Hillhouse. At first called Highwood and later Sachem's Wood, the house was, in its original design, in the form of a classical cube with a two-story Doric entry portico; the final executed design featured Ionic columns. Like many of his future designs, Highwood reflected the influence on Davis of his studies of books on classical antiquities. Unlike his partner, Davis never traveled in Europe and therefore did not have firsthand experience of the ancient Greek and Roman structures. He relied instead on Town's mammoth library, where he could study classical details in such books as Stuart and Revett's *Antiquities of Athens.*

Davis, however, did not settle for simply copying the designs of antiquities, but rather developed new classical vocabularies that combined elements from the Greek and Roman with some from his own imagination to create innovative forms. One of the most important innovations to come out of the Town and Davis office was the evolution of the Greek anta form into deeply projecting pilasters or piers that took the place of columns along building exteriors. These thick piers, or pilastrades, with the deep shadows they cast, gave structures an impression of strength and permanence that seemed particularly well suited to public buildings. This is seen on countless designs executed by the firm, including two of their state capitols. For the Indiana statehouse, a commission that Town had procured while traveling selling his bridge truss, a Doric temple form was combined with a Roman dome (fig. 12). This was topped by a cupola copied from Stuart and Revett's drawing of the Choragic Monument of Lysicrates (fig. 13).

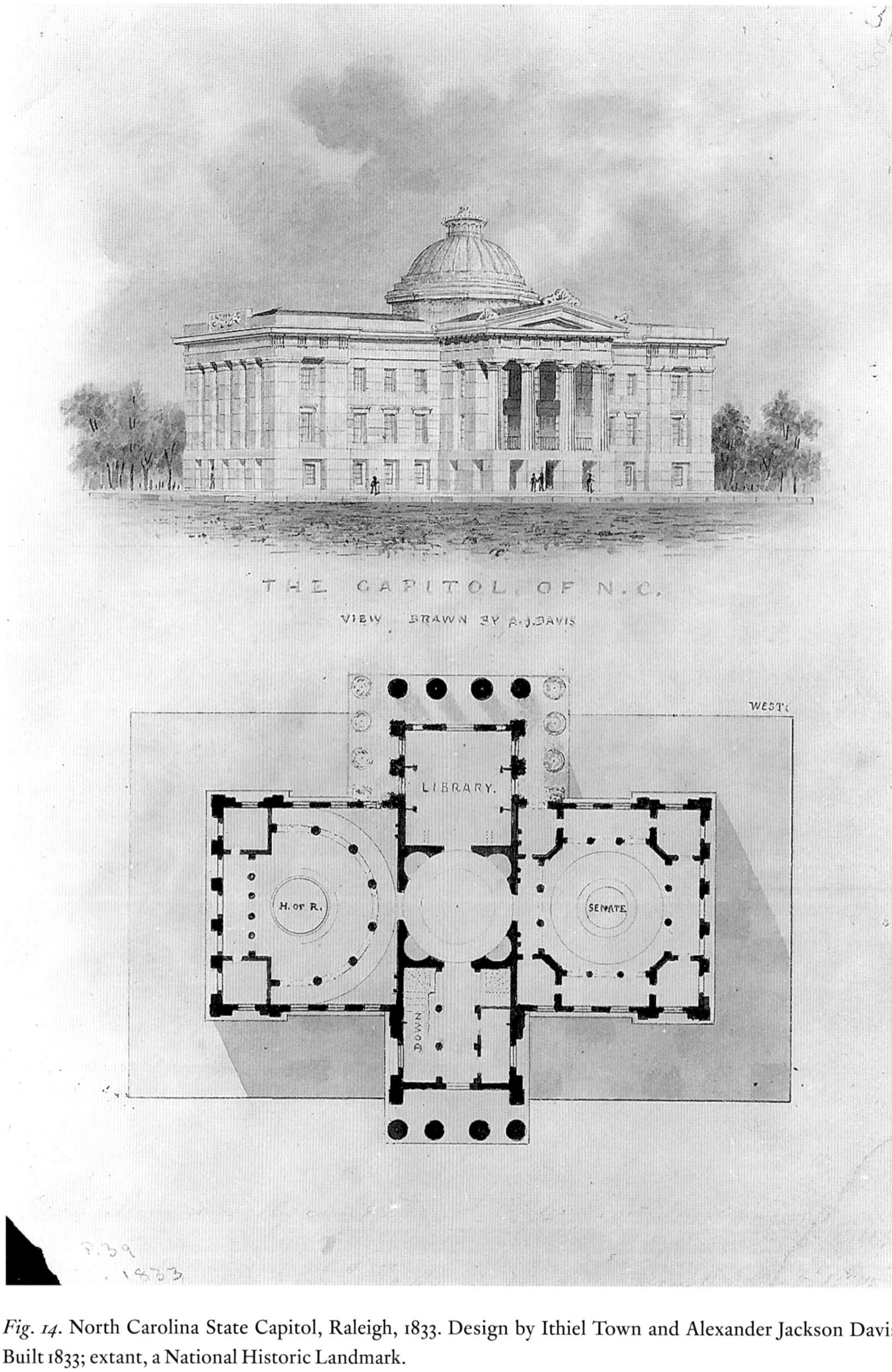

Fig. 14. North Carolina State Capitol, Raleigh, 1833. Design by Ithiel Town and Alexander Jackson Davis. Built 1833; extant, a National Historic Landmark.

Metropolitan Museum of Art, Harris Brisbane Dick Fund, 1924 (24.66.1401 [23], vol. 2, leaf 29).

The deep antae or pilastrade was also employed in Town and Davis's design for the capitol of North Carolina, the only one of their capitols to survive. At Raleigh, the cruciform shape was utilized, along with a low dome and Doric entry portico (fig. 14). Here again, the influence of pattern books is seen, as the portico reflects that drawn by Stuart and Revett and widely published in the books of Benjamin, Lafever, and others. This design element of pilastrades would also be used to great effect in Town and Davis's design for the U.S. Customs House on Wall Street in New York City, built 1834–42. Constructed of marble, this Doric temple was modified in execution by others, primarily in the deletion of the dome and the reduction of the depth of the portico. Now the Federal Hall National Monument, most of the interior ornamentation was executed by Town and Davis's friend, the sculptor John Frazee. These and other Town and Davis buildings in a similar vein were widely admired and greatly influential in the designs of other architects, such as Ammi Burnham Young, as evidenced by his Vermont statehouse (see fig. 4) and Boston customhouse (see fig. 5).

One of the most unusual features developed by Davis was a type of window fenestration which he called Daviséan. In the spaces between the deep antae Davis placed multistoried vertically stacked and recessed windows that were separated at floor levels with narrow flat horizontal panels. The window lights were separated by tall narrow piers or mullions that ran the height of the windows and reinforced the sense of verticality. This device was used by Davis not only in classical buildings, but also Gothic and Tuscan (see figs. 25, 60, and 61). Davis ultimately developed his Daviséan windows to be prominent features of buildings and anticipated, by several decades, the industrial glass curtain wall (e.g., in his design for the Commercial Exchange, New York City, 1862).

Two other variations on the Greek temple ideal by Town and Davis were particularly well suited for churches. One combined a simple classical Ionic portico with a Roman dome, such as in the French Church or Eglisé du Saint Esprit, 1831–34 (fig. 15). This delicate building is topped by a copy of the Choragic Monument, similar to the Indiana Capitol (see figs. 12 and 13). For the South Congregational Church in Middletown, Connecticut (1829), Town and Davis created a variation of the Doric portico by recessing the door behind two Doric columns and making the antae on the side more prominent (fig. 16). The *distyle-in-antis* design (literally two columns between antae) became a widely copied pattern in church architecture in America.

This device for the layout of churches was not Town and Davis's only original and influential innovation. In fact, Davis claimed fourteen "firsts" for the firm, including the first Greek orders for doorways for town houses ever known and executed in New York City.[48] The reference to Greek orders meant the use of pilasters or columns flanking the door and carrying a full entablature. One popular version of this entry has previously been illustrated as occurring on the Washington

48. Newton, *Town and Davis*, 61–64. Davis cites as an early example the Curtis House built in 1829.

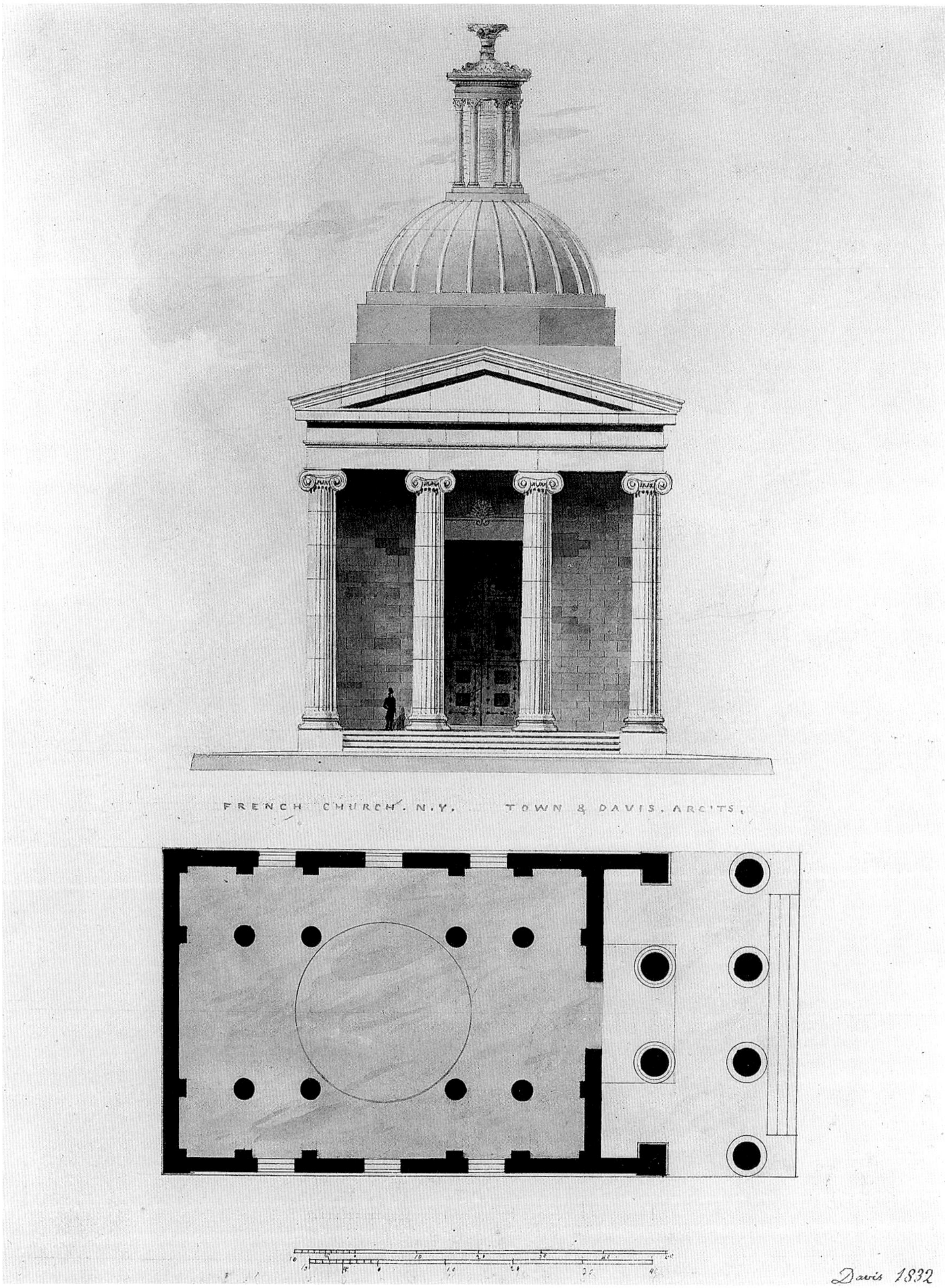

Fig. 15. Eglisé du Saint Esprit (French Church), New York City, 1832. Design by Ithiel Town and Alexander Jackson Davis. Built 1831–34; demolished 1864.

Fig. 16. South Congregational Church, Middletown, Connecticut, 1829. Design by Ithiel Town and Alexander Jackson Davis. Built 1829; demolished 1867.

Drawings and Archives, Avery Architectural and Fine Arts Library, Columbia University in the City of New York (1940.001.00364A).

Square North town houses designed by Martin Thompson (see fig. 11). Since Davis worked for and with Town and Thompson prior to his entering into partnership with Town, it is certain that the development of the classic entry for houses in New York City came out of the think tank of this talented triumvirate. There were many variations on this theme, including the rounded portico, which eventually grew to become a two-story half-round portico, as seen on the Whitney house with Corinthian columns (see fig. 41).

Among the other "firsts" claimed for Town and Davis, mostly in relation to their work in New York and New Haven, were the first rusticated basements (1831); first Greek temple building with portico *in antis,* elevated on a basement (1828, e.g., Highwood); first church in Greek temple form (in designs exhibited in 1828); first block development in New York (1828); first English Perpendicular Gothic villa with barge boards, brackets, oriels, and tracery in windows (1832, Glen Ellen); first vertical stone piers for ground-floor shop fronts, replacing solid walls pierced with openings (1829); and first iron shop fronts in New York (1835).[49] The last two are especially notable as they would have widespread influence in storefront design.

In 1831, Davis's good friend John Trumbull asked Town and Davis to design an art gallery for Yale College, which would house a collection of Trumbull's works. The resulting design, in the mode of a Doric temple, was not executed, but probably influenced the design that was built, which was drawn by Trumbull himself. This was, however, the beginning of Davis's long career of providing designs for colleges and universities. (Davis would, in fact, provide designs for Alumni Hall at Yale, built 1851–53.) The first major collegiate commission for the firm of Town and Davis was that for the newly formed New York University in 1831, then called the University of the City of New York. Several designs were produced by the firm, and the variation finally selected was a result of the collaboration of Town and Davis, with James Dakin and David Bates Douglass.

During their partnership, Town and Davis employed a number of draftsmen and apprentice architects. One of the most gifted was James Harrison Dakin, who was hired as an apprentice by Davis in 1829. Dakin was born in New York State on August 24, 1806. He had the same innate artistic talent as Davis and a sense of originality and creativity in his drawings. Under Davis's tutelage, Dakin became a superior renderer and draftsman, with a style quite resembling his mentor's. His talents were such that in 1831 Dakin was commissioned to provide illustrations for a book of *Views in New-York,* published by Theodore Fay.[50]

On May 1, 1832, James Dakin became a partner, and the firm's name was changed to Town, Davis and Dakin, Architects. The addition of a third partner was partly a result of Town's ambitious, though short-lived, plan to open branch offices in Washington, D.C., and Baltimore. Davis headed the Washington office for its brief existence. In addition to New York University, one of Dakin's most important commissions while with the firm was for the Rockaway Marine Pavilion on Long Island in 1833, a Greek Revival building featuring pilastrades, a Doric entry, and a tower (fig. 17). This and several other commissions made Dakin one of the most noted early hotel and resort designers. Shortly after he became a partner, Dakin hired James Gallier as a draftsman. Gallier (1798–1866), later to become famous as an architect in New Orleans, was newly arrived in America, and had quickly discovered that the professional architect was still something of a novelty. In his autobiography, Gallier wrote, "There was at that time, properly speaking, only one architect's office in New York, kept by Town and Davis. . . . There was a Mr. Dakin, a young man of genius, who had been a carpenter and had studied architecture in Town's office . . . from him I obtained the first employment I had in America."[51] Hired by Dakin on May 15, 1832, Gallier remained with the

49. Ibid.

50. Theodore S. Fay, *Views in New-York and its environs from accurate, characteristic, & picturesque drawings, taken on the spot, expressly for this work, by Dakin, architect* (New York: Peabody, 1831); and Scully, *James Dakin, Architect,* 6.

51. James Gallier, *Autobiography of James Gallier, Architect* (1864; reprint, New York: Da Capo Press, 1973), 18–19.

Fig. 17. Rockaway Marine Pavilion, Long Island, New York, 1833. Design by James H. Dakin. Built 1833–34; burned 1864. Collection of The New-York Historical Society (neg. 3166).

firm about a year. One of the most noted designs to come out of the joint effort of Davis, Dakin, and Gallier was for the Second Avenue Presbyterian Church in New York, 1832.

After leaving Town, Davis and Dakin in 1833, James Gallier entered into a short-lived and disastrous partnership with Minard Lafever, a well-known architect in New York. Lafever's true fame came from his popular and widely read builder's handbooks. His most important work was *The Modern Builder's Guide,* first published in 1833, which contained ten illustrations by James Dakin, including a notable and original design for an entrance doorway in the classical mode (fig. 18). Lafever's book also included a design for a country residence drawn by his partner James Gallier and used as the frontispiece. In addition, Dakin would provide illustrations for Lafever's 1835 book *The Beauties of Modern Architecture.*[52] Lafever acknowledged Dakin's contribution to the book, and it is evident that there was a general flow of ideas from and between Town and Davis, Dakin, Gallier, and Lafever.

In 1833, James Dakin, still in partnership with Town and Davis, hired his brother Charles as a draftsman. Here Charles Bingley Dakin (1811–39) met James Gallier. After his unsuccessful association with Lafever during part of 1833 and 1834, Gallier formed a partnership with Charles Dakin, and in October 1834 they moved to New Orleans to open a practice. James Dakin, for his part, gave up his partnership with Town and Davis on November 1, 1833. While on his own in New York City, he designed in 1834 the First Presbyterian Church in Troy, New York, in the form of a Doric tem-

52. Scully, *James Dakin, Architect,* 26–28.

Fig. 18. Design for a front door in Greek Revival style. Designed and drawn by James H. Dakin for Minard Lafever's *Modern Builder's Guide* (New York, 1833), plate 63.

Courtesy of Rare Book Room, Media Union Library, University of Michigan.

Fig. 19. New York University and South Dutch Reformed Church, Washington Square, New York City, engraving 1850 by William Howland after a drawing by William Wade. New York University designed by Ithiel Town, Alexander Jackson Davis, James H. Dakin, and David B. Douglass, built 1835–37; demolished 1894. Church designed by Minard Lafever, built 1835; demolished 1895.
Collection of The New-York Historical Society (neg. 30190).

ple. One of his most admired (and copied) designs from this period was the Bank of Louisville, which featured Ionic columns *in antis,* set within a portico with battered walls, a drawing of which was included in Minard Lafever's *Beauties of Modern Architecture.* Dakin has often been credited with the design of the South Dutch Reformed Church, which stood next to the New York University building on Washington Square, which had been designed by Town, Davis, Dakin, and Douglass (fig. 19). However, evidence exists that more clearly identifies Minard Lafever as the designer of the church.[53] During this time, 1833–35, Dakin worked on a number of illustrations for Lafever's books, mostly for original designs by Dakin, leading Dakin biographer Arthur Scully to conclude that Lafever was influenced by Dakin rather than vice versa.[54] Whether Dakin had any influence on Lafever's design of the Dutch Reformed Church is unclear, but quite possible.

In November 1835, James Dakin moved to New Orleans, where he maintained a successful career, obtaining as his highest achievement the design of the old Louisiana State Capitol at Baton Rouge.[55] Built 1847–49, the capitol was a complete departure from the usual pedimented and porticoed classical statehouses. Dakin designed for Louisiana a castellated Gothic building, which sur-

53. Jacob Landy, *The Architecture of Minard Lafever* (New York: Columbia University Press, 1970), 65–67.

54. Scully, *James Dakin, Architect,* 32.

55. When James Dakin arrived in New Orleans, his brother Charles was still in partnership with James Gallier. James Dakin joined the firm, but shortly thereafter Gallier withdrew from the partnership, and the Dakin brothers continued to practice together until Charles's death in June 1839.

Fig. 20. Louisiana State Capitol, Baton Rouge, photo ca. 1990. Designed by James H. Dakin. Built 1847–49; extant, a National Historic Landmark.
Courtesy of Louisiana's Old State Capitol.

vives today as a museum (fig. 20). Only one other antebellum state capitol would be executed in the Gothic Revival style, that at Milledgeville, Georgia. James Dakin, friend and protégé of A. J. Davis, died in 1852.

The University of the City of New York was founded in the fall of 1830 and incorporated by an act of the state legislature in April 1831.[56] Later called New York University, the institution was inaugurated in September 1832 and held classes in space temporarily obtained in Clinton Hall (designed by Town and Davis, built 1829). A building committee appointed in January 1833 selected the firm of Town and Davis to provide designs for the university's first building, to be constructed on land acquired on Washington Square. Evidence in Davis's diaries suggests the firm was working on designs in 1832 and perhaps as early as 1831. The first design produced was by Davis in the classical revival mode (fig. 21). This design featured several Davis hallmarks, including strong antae or pilastrades, a Doric-columned entrance *in antis,* and Daviséan windows. The rectangular

56. Theodore Francis Jones, ed., *New York University, 1832:1932* (New York: New York University Press, 1933), 21, 27–28.

Fig. 21. New York University, 1832. Design by Alexander Jackson Davis. Not executed.
Collection of The New-York Historical Society (neg. 30014).

building was surmounted with a copy of the Tower of the Winds, as drawn by Stuart and Revett (fig. 22). This design, however, was rejected by the university in favor of one in the newly emerging Gothic Revival style.

Considering that Davis was to become one of the foremost proponents of the Gothic Revival and picturesque styles, it seems surprising that his design for New York University would be Greek, and that the approved Gothic design for NYU should come from the pen of his associate. Generally thought to have been the work of Davis, evidence survives that reveals that the castellated Gothic design selected for NYU came mostly from the hand of James Dakin.[57] Letters written by Dakin to Davis show that Dakin met with the university's board of trustees, and in his letters Dakin sketched the design the trustees wanted, which was castellated Gothic. It is apparent that the partners all contributed to the NYU project, and Davis noted in his diary on November 1, 1832, that "many designs were made and finally one adopted and built in which Town, Davis, Dakin, and Professor Douglas [*sic*] had a hand."[58] The professor referred to was David Bates Doug-

57. Scully, *James Dakin, Architect*, 17–18.
58. Newton, *Town and Davis*, 230; and Glenn Patton, "Chapel in the Sky: Origins and Edifices of the University of the City of New York," *Architectural Review* 145 (March 1969): 178.

Fig. 22. Octagonal Tower of Andronicus Cyrrhestes or Tower of the Winds (restored). Drawn by James Stuart and Nicholas Revett, in *The Antiquities of Athens and Other Monuments of Greece* (London, 1762), vol. 1, chap. 3, plate 3.

lass, professor of natural philosophy and civil engineering, one of NYU's original faculty. Douglass (1790–1849) would teach at the university only a short time, moving in 1840 to Kenyon College in Gambier, Ohio, where he would become president of that institution. Other original faculty members at NYU included Samuel F. B. Morse and Henry Philip Tappan, who was appointed as professor of philosophy and belles-lettres.[59]

Built of marble from Sing Sing, the NYU building began construction in the summer of 1833. Although not completed until 1837, it was far enough along for the university to move its offices and activities into the structure in the fall of 1835 (see fig. 19). Among the first tenants of the new building were Ithiel Town and A. J. Davis, who were forced to move their offices when the Merchants Exchange burned down in the great fire of December 1835. Dakin had left the firm in late 1833, and Town and Davis's partnership had been dissolved in May 1835, but they continued to work in association on some projects and shared an office at NYU. The final part of this university commission was for the chapel's interior, for which Davis provided a breathtaking design in the Gothic Revival style, completed in 1837.

During the time Town and Davis's designs for NYU were being executed, they were persuaded to take on, as a student of architecture, the nephew of their friend Thomas Cole. Cole (1801–48) had become one of the leading painters in America after his work was "discovered" by artists John Trumbull and William Dunlap in 1825. Not merely a great landscape painter, Cole was also interested in architecture and found his work greatly influenced by Town, Davis, and Dakin's Gothic design of NYU, and this style of architecture began to appear in his paintings. In 1838, Cole entered a design of his own in the widely publicized competition for the Ohio State Capitol. A. J. Davis also entered the competition. In the end, the first prize went to Henry Walter of Cincinnati, with second prize going to Martin Thompson of New York, Ithiel Town's old partner. Thomas Cole took third prize, but none of these designs was executed as drawn. In 1839, Davis was asked to produce a new design using elements taken from the top three winners. This design was also rejected as being too costly to execute. Finally, Cole's design was adopted and built by Walter. At this time, Thomas Cole was legal guardian of his nephew Henry Bayless, who became a student of architecture in Town and Davis's office in February 1835. Bayless wrote to his uncle in January 1837, saying he was occupied with drawings of NYU for both Town and Davis, in their office at the university.[60] These drawings would have been for the chapel and other interior details.

Greatly drawn to Thomas Cole's artistry, Ithiel Town invited Cole to visit his house and library in New Haven in March 1839. Here Town commissioned a landscape painting from Cole, for which the artist would be paid in cash and books.[61] The resulting painting, entitled *The Architect's Dream,* was completed in April 1840 at the large size of seven feet (54" x 84"). Cole had apparently made it so large to compete with all the other things in Town's mammoth library. A bril-

59. Jones, *New York University,* 39.

60. Elwood C. Parry III, *The Art of Thomas Cole: Ambition and Imagination* (Newark: University of Delaware Press, 1988), 199.

61. Ibid., 217.

liant allegorical scene, *The Architect's Dream* shows in the foreground a man reposing on a column, on which has been inscribed the legend "PAINTED BY T. COLE FOR I. TOWN ARCH 1840." In the vistas behind the man, meant to be an architect, are portrayed images of great architecture through the ages. To one side, buildings of the ancient world—Greek, Roman, and Egyptian—are drenched in sunlight, and to the other side a great building in the Gothic style lurks in the shade, with the sun glowing through the traceried windows. To Cole's great dismay, the painting was rejected by Town because it was not what he wanted, which was a landscape in the manner that had made Cole famous. Although Town admired Cole's portrayal of architecture, he would not accept the painting. "I like the mixture of different ages and styles in the same imaginary picture," wrote Town, "but I wish the landscape to *predominate*—the Architecture, History, etc., to be various and subservient—or, mainly to enrich a very bold and richly various landscape."[62] Due to its large size, Cole was never able to sell the painting. Today this masterpiece resides at the Toledo Museum of Art.

When New York University moved into its new building in late 1835, Professor Samuel F. B. Morse took rooms in the northwest tower overlooking Washington Square. Already a well-known artist and founder of the National Academy of the Arts of Design, Morse (1791–1872) was appointed professor of sculpture and painting in 1832 at the newly founded NYU. He was also to become one of the members of the Hudson River school of artists, which included Jasper F. Cropsey, Asher B. Durand, and Thomas Cole, its founder. In 1835, Morse's title was changed to professor of literature of the arts of design. Here in the new NYU building, Morse was in frequent contact with his friends Ithiel Town and A. J. Davis. During these early years at the university, Morse continued to work on the electromagnetic telegraph that he had developed earlier, as well as a code that used dots and dashes to identify letters of the alphabet. The telegraph was demonstrated with success in early 1838, and Town, Davis, and Henry Tappan were among those who gathered by formal invitation at NYU on January 24, 1838, for a demonstration of the telegraph, at which the first version of Morse code was used.[63]

Morse also became interested in an invention that he felt had great implications for the design arts, which was the daguerreotype. Morse learned of it while traveling in Europe in 1838 with his telegraph, where he met Louis J. Daguerre (1787–1851) in Paris, shortly after Daguerre had announced his discovery.[64] Morse embraced the technology and was the second person in America to make an image by the daguerreotype method, in September 1839. The view was of the Unitarian Church, taken from the staircase at NYU. Morse was also one of the first of two to take a human

62. Letter Ithiel Town to Thomas Cole, New York, May 20, 1840 (Cole Papers, New York State Library, Albany), quoted in Parry, *Art of Thomas Cole*, 247.

63. Carleton Mabee, *The American Leonardo: A Life of Samuel F. B. Morse* (New York: Alfred A. Knopf, 1943), 201; and invitation from Professor Morse to witness operation of the telegraph, January 1838, folder P, Ithiel Town Collection, MSS 105, New Haven Colony.

64. Mabee, *The American Leonardo*, 227. After seeing Daguerre's discovery in Paris, Morse in April 1839 wrote for his brother's newspaper about this process for obtaining a photographic likeness. This was the first report on the daguerreotype process written by an American, and it was widely reprinted. Morse was taken by the beauty of the daguerreotype and its implications for the design arts. He wished to acknowledge Daguerre's contribution to art and proposed him for honorary membership in the National Academy, which was enthusiastically approved.

Fig. 23. Kenyon College, Gambier, Ohio, photo 1990 by Gordon Campbell. Designed by Norman Nash; spire by Charles Bulfinch. Built 1827–34; destroyed by fire and rebuilt 1949; extant.
Courtesy of Greenslade Special Collections, Olin Library, Kenyon College Archives.

portrait by this method and set himself up to do portraits on the roof of NYU as a professional daguerreotypist. Although best remembered by history for his invention of the telegraph, Morse thought of himself first and foremost as an artist and professor of art. In 1836, he produced an interesting allegorical painting of NYU that showed Town and Davis's building not in the center of a bustling metropolis, but overlooking a scenic lake. Morse's friendship with Davis would continue for many years, and in 1851–52 they worked together to produce a design that transformed Morse's country house in Poughkeepsie, called Locust Grove, into an Italian villa complete with tower.

New York University has generally been considered the first nineteenth-century American college building in the Gothic Revival style, although this is not precisely accurate. James Renwick Sr., an engineer and father of the more famous architect James Renwick Jr., designed a Gothic building for Columbia University in 1813, which was not executed, but whose plans were known. The earliest nineteenth-century Gothic structure to be built for an American institution was that for Kenyon College, built in 1826 with a spire designed by Charles Bulfinch,[65] in Gambier, Ohio (fig. 23). The ap-

65. Harold Kirker, *The Architecture of Charles Bulfinch* (Cambridge: Harvard University Press, 1969), 383.

pearance of this structure, with its simple lines and unadorned facade, was not reflective of the more evolved "Collegiate Gothic" style seen at NYU. But if New York University was not the first, it was certainly the most influential. The design was widely publicized, and its location in New York added to its becoming well known. In addition, Town, Davis, Dakin, and Douglass exhibited their designs for NYU at the American Academy of Arts in 1833, and their friend Samuel Morse helped further publicize it through his allegorical landscape.

At this time, in the 1830s when New York University was being designed, the emergence of the professional architect led to the desire on the part of several of the men to form a professional organization. By invitation of three men, Alexander Jackson Davis, William Strickland, and Thomas U. Walter, a group of eleven architects met in New York City on December 6, 1836, to discuss the possibility of forming this society.[66] In addition to those mentioned, others attending included Isaiah Rogers and John Haviland. They also had letters of support from other architects, including Ammi Young, James Dakin, Minard Lafever, Asher Benjamin, and Alexander Parris. Strickland was elected president and Walter secretary of the new organization called the American Institution of Architects. By May 1837, the Institution contained twenty-three professional members and twenty-five honorary members. But the society did not prosper, in particular because the members were scattered so widely and convening meetings was difficult. Although the organization gradually dissolved, it had laid the seed necessary for a professional society, and in 1857 it was reinvented as the American Institute of Architects, an organization that continues to this day. A. J. Davis was also a founding member of the 1857 A.I.A.

Davis and Town had terminated their official partnership on May 1, 1835, although they would on occasion work together on certain projects. They revived their partnership from May 1, 1842, to July 13, 1843, after which Town retired to his home in New Haven. Ithiel Town died on June 13, 1844, at age fifty-nine. Town's magnificent library was sold at auctions held prior to and after his death. Davis had benefited greatly from Town's library, not just through studying in it, but because he was able to purchase many books from Town over the years of their friendship.

After the dissolution of the Town and Davis partnership in 1835, Davis was associated briefly with Russell Warren (1783–1860), a native of Rhode Island who executed most of his works in that state. Together Davis and Warren produced several designs for the newly founded Bristol College in Pennsylvania. Offering designs in both Greek and Gothic Revival styles, one of the classical designs, featuring an Ionic entry portico, was ultimately built in a modified form (fig. 24). These designs for Bristol will be discussed in more depth later (see figs. 59 and 60). Another important commission executed by Davis and Warren was for the Dutch Reformed Church in Newburgh, New York, a Greek Revival building with an Ionic portico and high dome.

The association with Warren was short-lived, and from 1836 to 1878, Davis worked primarily

66. Newton, *Town and Davis,* 103–4; and Hamlin, *Greek Revival Architecture,* 60–61.

Fig. 24. White Hall, Bristol College, Bristol, Pennsylvania. Etching ca. 1860s. Designed by Alexander Jackson Davis, built ca. 1836; demolished. As executed, the entry portico actually had Ionic columns.
Etching from *The Bristol Pike* (1893), 342.

alone, except for the brief resurrection of the partnership with Ithiel Town during 1842–43. Occasionally Davis would hire additional draftsmen when needed, but for the next forty years Davis was the sole architect on the hundreds of designs he produced. Having moved his office to NYU in December 1838, he moved back to the new Merchants Exchange in 1842. Davis maintained his office at the Merchants Exchange until 1862, then returned to NYU, where he remained until 1878, at which time he retired to his home overlooking the Hudson River.

New York University and Bristol College were only two of the more than a dozen colleges and universities for whom A. J. Davis would design buildings. So prolific and well received were Davis's designs that he became known as the leading collegiate architect of the nineteenth century. Spanning the years 1831–70, his collegiate designs embraced the most popular styles of the day, from Greek (e.g., NYU, Girard, Bristol) and Gothic Revival (e.g., Michigan, Yale, Virginia Military), through to his later inventive adaptations in the bracketed and Tuscan Revival styles (e.g., Davidson College, New York Agricultural). Although about only half of his college designs were executed, most were publicized and well received. His designs for the University of Michigan in 1838 in the Collegiate Gothic style were especially noted and widely admired for their beauty, power, and originality (see plates). Davis himself is generally credited with coining the term *Collegiate Gothic*[67]

67. Turner, *Campus*, 124.

and for the transformation of the Gothic Revival style from the castellated form into one that seemed to reflect back on medieval sources and embrace ecclesiastical motifs, while yet endeavoring to produce new and original forms.

The years surrounding the Michigan designs were an extraordinary time for Davis. Not only were numerous important commissions executed—from residences to colleges to state capitols—but the year 1838 saw the publication of Davis's own pattern book entitled *Rural Residences, Consisting of Designs, Original and Selected, for Cottages, Farm-Houses, Villas, and Village Churches: with Brief Explanations, estimates, and a specification of materials, construction, etc.*[68] Enamored for years of the newly emerging Gothic Revival style, Davis felt it to be particularly suited for country residences, from small picturesque cottages to large estates, where the relation of the house to its natural environment was a prime concern. Intended to run to six volumes and include the work of other architects, only two volumes were published together in 1838, and all the designs contained therein were by Davis.[69] *Rural Residences* is considered the first true American pattern book, in which, unlike earlier builder's handbooks, designs were provided showing not only elevations, but also floor plans and notations on materials to be used and the probable cost of construction. It was also the first American architectural book to focus on country houses, and the first to be published in color. The designs, which were printed by the noted lithographers John H. Bufford and Nathaniel Currier,[70] were hand-colored. Davis also asked Samuel Morse to paint an original rural view for use on the title page, a romantic vignette that included a castellated Gothic villa.

Partly through the publication of *Rural Residences* and partly through several notable commissions for major country houses, Davis was to launch what has been referred to as American Picturesque architecture. Marrying building design with natural settings, this style would become extremely popular in the mid–nineteenth century and see the emergence of some of the greatest landscape architects. Beginning with the seeds of Gothic Revival, Davis sought ways to relate the buildings to their surroundings. In this he was influenced by the Hudson River school of artists, whose members included Davis's friends Samuel Morse and Thomas Cole. Davis also devised new forms based on Italian and Tuscan models, which he felt were equally as suited to rural scenes as the Gothic. Davis created the American bracketed style for residences, which combined elements of Gothic, Italian, and Tuscan. His designs and the publication of *Rural Residences* brought him to the notice of another man of immense talent and taste, Andrew J. Downing.

One of America's greatest landscape architects, Andrew Jackson Downing (1815–52) approached A. J. Davis in 1838 about providing illustrations for a book Downing was preparing for publication. The two men found they had strong similarities in taste in the area of rural and picturesque architecture. Downing provided Davis with rough sketches for illustrations he desired, from

68. Alexander Jackson Davis, *Rural Residences, Consisting of Designs, Original and Selected, for Cottages, Farm-Houses, Villas, and Village Churches: with Brief Explanations, estimates, and a specification of materials, construction, etc.* (New York: By the author, 1838).

69. The title page gives 1837 as the date of publication, but it was not actually published until 1838.

70. Jane B. Davies, introduction to *Rural Residences,* by Alexander Jackson Davis (New York: Da Capo Press, 1980).

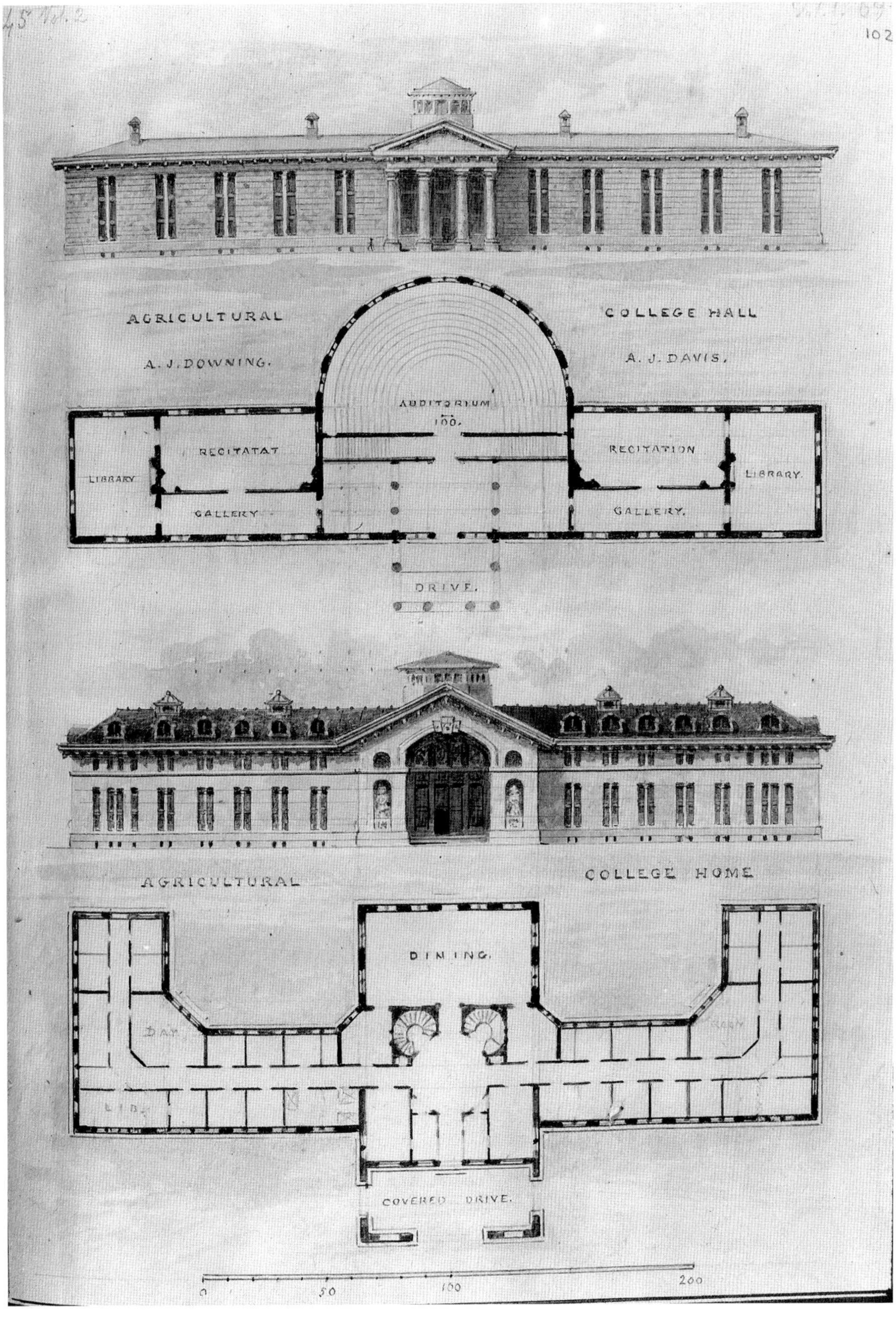

Fig. 25. Agricultural college, New York, 1849. Design by Alexander Jackson Davis and Andrew Jackson Downing. Not executed.

which Davis created artistic renderings, which were used in Downing's first book, *Landscape Gardening and Rural Architecture,* published in 1841.[71] Davis included illustrations of his own house designs, many of which had already been built. Until 1850, Downing and Davis would work in close collaboration, with Davis providing illustrations for all of Downing's books, as well as for his magazine, the *Horticulturist*. Downing in turn helped develop Davis's understanding of landscape design, and together they widely influenced the development of the American Picturesque style. In 1849–50, the two men worked together to produce designs for buildings for an agricultural college in New York. Featuring a central focal element with wings, as well as Daviséan windows, the designs for two buildings were in the Tuscan Revival style (fig. 25). The college was apparently never founded and the designs were not executed; it is not known what locale was intended for the college. Davis and Downing's fruitful collaboration would probably have continued for some years if Downing had not been tragically killed in the destruction by fire of the steamboat he was traveling on in 1852.

In 1838, A. J. Davis received a commission for what would be one of his most famous designs, a house called Knoll, built 1838–42 for William and Philip Paulding in Tarrytown, New York. Designed in the Gothic Revival style, this grand mansion would gain more fame when its second owner, George Merritt, asked Davis in 1864 to design an addition that would double the size of the house. Davis's design for the enlarged residence, renamed Lyndhurst, respected the original majesty of the house's Gothic style (fig. 26). Davis was so consumed by this project that he not only designed the elaborate interiors, but also much of the furniture. Today Lyndhurst, one of Davis's most pristine surviving buildings, is owned by the National Trust for Historic Preservation. Lyndhurst embodies in a grand manner Davis's love for the Gothic and Picturesque styles. Over the course of his long career he designed countless residences across the spectrum of the picturesque. These ran from Gothic mansions such as Glen Ellen (1832–34, Townson, Md.) and Ericstan (1855–59, Tarrytown, N.Y.), to Italian villas such as Grace Hill (1854, Brooklyn), and on down to small picturesque cottages dressed in Gothic, Tuscan, and bracketed forms.

In 1856, Davis began building a summer cottage for himself in West Orange, New Jersey. The Gothic Revival house, called Wildmont, was enlarged several times, in particular in 1878, when it became more a villa than a house, and included a tall conical tower. Davis remained a bachelor until after age fifty. In 1853, he married Margaret Beale, and they had two children, Flora Foster Davis (born 1854) and Joseph Beale Davis (born 1856). In 1878, after a career spanning half a century, Davis retired to his home at Wildmont. He spent his declining years gathering together his drawings, office diaries, and correspondences. He would make so many notations on his drawings and papers, and re-create some designs from memory, that it has been difficult for later researchers to

71. Andrew Jackson Downing, *A Treatise on the Theory and Practice of Landscape Gardening, Adapted to North America; with a view to the Improvement of Country Residences* (New York: Wiley and Putnam, 1841). In reprints often called *Landscape Gardening and Rural Architecture* (New York: Dover, 1991).

Fig. 26. Lyndhurst, George Merritt House, Tarrytown, New York, 1865. Design by Alexander Jackson Davis. Original section of house (called Knoll) built 1838–42; enlarged as Lyndhurst 1865; extant, a property of the National Trust for Historic Preservation.

Metropolitan Museum of Art, Harris Brisbane Dick Fund, 1924 (24.66.14).

determine when some of his drawings were actually executed, and if he did not in fact write up parts of his diaries in the 1880s. Davis also began compiling numerous albums in which his designs were to be grouped by styles and so forth, although most were far from complete at the time of his death, and his system for compiling these albums has been indecipherable to later historians.

Wildmont was several times struck by lightning, and in 1884 it burned down. Sadly, a great deal of Davis's papers and drawings were lost in the fire, in particular, Davis indicated, his albums pertaining to Ithiel Town. Since a large number of Davis's drawings survive, not to mention office diaries and volumes of correspondence, it challenges the imagination to picture the vastness of his collection before the fire. It is tempting, yet fruitless, to speculate on the nature of the documents that were lost. Davis made drawings to have Wildmont rebuilt, but these were not carried to fruition. He moved into his son's house nearby, where he spent his remaining years. On January 14, 1892, Alexander Jackson Davis, architectural composer, father of American Picturesque architecture, and first architect of the University of Michigan, died at home. He was eighty-eight years old.

In the course of his growth as an architect, the gifted Alexander Jackson Davis was inspired and influenced by a talented group of architects and artists whose spheres of influence revolved with his. These most notably included architects Ithiel Town, Martin Thompson, and James Dakin, as well as landscape architect Andrew Jackson Downing, and artists John Trumbull, Samuel Morse, and Thomas Cole. Out of this melting pot of ideas, imagination, and great talent came the sources of the University of Michigan's earliest buildings.

The Ann Arbor Campus 1838–50

THE REGENTS OF THE UNIVERSITY OF MICHIGAN had determined by late summer 1838 that they would seek plans for the first buildings on the new Ann Arbor campus from Alexander Jackson Davis, and on August 7, 1838, Lieutenant-Governor Edward Mundy, representing the board of regents, visited Davis in his offices at New York University to discuss the designs.[1] Davis's name first appears in the regents' records on September 16, 1838, on which date the board adopted Davis's plan and resolved to build the first section of it (*RP*, 55). Four-and-one-half months later, on January 31, 1839, the regents terminated their contract with Davis and decided to build something completely different. It is important to know that for three-and-one-half of those four-and-one-half months (September 18, 1838–January 4, 1839) the regents did not meet. Still, in early January 1839 they were resolved to execute at least part of Davis's plan. But just three meetings later, on January 31, 1839, the regents did an about-face and seemingly abandoned Davis's plans. Instead of the large Gothic structures designed by Davis (see plates), the regents decided to build four houses for professors in a simple classical style (see figs. 37 and 44). The source of the design for these houses, and the emergence in the record of two builders, Isaac Thomson and Harpin Lum, is the mystery whose solution is being attempted here.

Beginning with the documentation most readily available to Michigan historians, the *Proceedings* of the regents' meetings, a sketch of the pertinent events of 1838–41 can be laid out. Considering that these *Proceedings* were to serve as the university's official records of the time, the paucity of information contained therein on the subject of buildings leaves the door open for many questions. What is recorded can be quickly summarized. On September 16 and 17, 1838, the regents adopted the plan provided by Alexander J. Davis (fig. 27), decided to begin building a portion of it immediately, and appointed Isaac Thompson builder for the university.[2] Regents George Morell and Zina Pitcher were asked to prepare a contract with Davis and Thompson, which was presented to the regents at their next meeting on January 5, 1839. There is no indication in the regents' minutes that Davis ever visited Michigan, nor was this contract transcribed into the minutes, and it does not survive among the university's documents in Michigan. (However, the contract survives elsewhere, as will be explained.)

1. Office Diary 1827–53, p. 189, A. J. Davis Papers, NYPL.

2. See note 24, this chapter.

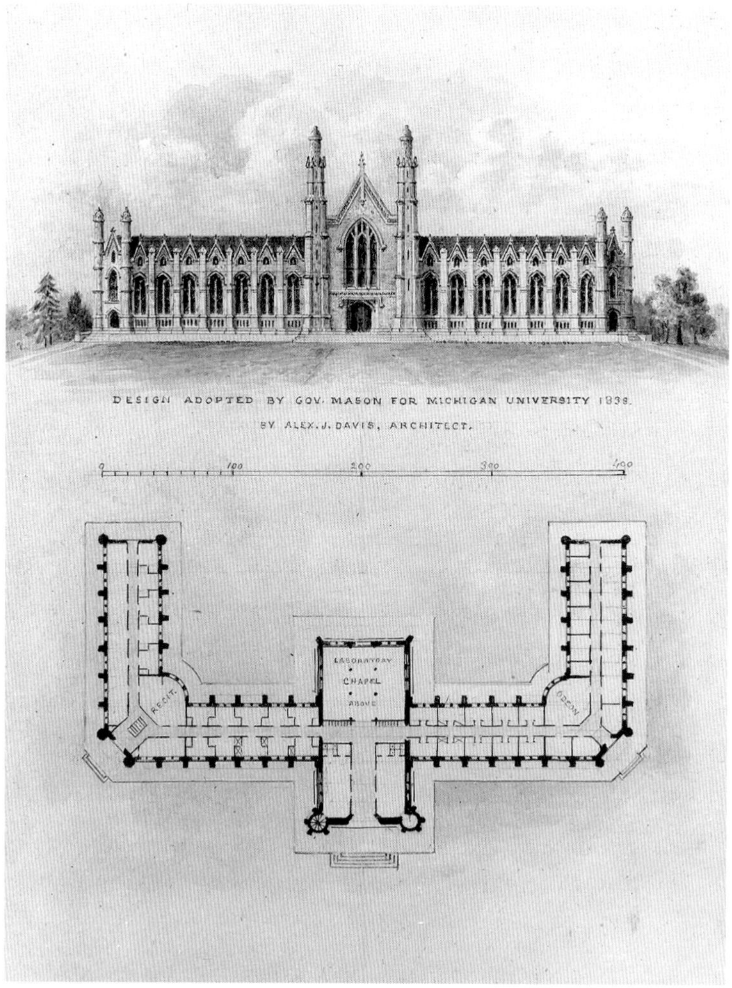

Fig. 27. University of Michigan, Ann Arbor, 1838. Design by Alexander Jackson Davis. Not executed.

Metropolitan Museum of Art, Harris Brisbane Dick Fund, 1924 (24.66.1406[81], vol. 7 scrapbook).

On January 31, 1839, the regents made two important decisions, which were to authorize the construction of the four houses for professors, and to annul the contract with Davis and Thompson and to enter into a new contract with just Thompson. The reasons for this change are not explained, nor are Thompson's duties, which however, can be presumed to continue as builder for the university. Whether Davis's plans were entirely abandoned is never made clear, but on February 11, 1839, the board adopted a new plan for the buildings they had authorized at their previous meeting, that is, the four houses for professors. The regents' minutes continue sparse, but by July 12, 1839, the houses were under construction, and the regents requested a full report from the Building Committee concerning the buildings under construction, including information on contracts, costs, and estimates. On the following day, July 13, the contract with Isaac Thompson was annulled, and a new contract was entered into with a Mr. Lum for the completion of the four houses. This is the first mention of Harpin Lum in the *Regents' Proceedings*,[3] although a report filed by the Building Committee the following year, on March 6, 1840, describes the committee as having contracted with Lum as early as February 1839 (*RP,* 124–27; see appendix). None of the contracts entered into with Thompson or Lum appear to have survived. In any case, Lum became superintendent of building for the university and saw the construction of the four houses to completion in the summer of 1840. A few months earlier, in April 1840, the regents had determined to construct the university's Main Building, and on April 8, 1840, they adopted a plan submitted by Harpin Lum (see fig. 46). Lum was also contracted to build the Main Building, which was begun by July 1840 and completed by autumn 1841.

This brief recitation of the facts as described in the *Regents' Proceedings* does little to shed light on the mystery at hand. What was the nature of the "plans" provided by Alexander Jackson Davis, and were they entirely abandoned? The regents provide virtually no description of these plans, but to mention a "Main Building," "North Wing," and later a "Chapel and Museum" (*RP,* 55, 60). Although at least one Gothic design was publicized, none of Davis's drawings survive at Michigan to illuminate this issue, except for two floor plans for a Gothic building (see figs. 34 and 35). Fortunately, several of Davis's drawings for Michigan survive in New York City, and although all are for Gothic designs, they nevertheless reveal that Davis provided not only specific building designs (e.g., Main Building, North Wing, library-chapel) but also campus plans (see plates). This will have significant bearing on the story as it unfolds. Relying solely on the *Regents' Proceedings* leaves innumerable questions about how the regents migrated from Davis's elaborate Gothic designs to the simple classical structures that were built. When the regents annulled their contract with Davis, did they in fact give up all intention of executing any part of his plans? With Isaac Thompson continuing on the job, there is no reason to suppose that Davis's plans were entirely abandoned. He was well paid for his work, so the regents would have been justified in having a design of his executed by someone else. There is also the mystery of who Isaac Thompson and Harpin Lum were, and how they became involved in the University of Michigan's building projects. What role might they have played in the design of the professors' houses and the Main Building that were actually constructed between 1839 and 1841? It is apparent that the *Regents' Proceedings* alone are not enough to answer these questions. However, sources outside Michigan exist, many of them previously unknown, that help unravel the mystery of how Davis's Gothic designs of 1838 metamorphosed into the five classical buildings that stood, newly completed, when the University of Michigan opened for class for the first time in the fall of 1841.

3. The minutes that make up the first volume of the published *Regents' Proceedings* (1837–64) were transcribed in 1915 by Professor Isaac Newton Demmon. As he describes, the original minutes are in two thick folio volumes of 1,129 closely written pages, in the handwritings of ten different men who served as secretary for the board of regents during this time. Prof. Demmon misread the spelling of Lum's first name, recording it as Haspier. However, other persons reading the original minutes were able to decipher the spelling as Harpin, which turns out to be correct. "Harpin Lum" will be used throughout this paper, as the misspelling was a result of Prof. Demmon's transcription, and not an error on the part of the Board secretary who originally wrote it down. This is not true in the case of the misspelling of Isaac Thomson's name, which is explained in note 24, this chapter. Board of Regents Records, Bentley.

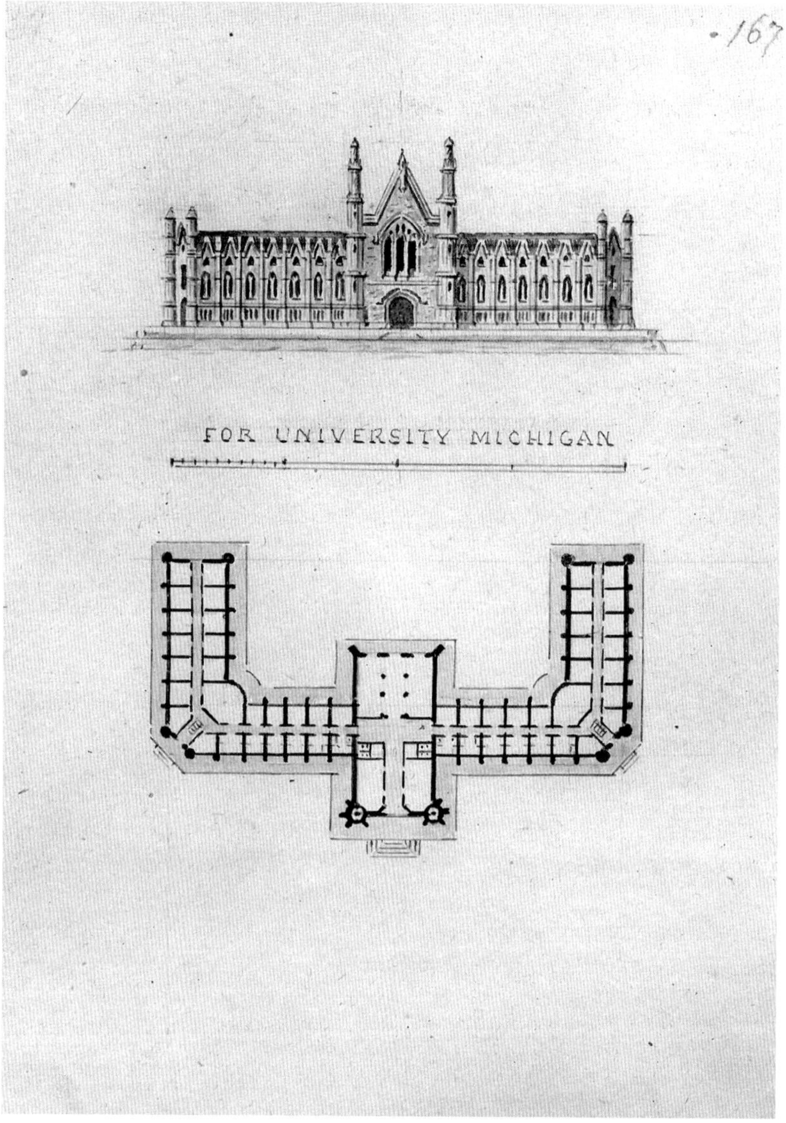

Fig. 28. University of Michigan, Ann Arbor, 1838. Design by Alexander Jackson Davis. Not executed.

Metropolitan Museum of Art, Harris Brisbane Dick Fund, 1924 (24.66.1401[144], vol. 2 diary, no. 167, blue-book folio P).

Following the visit of Lieutenant-Governor Edward Mundy in August 1838, Alexander Jackson Davis was assured of his position as architect for the University of Michigan, although he had earlier begun work on the project under the belief that the job would be his. It is possible that Davis had rough drawings to show Mundy when he arrived at Davis's office at New York University, such as the sketch in figure 28. There is also some evidence to suggest that Mundy spent several days in New York meeting with Davis. Surviving letters of Asa Gray's indicate that the regents had planned to meet in Detroit on August 16, 1838, to discuss the issue of the campus buildings, "but as Lieutenant-Governor Mundy had not arrived there was no quorum. It seems that Mundy has not managed well, and has allowed the plans to be delayed, and Davis, instead of sending the plans he promised, is coming out here to see for himself."[4] Asa Gray, a botanist, was the first professor appointed by the regents in 1838 and was keenly interested in the development of the campus site. Evidently the regents expected Mundy to return to Detroit with some drawings from Davis, but Davis apparently wished to have additional information on the actual site before developing the more elaborate plans he would present to the regents.

Toward this end, Davis undertook a trip to Michigan in September 1838. For many years it has been assumed that Davis remained in Michigan for six weeks, which seems an extraordinarily long time for Davis to stay at one project site, especially during one of his most prolific years. The source of this information is one of the volumes of Davis's diaries held by the Metropolitan Museum of Art. Although portions of his papers made their way to the Avery Library at Columbia University, as well as the New York Public Library and the New-York Historical Society, those at the Metropolitan Museum were more well known. One reason was the publication of Edna Donnell's monograph on Davis, which was based on the collection of Davis's drawings and diaries that had been newly acquired by the Metropolitan.[5] In her research for this paper, Donnell had been in contact with persons at Michigan, in particular Wilfred B. Shaw, director of alumni relations, delineator of views of university buildings, and erstwhile historian.[6] Frank E. Robbins, assistant to the university president, also corresponded with Donnell on this issue.[7] Shaw and Robbins were interested in the sources of the University of Michigan's earliest buildings and their possible relation to Davis. Edna Donnell was in touch with others at Michigan as well, writing in June 1936 to a Miss Paine about three watercolor drawings related to Michigan in the Metropolitan's collection, and her attribution of another unlabeled drawing to Michigan, which she planned to use in her monograph (see fig. 62).[8] In this letter Donnell mentioned an entry in Davis's diary that indicated he visited Ann Arbor in September 1838 and was absent six weeks.[9] Other historians have relied on

4. Letter Asa Gray to Mrs. Torrey, dated Detroit, August 16, 1838, *Letters of Asa Gray,* ed. Jane Loring Gray (London: Macmillan, 1893), 1:76–78. Mrs. Torrey was the wife of Dr. John Torrey, a famous New York botanist for whom Asa Gray worked as an assistant. Dr. Torrey was also a friend of Charles Whipple, secretary of the board of regents, with whom Asa Gray discussed the campus plans at length. As classes were not to commence for some time, the regents assigned Professor Gray the duty of procuring books for the university's library. Gray wholeheartedly embraced this task and sailed to Europe for this purpose. In 1842, after acquiring a significant number of books for the University of Michigan, Gray resigned from the university, before having ever taught a class, and went on to a distinguished career at Harvard.

5. Donnell, "Davis and Gothic Revival."

6. Alexander Jackson Davis Papers and Letters, etc., M–Z, file folder labeled "University of Michigan," Met. The Metropolitan Museum retains files related to Donnell's research, in particular, correspondence.

7. Frank E. Robbins Papers, box 1, Bentley. Among Robbins's papers are several related to his pursuit of information on the Davis connection to Michigan. These include the following letters: Frank E. Robbins (FER) to Frank Baldwin, secretary for the American Institute of Architects, December 16, 1930; Edward C. Kemper, executive secretary for the American Institute of Architects, to FER, December 23, 1930; Hobart Upjohn, architect in New York, to FER, January 6, 1931; FER to Hobart Upjohn, January 8, 1931; Hobart Upjohn to FER, April 27, 1931; FER to Edna Donnell, May 29, 1931; Edna Donnell to FER, June 11, 1931; and FER to Edna Donnell, June 15, 1931. Robbins wrote to the American Institute of Architects asking where Davis's papers might be located or how to reach surviving family members. The AIA referred Robbins to the New York architect Hobart Upjohn, and between them Robbins was led to the collections of Davis's papers that had been deposited recently in the Metropolitan Museum of Art and the New-York Historical Society, after the death of Davis's son. Robbins corresponded with Edna Donnell following Wilfred Shaw's visit with Donnell in New York.

8. Donnell, "Davis and Gothic Revival," 185. The illustration is labeled "Fig. 1,—Unexecuted design by Davis for the University of Michigan—A Project for Gothicizing a Building by Adding an Entrance in the Gothic Style."

9. Letter Edna Donnell to Miss Paine, June 26, 1936, Alexander Jackson Davis Papers and Letters, etc., M–Z, file folder labeled "University of Michigan," Met. Donnell's letter reads, "We have in the Print Department three large water-color drawings by A. J. Davis labelled as studies for the University of Michigan [she lists North Wing—east front, North

this source when discussing Davis's trip to Michigan, especially biographer Roger Hale Newton.[10] This diary entry reads:

Sept. 1838	Designs for University of Michigan	600.00
	Visit to Ann Arbor. Absent six weeks. Paid Isaac Thompson $200 for visit and estimates[11]	

Davis did not, however, visit Ann Arbor for six weeks. A more detailed account of his trip was recorded in another office diary of his, which is in the possession of the New York Public Library.[12] Davis left New York on September 2, 1838, and traveled by "steamboat Erie for Detroit, 10 A.M. touched at Dunkirk, Erie, Cleveland, Sandusky, Toledo, at Detroit 2 days and 2 nights. Am. Hotel. Detroit." Davis also recorded that he met with Governor Mason, Chancellor Farnsworth, and Dr. Zina Pitcher in Detroit. On September 7, Davis traveled with Isaac Thompson by railroad to Ypsilanti, then by stage to Ann Arbor, where they "Put up at Thompson's Exchange Hotel" for eight days. On September 15, Davis returned to Detroit, where he stayed for three days, departing the evening of September 18. In this diary, Davis recorded the rest of his six weeks' absence from New York. He traveled through Ohio and Virginia, then on to Washington, Philadelphia, and home to New York on October 11, 1838.

In the eight days he was in Ann Arbor, Davis would have had ample opportunity to get to know the town and the forty-acre parcel that had been deeded to the regents for the site of the new university. It must have been exciting to Davis to have the entire expanse of this site as a blank canvas upon which he could create whatever vision he chose for this important institution. Whether or not the regents provided any guidelines or parameters for Davis in executing his design is not known. Nothing concerning Davis's visit to Ann Arbor is recorded in the *Regents' Proceedings* or elsewhere. In fact, nothing survives to shed light on any deliberations or meetings that must have occurred between Davis and various members of the board. Did the regents provide any input or suggestions to Davis on what they envisioned for the university, or did they give Davis a completely free hand? The only indication to survive of any serious thought being given to the campus plan by someone at Michigan prior to Davis's arrival is contained in Asa Gray's letters. Gray is

Wing—west front, and library-chapel] and one drawing with no inscription which I believe to be a study for an entrance door for the University of Michigan and which I am reproducing as plate no. 1 in my forthcoming Studies article. There is only one notation in the Davis diary, as follows: [lists the entry for Sept. 1838 in which it is indicated Davis visited Michigan and was absent six weeks]. The question of whether or not Davis designed the buildings for the University of Michigan has come up again and again. I have had correspondence on this subject with Mr. Robbins and after going over the excerpts from the Regents Proceedings of the University of Michigan I have come to the conclusion that Davis had no part in the buildings that were executed."

10. Newton, *Town and Davis*, 236.

11. Vol. 1, Diary, p. 61, Alexander Jackson Davis Collection, Met, Harris Brisbane Dick Fund, 1924 (24.66.1400).

12. Office Diary 1827–53, pp. 191–92, A. J. Davis Papers, NYPL. The hotel in Ann Arbor mentioned by Davis was William R. Thompson's Ann Arbor Exchange, one of several inns in the town, as advertised in the *Michigan Argus*, in the late 1830s (per an index of the newspaper compiled by Louis Doll, Ann Arbor, 1941). Thompson's hotel, considered the finest between Detroit and Chicago, was more commonly called the Washtenaw House and was built in 1832 in "Lower Town," a section of Ann Arbor north of the Huron River (but at a lower elevation than the rest of the village). Chapman and Co., *History of Washtenaw County, Michigan* (Chicago, 1881), 440, 888.

never mentioned in any official records in terms of the physical development of the campus, yet his letters indicate that he was developing plans on his own that he wished the regents to adopt. In visits to Ann Arbor and Detroit in mid-August 1838, Gray met with Governor Mason and several regents on the topic of the campus plan and recounted that of the proposed site "all speak in glowing terms of the beauty of the location for the university."[13] Gray's strongest ally in his planning task was Charles Whipple, a Detroit lawyer who was serving as the first secretary of the board of regents, although he was not an actual appointed member of the board. Recapping his activities of August 16, 1838, to a friend, Gray wrote:

> I spent the whole morning with Mr. Whipple, who is really a downright clever fellow in both the English and the Yankee senses of the term. We compared notes fully about the university and everything about the matter we could think of. I obtained all the information he could afford me about what they were doing, and contemplated doing. I told him fully what I wished to do, and in everything I believe we understood each other and agreed wonderfully. This is important, because Whipple, although secretary of the board, is not a member; yet he is the moving spirit of the whole, and throws his whole energy into the work. We owe the plan adopted as to the arrangement of buildings, etc, to him, and he carried it over considerable opposition. As I know it is just what will please the doctor [John Torrey, botanist and friend of Gray's] I mention it here. It is to have the professors' houses entirely distinct from both the university building and the dormitories of the students. The grounds are nearly square, and are to be entirely surrounded by an avenue. He proposed to have a university building for lecture-rooms, library, laboratory, etc., but to contain no students and no families; to have two lateral buildings for students and the tutors who have the immediate charge of them. Then to build professors' houses on the other side of the quadrangle, fronting the main building, each with about an acre of land for yard and garden, by which the houses will not only be away from the students, but at sufficient distance from each other to render them retired and quiet. It is quite a point with him that the professors shall have retired, comfortable houses, so that they shall be subject to no annoyance.[14]

This letter raises certain questions about the planning endeavor. Gray mentioned a plan by himself and Whipple as having been adopted by the regents, yet there is no record of such a plan ever being discussed, much less adopted, in the regents' records. Other than these few obscure letters by Gray, nothing has been known of his attempt to have a plan adopted before the architect Davis was due to arrive in Ann Arbor. In another letter, dated from Ann Arbor, August 20, 1838, Gray wrote, "The grounds for the university are very prettily situated. The only possible fault I

13. Letter Asa Gray to Mrs. Torrey, August 12–14, 1838, *Letters of Asa Gray*, 1:75.

14. Letter Asa Gray to Mrs. Torrey, August 16, 1838, *Letters of Asa Gray*, 1:76–78.

can imagine is that they are too level. I have contrived a plan for the arrangement of the grounds which gives satisfaction to the members of the board here, and I think will suit all."[15] Gray further indicated that Davis was expected in Ann Arbor in about ten days' time and that the regents asked Gray to wait for Davis's arrival, but Gray wished to return immediately to New York, and so never met with Davis. Gray, however, apparently left more than one version of his campus plan with the regents, in the hope that it would have some influence on the plans Davis would develop. In route back to New York on August 20, 1838, Gray wrote to his friend:

> But before I could reach New York, Mr. Davis, according to his appointment, would be at Detroit, and it is possible that a very few days would enable us to settle almost everything about the arrangement of the grounds, the internal disposition of the university building, and the plan of professors' houses. I feel so strong a hope that the doctor [John Torrey] will be persuaded to take a professorship that I have fixed upon the place for his house, should my plan for the arrangement of the grounds be adopted. . . . I am anxious that the proper means should be adopted to supply the university and houses with water in abundance, and at such a level that it can be taken into the second story of the professors' houses; I think you may imagine one reason I am so solicitous about this matter. I was pleased to find on my arrival here that this subject had already received much attention and there is a determination, on the part of nearly all the regents I have conversed with, to effect this object at whatever expense. Of the different plans in contemplation only one, I think, will effectually answer the purpose. I have some hope that the subject will be acted upon at the first meeting after Mr. Davis arrives.[16]

Gray apparently included in his plans provisions for professors' houses, as well as indicating that buildings to house students should be separate from those that housed the classrooms. Whether or not any of Gray's plans were shown to Davis is unknown. Davis, in his subsequent designs, did allow for professors' houses on the opposite side of the campus from the main building, but in all the plans he developed, students were to be housed in the same large building as the classrooms, museum, and library. None of the plans that Asa Gray indicated he drew have survived, but it is probable that after his many discussions with the regents on the issue, some influence of his may have trickled down to Davis and been incorporated in his plans, even if it were simply in the idea to place professors' houses on the far side of the campus. Gray and Whipple's idea for separate classroom and dormitory buildings seems to have had no influence on Davis, who probably had a well-developed idea of his one large Gothic building in mind before venturing to Ann Arbor, a design that may have been the result of the meetings Davis had in New York with Edward Mundy. The regents, too, may not have been persuaded by Gray in this issue of buildings

15. Letter Asa Gray to Mrs. Torrey, August 20, 1838, *Letters of Asa Gray,* 1:80.

16. Ibid., 81–82. Frank Robbins was also intrigued by Gray's letters and the implications his supposed campus plans might have for later scholars tackling the issue of Davis's plans and his influence on the development of the professors' houses (Frank E. Robbins, "Asa Gray's Visit to Ann Arbor," in *Michigan Alumnus* 36, no. 25 [April 12, 1930]: 483–84).

and probably felt committed to accepting designs from the qualified, experienced, and highly regarded architect whom they had retained.

The issue of the University of Michigan's first buildings would have been of the highest concern to the regents. The design and execution of the structures would reflect on their leadership abilities and their decision to select this architect. And, as the first institution of higher learning founded under the state constitution, the physical embodiment of its ideals would speak to the nation on behalf of the state. The design of the first buildings must necessarily have been of the utmost concern to the regents, who with foresight had engaged such a prominent architect, and who must have had many dialogues with Davis during his stay in Ann Arbor. In particular, the members of the Building Committee (Farnsworth, Mundy, and Fletcher), the governor, and other very active regents such as Zina Pitcher and Jonathan Kearsley would have felt the design of their building to be vital to the success and soon-to-develop reputation of the university.

A. J. Davis did not fail them. It is apparent that during his visit to Ann Arbor he more fully developed his idea for a main building in the Gothic Revival style. He certainly painted some of his beautiful watercolors while in the city (see plates) and recorded the purchase of supplies necessary to this task—a drawing board, $2.50, T square, $1.00, and painting materials, $1.50.[17] It was important for Davis to present renderings to the regents that would reflect his fully realized concepts. Davis not only drew elevations for the main building, he also embraced the large site and provided a master plan that encompassed the university's forty acres (fig. 29). This plan placed the main Gothic structure facing west on the primary street (State Street) and set back to allow a generous lawn. Davis included extensive landscaping with a botanic garden, around which were clustered houses for professors. It is very interesting that Davis's plan provides for these houses (in a variety of footprints) but does not include possible locations for future university buildings. With the large main building set so far back from the street, placing other buildings so that they would relate to this structure would present an interesting challenge, especially if the professors' houses had been built on the far (east) side of the site. A U-shaped building seems to preclude the development of a row along the lines of Yale, although a mirror image U on the other side of the "public avenue" would have been a possibility.

The inclusion of a botanic garden is also notable and raises the question of whether the regents had some input into this and other aspects of the design. In must be remembered that by the time the regents acquired the forty-acre site there were few trees remaining, and the grounds were mostly covered by a wheat field, a peach orchard, and pastures.[18] A little bit of landscaping and a botanic garden would certainly have been desirable. Davis included more extensive landscaping in a second version of his plan (fig. 30).[19] This plan is similar to that in figure 29 except that in this one

17. Office Diary 1827–53, p. 192, A. J. Davis Papers, NYPL.

18. Peckham, *Making of University of Michigan*, 18.

19. This drawing is undated, and although probably executed at the same time as that in figure 29, it is also possible that it was drawn from memory by Davis in later years.

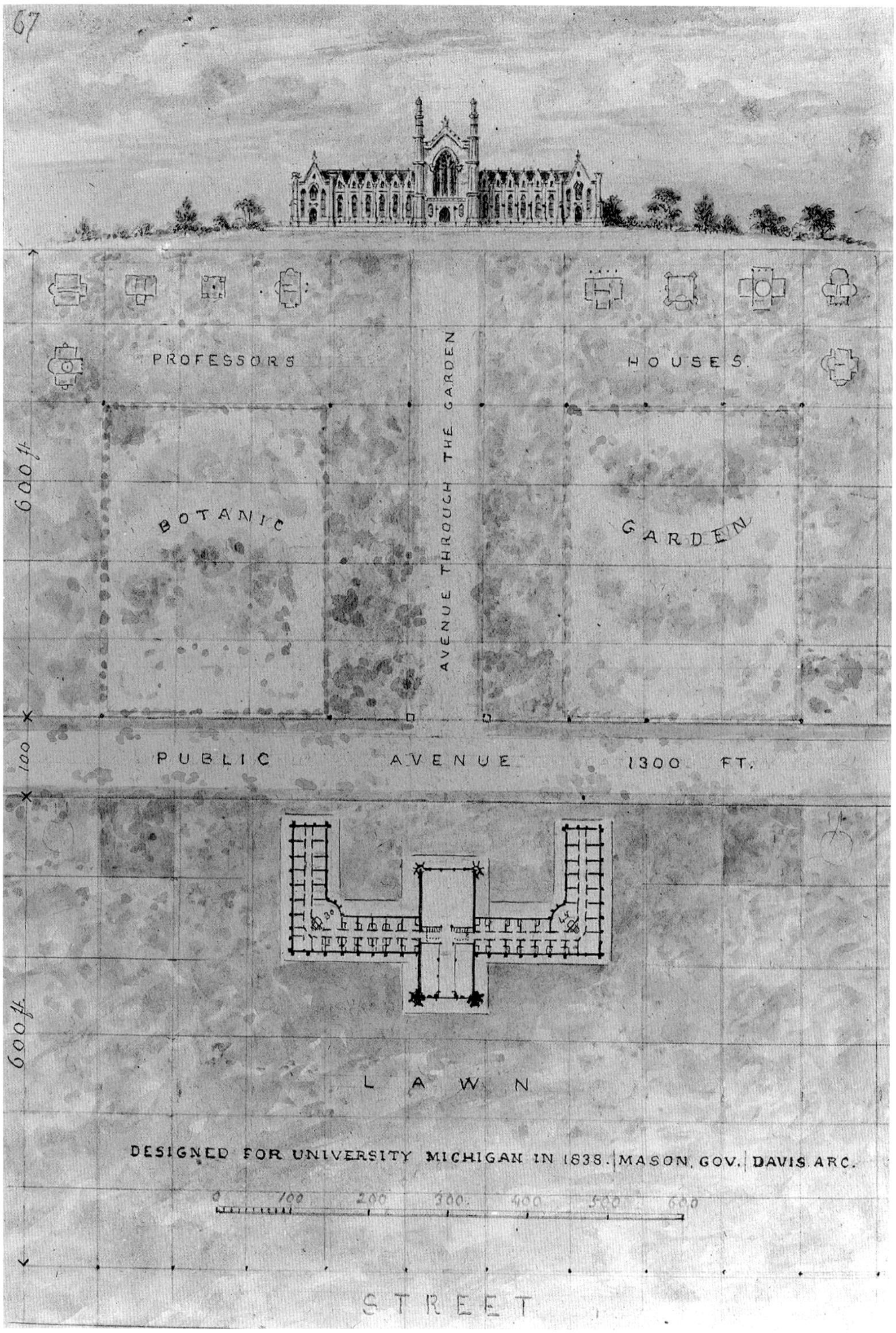

Fig. 29. University of Michigan, Ann Arbor, campus plan and elevation, 1838. Design by Alexander Jackson Davis. Not executed.

Metropolitan Museum of Art, Harris Brisbane Dick Fund, 1924 (24.66.1404, leaf 97v, vol. 5 diary, p. 67).

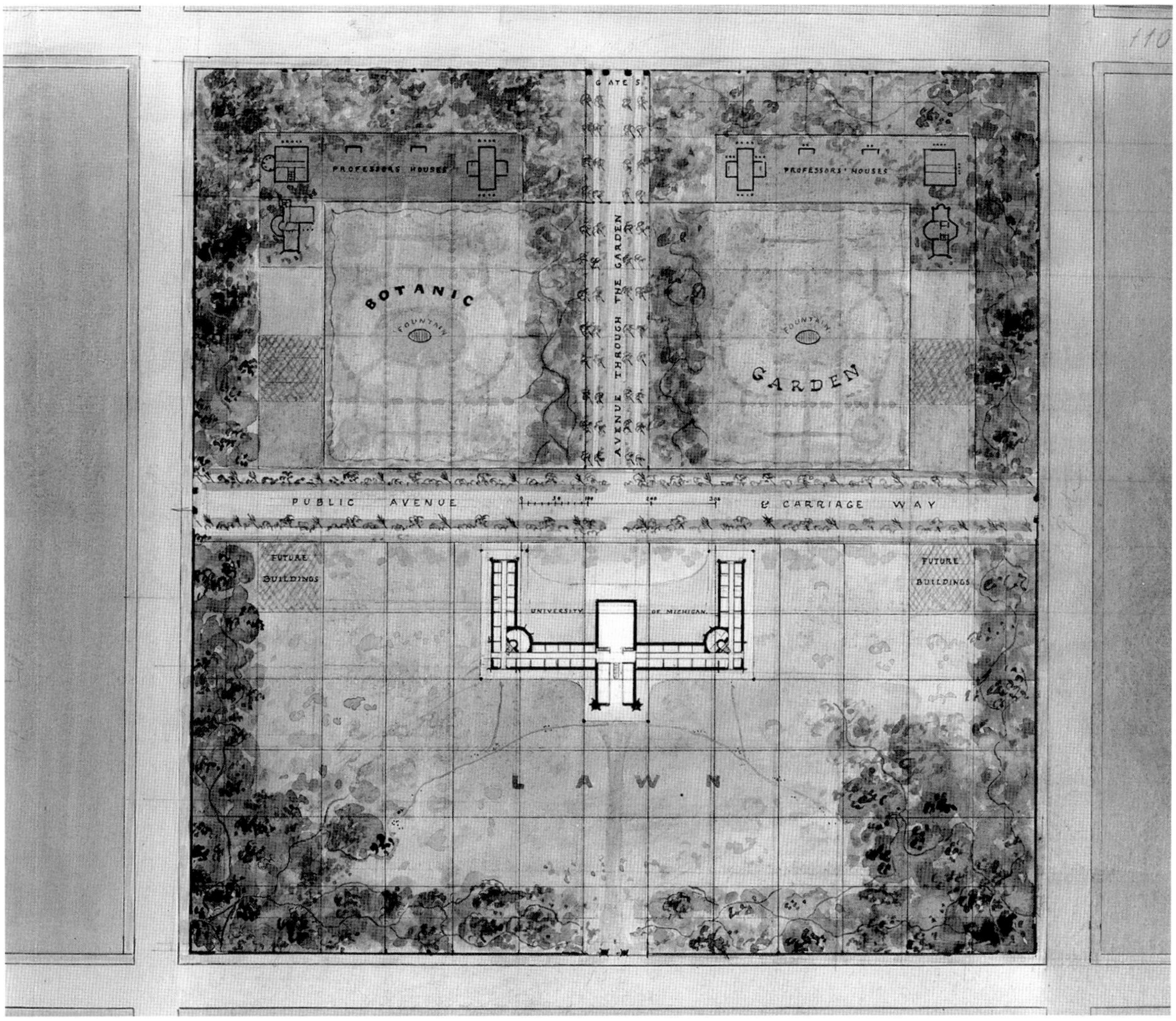

Fig. 30. University of Michigan, Ann Arbor, campus plan, 1838. Design by Alexander Jackson Davis. Not executed. Metropolitan Museum of Art, Harris Brisbane Dick Fund, 1924 (24.66.640).

Davis has provided possible sites for future buildings, which interestingly correspond roughly to the sites ultimately chosen for the four professors' houses built in 1840.

Davis left Ann Arbor on September 15, 1838, and his designs (probably including figs. 1, 27, and 29) were presented to the regents on September 16. Whether Davis attended this meeting and presented his own designs is not known; his presence was not recorded, but it was procedure for only board members present to be recorded, not other spectators. Davis was in Detroit on that day, where the regents' meetings were held at the state capitol, so it is likely he attended to submit his designs. The regents' reaction to Davis's plan was recorded as follows: "On motion of Justice Morell, the plan offered by Alexander J. Davis, Architect of New York City, was adopted by yeas and nays as follows [all voted yea]. . . . On motion of Dr. Denton, Resolved, That the Main Building and eight sections of the North Wing, as specified in the plan of Mr. Davis, be immediately commenced" (*RP*, 55). That this board, which habitually split on votes, unanimously approved Davis's plan can be taken to mean they enthusiastically approved of the design. They had good reason to be excited about the prospect of such a structure that would have had a profound visual impact on the still-young rural town. Davis's design embodied the qualities the regents would have held essential for the new university—strength, monumentality, beauty, and an aura of presence and permanence. Certainly few other new collegiate edifices of the time in America measured up in terms of grandeur and scope.

At the same meeting on September 16, 1838, nominations were made for the person who would act as builder for the university. Among those nominated were Charles Lum (by Zina Pitcher) and Isaac Thompson (by Lucius Lyon). The nominations were "laid on the table" and taken up the next day. Charles Lum was a builder and architect from Detroit. In fact, he was one of two Lums residing in Detroit at this time who had the same given profession; the other was David O. Lum.[20] On the following day, September 17, 1838, Isaac Thompson of Connecticut was appointed builder for the university by a vote of five to four, and "On motion of Judge Fletcher a Committee of two of the Board was appointed to prepare a contract between the Board and the Builder and Architect. Judge Morell and Dr. Pitcher were appointed said Committee" (*RP*, 56). Whether or not Isaac Thompson was in Michigan at this time is not made clear by the *Regents' Proceedings*, although the reference to the preparation of a contract would imply that both Davis and Thompson were in town [Detroit] to negotiate the terms. In fact, Davis confirms Thompson's presence in an entry in his diary for September 1838 that reads, "Plans for University of Michigan, inc. expenses of going, absent 6 weeks. $600. Paid I. Thompson. for accompanying 200 = 400."[21]

The regents, on September 17, 1838, approved a payment of $600 to Davis, which is also recorded in the financial report, as paid to A. J. Davis on September 18, 1838, by the Bank of Michigan (*RP*, 56, 104–5).[22] The payment of such a large sum to Davis for initial drawings (he would have produced presentation drawings and not working drawings at this early date) has been a source of considerable mystery and speculation to historians, especially since Davis often charged on a per drawing basis. Relying on the most widely used direct source of information, Davis's papers at the Metropolitan Museum of Art, the deduction has been that Davis must have prepared a large number of drawings. In his diary Davis listed his typical architect's fees, per drawing, for a medium building.[23]

20. MacCabe's Detroit City Directory 1837, listing for Charles Lum, architect and builder, on Congress at the corner of Brush St. (the directory also lists D. O. Lum, architect and builder, on Atwater St.), Bentley; Detroit City Directory 1845, listing for Charles Lum, David Lum, and William Lum, all carpenters at 85 Congress St., Clements Library, University of Michigan; Wellings Detroit City Directory 1846, listing for Charles Lum, architect, and David O. Lum and William Lum, joiners, Bentley; Shove's Detroit City Directory 1852–53, listing for Charles Lum, landscape painter, and David O. Lum of Lum and Ford, architects and draftsmen, Hatcher Graduate Library, University of Michigan; and Detroit City Directory 1853–54, listing for Charles M. Lum, artist, no address, and David O. Lum, architect, with an office in Masonic Hall, Burton Historical Collection, Detroit Public Library.

21. Office Diary 1827–53, p. 189, A. J. Davis Papers, NYPL.

22. The *Regents' Proceedings* as transcribed by Prof. Demmon show a payment of $60.00 to Davis on 9/18/1838, but this is most likely an error by Demmon in copying from the handwritten ledger, as the regents approved $600.00, and Davis recorded receiving that amount.

23. Vol. 6, Diary, folio R, p. 9, Alexander Jackson Davis Collection, Met, Harris Brisbane Dick Fund, 1924 (24.66.1405).

These ranged from $5 for sections and details, to $10 for secondary elevations, to $15 for principal elevations and plans. Even adding the 1 percent he listed for a first set of designs without working details, a fee of $600 implies a very large number of drawings, on the order of forty to fifty or more. It is unlikely Davis produced even a fraction of that number while in Michigan. The mystery was compounded by the fact that Davis and Thompson were paid an additional $625 in January 1839, and $616 in February 1839. This totaled more than $1,800 in less than five months' time, during which there were more than three months of no activity.

The mystery of the high fees paid is solved only by the introduction of a new piece of evidence, heretofore unknown to Michigan historians. This is the actual contract executed between the regents and Davis and Thompson. The regents appointed a committee of two on September 17, 1838, to prepare this contract, and on January 5, 1839, "Dr. Pitcher presented a contract entered into between the Board and Messrs. Davis and Thompson" (*RP,* 60). However, the terms of the contract are not entered into the *Regents' Proceedings,* and no copy of the document appears to have survived in Michigan. Fortunately, an original signed copy was kept by Davis and is among his papers preserved in the Avery Library at Columbia University.

The contract was entered into not only by the regents and Davis, but also the selected builder of the university, Isaac Thompson [*sic*]. Not much has been known about the gentleman except that he was from Connecticut. In fact, Isaac *Thomson*[24] was from New Haven, where he had a long career as a builder, and also referred to himself as an architect. He apparently worked on a number of projects for Davis and Ithiel Town, and was a logical choice to accompany Davis to Michigan. Isaac Thomson was born in either 1797 or 1798, as he died on April 21, 1873, at age 75, and was buried in the Grove Street Cemetery in New Haven.[25] From New Haven's earliest city directories (1843–44) through until 1872 (one year prior to his death), Isaac Thomson is regularly listed with his occupation variously given as architect and builder (1843–44), mason and builder (1862), or as part of the firm of Thomson, Smith and Sperry, contractors and mason builders (1872). A street guide for 1841 also lists Isaac Thomson as architect and builder, and in fact Thomson Square in New Haven is named for him.[26]

The day after authorized to do so, Regent Pitcher prepared a contract with Alex J. Davis, architect, and Isaac Thomson, builder. Signed on September 18, 1838, by Davis, Thomson, and Governor Stevens T. Mason on behalf of the board, the contract is a remarkable and informative

24. The correct spelling of his name was *Thomson,* without the *p*. Despite the fact that this was how he signed the contract with the University of Michigan, the records of the regents persisted in spelling it *Thompson*. Surprisingly, A. J. Davis also consistently misspelled the name, even though Davis had known Thomson for many years and even though Davis received letters signed "Thomson." It is actually a common spelling of the name, but in the official records the misspelling persists. This was not a transcription error by Prof. Demmon, but the way the name was actually recorded by board secretaries. In this book, from this point forward, when quoting from the *Regents' Proceedings* or Davis's papers, Thompson will be used. In all other instances, Thomson will be spelled correctly.

25. Grove Street Cemetery tombstone engravings, "Thomson, Isaac, died April 21, 1873, age 75 yrs.," New Haven Colony. Thomson's wife, Sarah A. Treat, and some of their children were buried alongside Isaac.

26. Originally called Spireworth Square, it was purchased by Isaac Thomson and deeded to the city in 1860, which in turn named it for him. New Haven City Directory 1843–44, p. 84; New Haven City Directory 1862, p. 315; New Haven City Directory 1872, 10, 375; MSS C-1, box 87, photo of Isaac Thomson, New Haven Colony; Arnold Guyot Dana, "New Haven Old and New," vol. 3, street directory, p. 9, New Haven Colony; and Dana, vol. 102, p. 27, New Haven Colony.

document (fig. 31; see appendix for transcription).[27] It is also a historic treasure in that it is the first contract ever entered into by the regents with a professional architect; and that it is signed not only by the "boy" governor, but also by such a distinguished architect as Davis, adds to its priceless quality.[28] The terms of the contract may seem simplistic today, but each of the parties well understood the scope of their duties. Davis and Thomson were to "jointly act and do the duties of Architects and superintendants [*sic*] of the University of Michigan." Davis was to provide working drawings, specifications, and details, while Thomson was to reside in Ann Arbor at least six months per year to supervise the construction. Thomson's duties also indicated that he was to determine what materials were needed, receive proposals for the materials, and hire the necessary workmen. In addition, Thomson was to employ "at his own expense" someone to act as foreman all year round, especially during Thomson's absences. In this capacity as foreman is doubtless how Harpin Lum entered upon the scene.

The contract went on to specify the fees that would be paid to the architect and builder. "Thompson and Davis shall be paid in full the just sum of Twenty five hundred dollars for each and every year, in current money of the United States, in quarterly installments." Here then is the explanation of the seemingly large sum paid to Davis in September 1838. A quarterly installment of the total $2,500 would have been $625. On September 17, 1838, the regents had authorized a payment to Davis of $600. The reason the amount was given as $600 and not $625 is not clear, but may have been due to the regents covering Davis's expenses while in Ann Arbor. The next quarterly payment would have been due in mid-December 1838, but was not paid until January. The Treasurer's report shows $625 paid to Davis and Thomson on January 11, 1839. It is no wonder Thomson decried in a letter to Davis in early January that "I have been trying for several days past to get a payment of salary but have not succeeded as yet."[29]

The day after the regents adopted Davis's plan, September 17, 1838, they passed a resolution that the plans be presented to the governor and the superintendent of public instruction for their approval "in accordance with certain provisions of the Revised Statutes." Although the governor was serving as the president of the board and had given his assent to Davis's plan in that capacity, it was evidently necessary for him to formally assent again in his role as governor. The approvals were obtained in short order, for at the regents' meeting reconvened that evening, "The President announced the assent of the Governor and the Superintendent of Public Instruction to the plan of the University Building as required by law" (*RP*, 56, 58).

The activities of the board of regents, especially in regard to new buildings for Ann Arbor,

27. Contract between the Regents of the University of Michigan, Alex J. Davis and Isaac Thomson, September 18, 1838, Alexander Jackson Davis Collection I, file N-6, item 40-9416, Avery; see appendix.

28. At the time, A. J. Davis was thirty-five years old, and Stevens Mason was twenty-six. It is interesting to speculate on how the two men reacted to each other. It seems likely that the young governor would have had an appreciation for the obvious talents and powerful personality of the famous architect, whose reputation certainly preceded him.

29. Letter Isaac Thomson to Alexander Jackson Davis, dated Ann Arbor January 11, 1839, Letterbook 1821–90, p. 236, A. J. Davis Papers, NYPL.

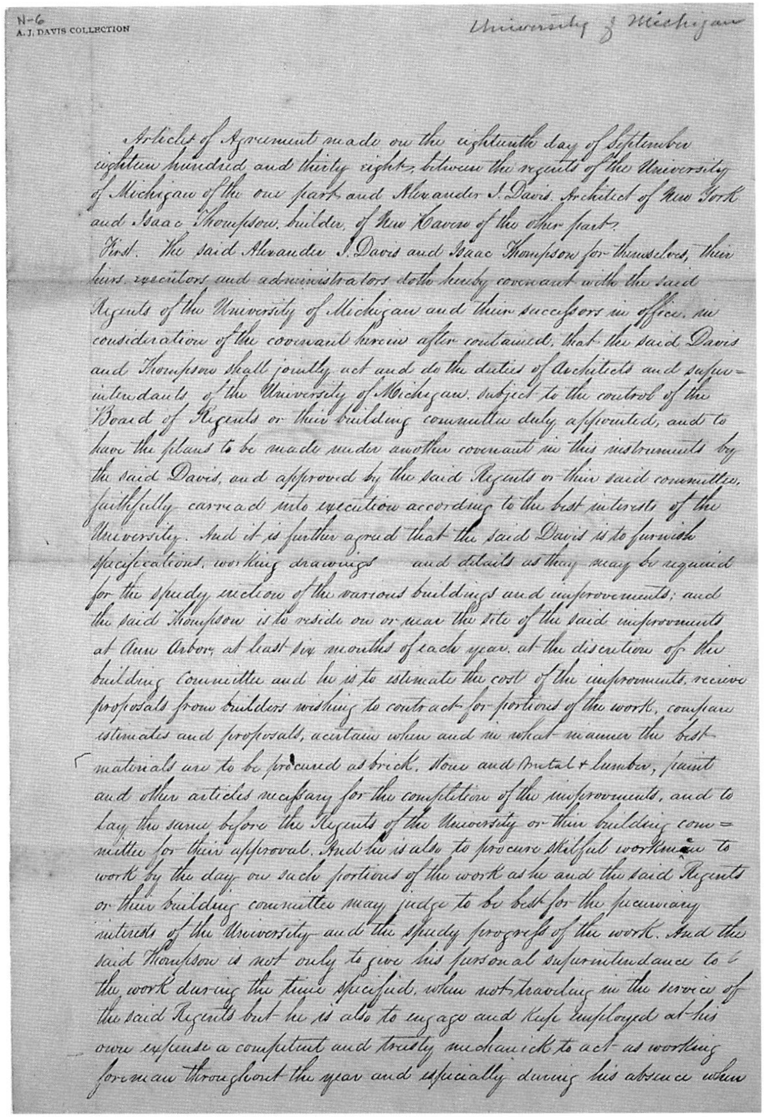

University of Michigan

Articles of Agreement made on the eighteenth day of September eighteen hundred and thirty eight, between the Regents of the University of Michigan of the one part and Alexander J. Davis Architect of New York and Isaac Thompson builder of New Haven of the other part.

First. The said Alexander J. Davis and Isaac Thompson for themselves, their heirs, executors, and administrators doth hereby covenant with the said Regents of the University of Michigan and their successors in office, in consideration of the covenant herein after contained, that the said Davis and Thompson shall jointly act and do the duties of Architects and superintendants of the University of Michigan, subject to the control of the Board of Regents or their building committee duly appointed, and to have the plans to be made under another covenant in this instrument by the said Davis, and approved by the said Regents or their said committee, faithfully carried into execution according to the best interests of the University. And it is further agreed that the said Davis is to furnish specifications, working drawings and details as they may be required for the speedy erection of the various buildings and improvements; and the said Thompson is to reside on or near the site of the said improvements at Ann Arbor, at least six months of each year, at the discretion of the building committee and he is to estimate the cost of the improvements, receive proposals from builders wishing to contract for portions of the work, compare estimates and proposals, ascertain when and in what manner the best materials are to be procured as brick, stone and metal + lumber, paint and other articles necessary for the completion of the improvements, and to lay the same before the Regents of the University or their building committee for their approval. And he is also to procure skilful workmen to work by the day on such portions of the work as he and the said Regents or their building committee may judge to be best for the pecuniary interests of the University and the speedy progress of the work. And the said Thompson is not only to give his personal superintendance to the work during the time specified, when not traveling in the service of the said Regents but he is also to engage and keep employed at his own expense a competent and trusty mechanick to act as working foreman throughout the year and especially during his absence when

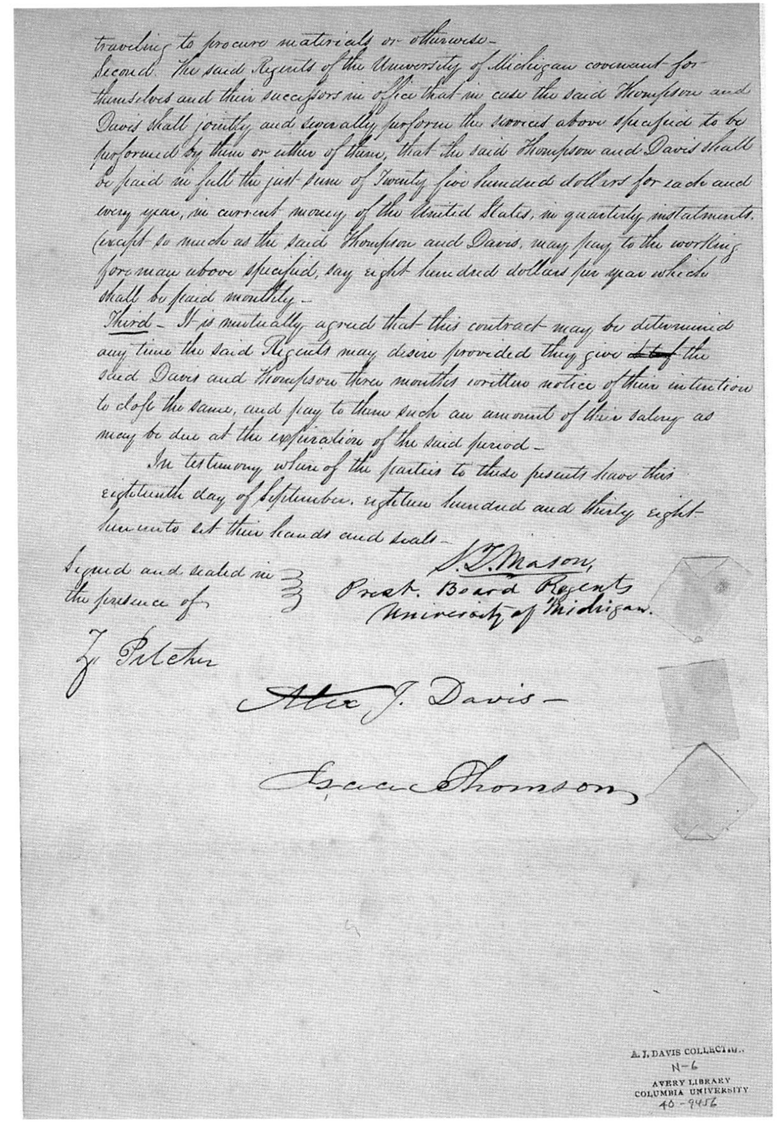

traveling to procure materials or otherwise.

Second. The said Regents of the University of Michigan covenant for themselves and their successors in office that in case the said Thompson and Davis shall jointly and severally perform the services above specified to be performed by them or either of them, that the said Thompson and Davis shall be paid in full the just sum of Twenty five hundred dollars for each and every year, in current money of the United States, in quarterly instalments. (except so much as the said Thompson and Davis, may pay to the working foreman above specified, say eight hundred dollars per year which shall be paid monthly.

Third. It is mutually agreed that this contract may be determined any time the said Regents may desire provided they give ~~to~~ the said Davis and Thompson three months written notice of their intention to close the same, and pay to them such an amount of their salary as may be due at the expiration of the said period.

In testimony whereof the parties to these presents have this eighteenth day of September, eighteen hundred and thirty eight hereunto set their hands and seals.

Signed and sealed in the presence of

J. Pilcher

S. T. Mason,
Prest. Board Regents
University of Michigan.

Alex J. Davis

Isaac Thomson

Fig. 31. Contract executed between the Regents of the University of Michigan and Alexander J. Davis and Isaac Thomson, September 18, 1838 (see appendix).
Drawings and Archives, Avery Architectural and Fine Arts Library, Columbia University in the City of New York (collection 1, folder N-6, p. 4, 40-9416).

would have been of great interest to the people of Michigan. This was, after all, the first institution of higher learning in the state, a creation dictated by the state constitution. As today, the regents' meetings of 1838 would have been open to the public, and certainly some decisions of the board were publicized. It soon became known that the regents had accepted a plan by Davis and that Thomson would act as builder. One article to this effect appeared in the widely read *Michigan Argus,* on September 20, 1838:

> University of Michigan—It affords us great pleasure to be enabled to announce to our readers that the Board of Regents, at their recent session, have concluded upon the plans for the College and that the work is to be entered upon immediately under the superintendance [*sic*] of Mr. Isaac Thomson, of New Haven, CT. The plan is of the Gothic style, and furnished by Mr. Alexander J. Davis, of New York, consisting of a central building with two wings. One wing only is to be erected for the present, and that to be completed within a year.[30]

The plans so described would have been made available for viewing by interested parties, probably wherever Isaac Thomson was staying in Ann Arbor. Masons and other building suppliers would have wished to study the plans in expectation of bidding on portions of the work. Although Davis left Michigan on September 18, 1838, Thomson would have stayed on in anticipation of beginning the building project. Evidence survives, however, to indicate that Thomson returned to New Haven sometime in the fall and came back to Michigan in December. The plans that were made public following the regents' meeting in September were not entirely well received by the public. A letter to the *Detroit Daily Advertiser,* in late September 1838, decried the use of out-of-state talent, and the presumed expense of executing the Gothic design.

> For the Advertiser.
>
> *Mr. Whitney.*—An article appeared in your paper a few days since, stating the necessity of giving encouragement to our own manufacturers and Mechanics. I am sorry such a useful lesson did not appear at an earlier day, for the benefit of the Mechanics of Michigan. It is hoped some of your readers will be able to explain the reason why there was not a general invitation given, by advertisement, to the Mechanics of this State, for plans and elevations for the University, by offering prizes; for the best, $300, for second best, $150, for the third, $100, for the fourth, $50—the amount already sent out of this State for the plans approved for said building. It is well known our own mechanics' have taste and abilities sufficient to plan and execute any edifice which the wants of Michigan require. When will the Executive of New York degrade his Mechanics' by sending to Michigan for what his own citizens are capable of doing? Why did not the Lieut. Governor of this State give his own citizens a fair trial before he went out of the State for his plans &c.? I suppose it was because the Mechanics of Michigan do not assume that dignified name called *Architect!* or any

30. *Michigan Argus,* September 20, 1838, Bentley. The *Michigan Argus* was published in Ann Arbor between February 1835 and July 1839. It became the *Democratic Herald,* which was published from September 1839 through December 1842.

> of those *lofty* titles as *Esq'rs.*, &c. The elevation approved, is of the Gothic style of architecture, painted up to the eyes, splendid in appearance, but will be paltry in the execution, on account of the limited means. I don't know what there is that is so very attractive about this Gothic elevation, without it is those towers of Babel between 200 and 300 feet high. . . . Pray, why does Michigan want to imitate the fooleries and splendid extravagances of Europe? The whole of the funds appropriated will be expended before there will be conveniences for a single Professor. Why are those four mammoth windows necessary, and the large chapel which will require a fortune to provide fuel to keep it comfortably warm in winter. Respectfully yours, QUIZ.[31]

These sentiments notwithstanding, the project for the Gothic building seemed under way. That was in mid-September 1838, but three-and-a-half months of inaction followed. The regents did not meet again until January 5, 1839, and although this may seem an inordinate amount of time between meetings, the regents' by-laws at the time called only for quarterly meetings. Activity related to building seems also to have been suspended during this time, and Isaac Thomson apparently returned to New Haven. The only indication of any activity during this gap is recorded by A. J. Davis in his diary, for December 3–6, 1838, which states "University of Michigan. Working Drawings for Isaac Thompson, who left for Detroit Dec. 7 '38 with Peck & Lumm."[32] Davis also listed the drawings he sent:

General Plan of Ground	General Plan of Building, with Terrace
1. Basement plan, north wing	
2. Principal floor "	Plan of section of Basem't window ½ size
3. Gallery floor "	Plan of section great windows ½ size
4. Elevation of west front.	Great window jamb full size
5. Elevation of east front.	Splay and jamb Great doorway ½ size
with 2 sections "on margins"	

Of these drawings, only two or three appear to have survived. It is known that when the regents approved Davis's plans in September 1838, they resolved to build the main building (i.e., the center portion) and eight sections of the North Wing. The "elevation of west front" and "elevation of east front" as listed in Davis's diary entry probably refer to the two watercolor renderings of the North Wing that survive (figs. 32 and 33; see also plates). In addition, the "general plan of ground" may refer to the plan shown in fig. 30, although the drawing itself is undated. It should be noted that the watercolor drawings of the North Wing are not dated either, but in view of the fact that the regents approved the North Wing, it is very likely that Davis spent the fall developing the design and executing the renderings that he gave to Isaac Thomson in December 1838. All of the Davis

31. *Detroit Daily Advertiser*, circa late September 1838, published by George L. Whitney. Copy in Alexander Jackson Davis Collection I, folder P-3, p. 8 (undated), Avery. *Quiz* was a common way for anonymous letters to be signed.

32. Office Diary 1827–53, p. 195, A. J. Davis Papers, NYPL.

Fig. 32. North Wing (west front), University of Michigan, Ann Arbor, 1838–39. Design by Alexander Jackson Davis. Not executed.

Metropolitan Museum of Art, Harris Brisbane Dick Fund, 1924 (24.66.40).

drawings related to the University of Michigan that have so far been illustrated are among the Davis collection at the Metropolitan Museum of Art. One additional, clearly attributable drawing survives in Michigan. This is a floor plan for a Gothic building (fig. 34), which closely resembles the one illustrated on the plan approved by the regents in September 1838 (see fig. 27), as well as that shown in figure 1. This floor plan is signed "Alex J. Davis" and dated December 1838.[33] It certainly must have been among those sent out in December 1838, although it does not seem to correspond to any drawing listed in Davis's diary. Perhaps Davis made the list of drawings from memory in later years and did not accurately recollect all the drawings he had produced. One of the most important things to notice about this floor plan is that the section left (north) of the central pavilion matches the rendering of the west front of North Wing in figure 32. Although probably not intending at this time for North Wing to be L-shaped, the floor plan certainly pertains to this section.[34] A second drawing that survives at Michigan is unquestionably by Davis, as the handwriting on it is recognizably his (fig. 35).[35] This is also a floor plan for one of the Gothic structures, but shows a wing much longer than depicted in any of the surviving elevations. This drawing is undated but probably was executed at the same time as the other Davis floor plan it survives with.

33. It was common for Davis to sign his works as *Alex J. Davis*. This can be seen on figures 1 and 27, as well as on the contract signed with the University of Michigan.

34. In this floor plan, the eastern portion of the L has not been completely laid out with rooms, etc., which perhaps implies that it was not to be built at that time.

35. Davis biographer Jane Davies concurs (phone conversation between Mary M. Culver and Jane B. Davies, March 28, 1996, transcript in possession of author).

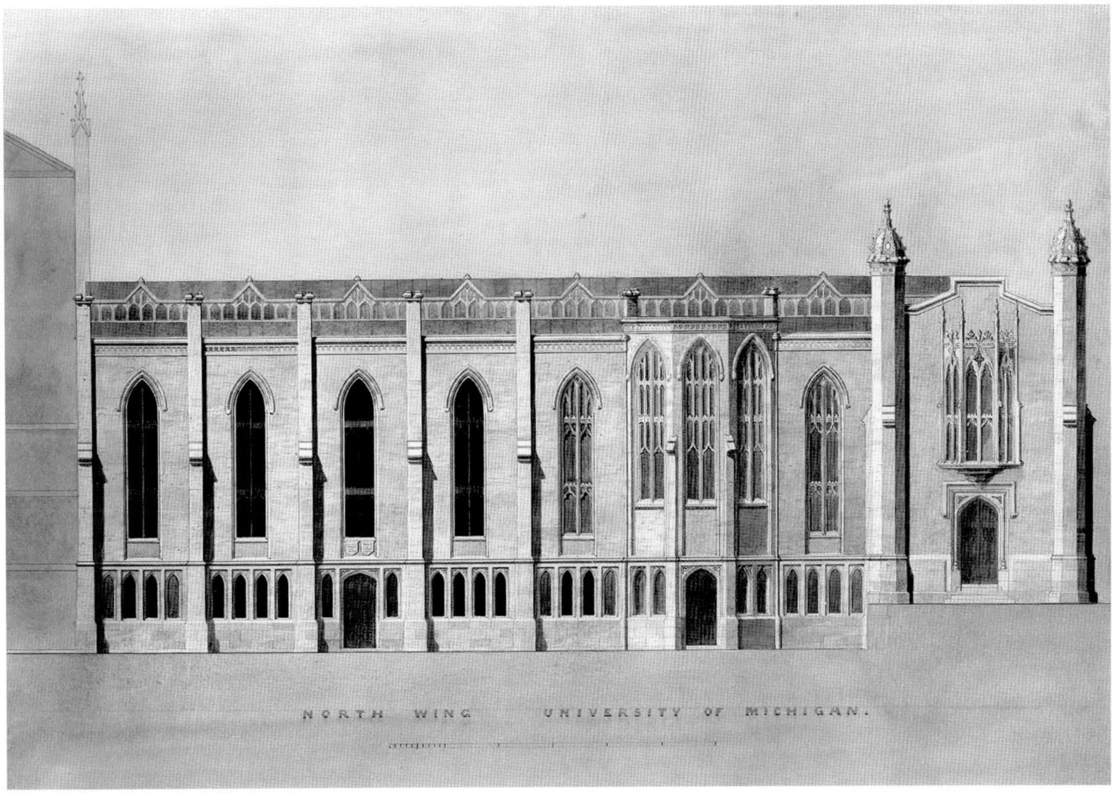

Fig. 33. North Wing (east front), University of Michigan, Ann Arbor, 1838–39. Design by Alexander Jackson Davis. Not executed.

Metropolitan Museum of Art, Harris Brisbane Dick Fund, 1924 (24.66.39).

Although none of Davis's watercolor renderings of Gothic elevations or campus plans are known today to survive at Michigan, this has not always been the case. At least one drawing survived for many years, kept in a prominent location. Andrew Ten Brook, writing in 1875, indicated that "the plan of the principal building [the central portion of Davis's Gothic design] which was to absorb this fund now hangs in the Museum."[36] The museum at that time was located in North Wing, and the fund referred to was the one-hundred-thousand-dollar loan made by the state to the regents in 1838. In addition, a description of the plan was made in the student newspaper of that time, the *Chronicle,* in an article dated March 26, 1870, about illustrations of the university on display in the museum: "There is a passage-way in the museum containing a collection of relics, which include the faces of certain graduates of very early classes, specimens of diplomas, and two large architectural designs for the University. One of these, dated 1838 and proposed by Alexander J. Davis, the architect of the University of New York, represents a very handsome building of the Gothic order, 400 feet long, and covered with towers, turrets, pinnacles, and spires. Sixteen highly ornamental windows adorn the front, besides a very large one over the central entrance."[37]

36. Ten Brook, *American State Universities,* 136.

37. "Pictures of the University," *Chronicle* (University of Michigan), March 26, 1870, 194–95.

A reference to the plan was also made in a later publication, in which it was stated that "one set of plans which Davis drew is deposited in the Metropolitan Museum of Art in New York; the set which was submitted for the approval of Governor Mason, after many vicissitudes, found its way back to the archives of the University."[38] Although this seems to refer to a representation of the campus and building elevation, it may also refer to a floor plan, as a newspaper article of 1936 mentions the floor plan as hanging in the president's office.[39] However, it was not a floor plan alone that was presented to the governor for approval; it was one or more of Davis's elaborate renderings, as indicated by Davis himself on one drawing (see fig. 27), which corresponds to the drawing described by both Ten Brook and the student newspaper. The 1936 article stated that "up to the present the only original drawing made by Mr. Davis in the University's possession has been a floor plan for the projected building identical with the copy in the museum. This was discovered some years ago in Lansing and brought to Ann Arbor by Regent Junius E. Beal. It now hangs in the president's office in Angell Hall." The floor plan referenced here does survive (see fig. 34), but the ultimate fate of any other plans that might have been in the museum at Michigan, especially that referred to by Ten Brook and the *Chronicle,* remains unknown.[40]

In early December 1838, Isaac Thomson returned to Ann Arbor with more working drawings provided by Davis. Still the regents had not met in three months, and Thomson was probably occupying his time in preparing the site, determining what materials would be needed, and generally just waiting. In fact, a brief newspaper item on December 20, 1838, indicated that some work was being done at the site: "We rejoice to learn that operations are to be forthwith commenced upon the University buildings. A large amount of materials has been already collected; and the foundations will be laid as soon as the state of the weather permits."[41] Davis had indicated that Isaac Thomson returned to Ann Arbor with "Peck and Lumm," but who were these persons and for what purpose did they accompany Thomson to Michigan? Peck was almost certainly John Peck, a mason from New Haven who is known to have worked on projects in that city for Harpin Lum.[42] Peck never enters the official record at Michigan, may not have stayed long, and does not appear to play a significant part in this story. "Lumm," however, will play an important role, and unraveling his identity is critical to understanding what unfolded over the next few months.

The name Harpin Lum entered the official record on July 13, 1839, when he took over as superintendent of building from Isaac Thomson. However, the treasurer's report of December 18, 1839,

38. Frank E. Robbins, "First Buildings," in *The University of Michigan: An Encyclopedic Survey,* vol. 4, ed. Walter A. Donnelly (Ann Arbor: University of Michigan Press, 1958), 1619.

39. George A. Stauter, "First Building for 'M' Campus Never Erected," in *Ann Arbor Daily News,* August 22, 1936. The president's office at the time was located in Angell Hall.

40. The extent of documents and drawings related to the University of Michigan that may have been lost in a devastating fire at the State Office Building in Lansing in 1951 is unknown. Most of the records of the State Archives of the Michigan Historical Commission were destroyed or damaged. However, if other drawings related to the university's early buildings were among official documents in Lansing, it is probable they too would have been returned to Ann Arbor by Regent Beal, with the drawing referred to in the 1936 article.

41. *State Journal,* December 20, 1838, Bentley. The *State Journal,* sometimes called the *Michigan State Journal* or the *Ann Arbor State Journal,* was published in Ann Arbor between September 1835 and March 1847.

42. Invoice Harpin Lum and John Peck, for mason's work on railroad, October 1847, folder L; receipt Harpin Lum to Peck and Baldwin, March and June 1847, Harpin Lum Papers, New Haven Colony, MSS 82; and New Haven City Directory 1840, p. 68, listing for "Peck, John, mason," New Haven Colony.

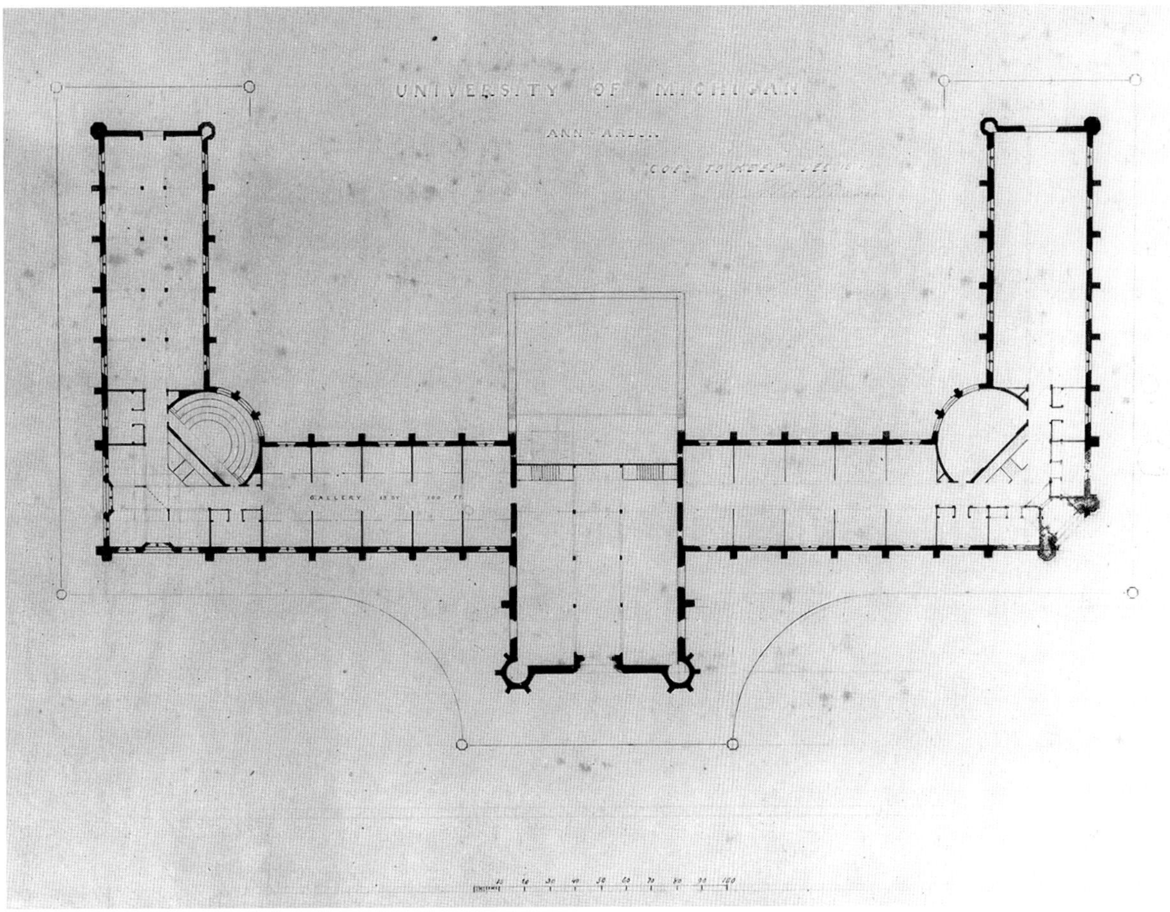

Fig. 34. Floor plan for a Gothic structure, University of Michigan, Ann Arbor, 1838. Design by Alexander Jackson Davis (signature "Alex J. Davis" faintly visible). Not executed.

Bentley Historical Library, University of Michigan (University of Michigan Architectural Drawings, folder 5).

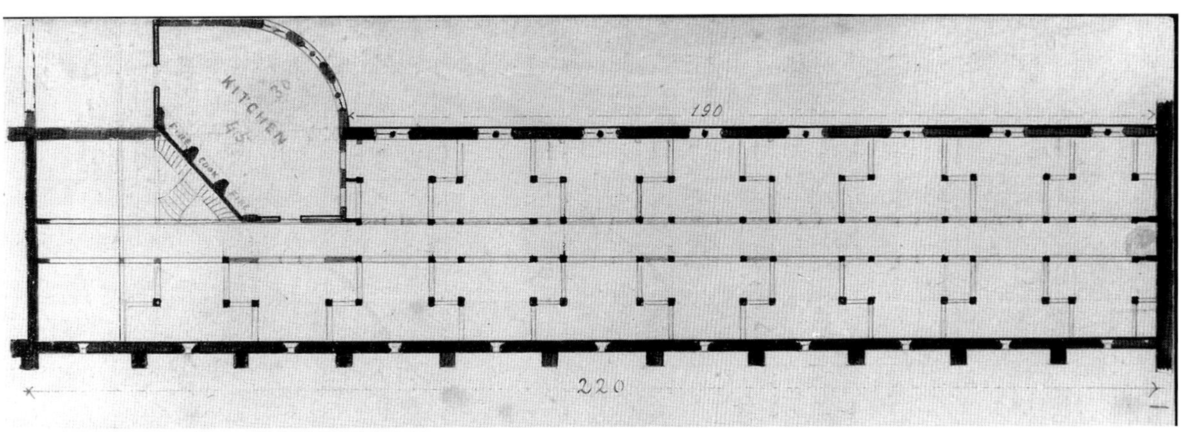

Fig. 35. Floor plan for a Gothic structure, University of Michigan, Ann Arbor, ca. 1838. Design probably by Alexander Jackson Davis. Not executed.

Bentley Historical Library, University of Michigan (University of Michigan Architectural Drawings, folder 5).

shows Harpin Lum as having been paid for services as early as February 1839, when he was paid $1,000. According to this abstract of expenditures, by the time Lum is first mentioned in the *Regents' Proceedings,* on July 13, 1839, he had already been paid a staggering $13,700 (*RP,* 104–5). Harpin Lum, who would become builder of the first five buildings on the university grounds in Ann Arbor, was long presumed to have been a local builder. Historians have assumed that he must have been from Ann Arbor or Detroit, though no proof was provided. This was not, however, a bad assumption. There were, at this time, at least two Lums in Detroit who gave their occupation as architect and builder. As noted, they were Charles and David Lum.[43] In fact, Charles had been nominated for builder by Regent Pitcher in September 1838. It would seem logical that if there were another builder named Lum working in the Detroit–Ann Arbor area, he would surely be related to those as listed in Detroit.

The fact that there were two architect-builders named Lum in Detroit, however, piqued the curiosity of this writer, who felt that if a third Lum named Harpin existed in that city, he too would certainly have been listed in the directories, especially in his professional capacity. Since he was not so listed, the suspicion began to form that perhaps Harpin Lum was from New England and came to Michigan at the behest of Davis, as did other workers such as Isaac Thomson, and later on, George Gill. The first clue that this might be true was the discovery of the entry in Davis's diary indicating he had given drawings to Thomson "who left for Detroit . . . with Peck & Lumm."[44] Could this "Lumm" be Harpin Lum, and could he, too, have been from New Haven? This indeed turned out to be the truth, and a mysterious person from the university's past is finally revealed.

Harpin Lum was born on October 27, 1806, in Woodbury, Connecticut. He was descended from John Lum of Yorkshire, England, who was one of the pioneer settlers of Stamford, Connecticut, in 1642. Harpin Lum spent most of his short life in New Haven, where he was married on January 15, 1846, in Trinity Church to Nancy Maria English. Nancy (1823–1904) was the sister of Connecticut governor James E. English. Harpin and Nancy had two children, Harpin Meigs Lum and Charles English Lum. Starting with one of the earliest New Haven city directories (1843–44) and continuing yearly through the 1849–50 edition, Harpin Lum is listed as a builder. Tragically, Harpin Lum died of dysentery on October 15, 1849, at the young age of forty-two. He was buried in Grove Street Cemetery in New Haven.[45]

Isaac Thomson returned to Michigan in early December 1838, accompanied by Harpin Lum and John Peck. They found that the regents had not met since Thomson and Davis had visited in September, and in fact their arrival in early December was probably meant to coincide with what

43. It should be noted that no previous historian of University of Michigan buildings had identified any Lums, either in Ann Arbor, Detroit, or elsewhere.

44. Office Diary 1827–53, p. 195, A. J. Davis Papers, NYPL.

45. Harpin Lum Papers, New Haven Colony, MSS 82, includes bills from George Gill (folder G), John Peck (folder P), Peck and Baldwin (folder P), and Isaac Thomson (folder T); *Vital Records of New Haven, 1649–1850,* part 2 (Hartford: Connecticut Society of the Founders and Patriots of America, 1924), p. 962, marriage Harpin Lum to Nancy Maria English, January 15, 1846, p. 878; internments in city burying ground in 1849 included "Oct. 15—Harpin Lumm, Age 42, dysentery"; Grove Street Cemetery tombstone engravings, "Lum, Harpin, died Oct. 15, 1849, age 42 yrs."; and New Haven City Directory 1843–44, p. 59, listing for "Lum Harpin, builder," New Haven Colony.

should have been the regents' next quarterly meeting. Whether there was any communication between the regents and Thomson and Davis between September and December is unknown. The only record of any activity during the fall of 1838 is a line item in the treasurer's report indicating that one thousand dollars had been paid for bricks on November 1, 1838 (*RP,* 104–5). With this three-month gap in activity, and with the financial crisis of bank closings and approaching depression, it must have seemed evident that the construction of the campus buildings was not to shortly or smoothly commence. Thomson and Davis must have communicated during December, but the only extant remnant is an envelope for a letter from Thomson to Davis dated Ann Arbor, December 28, 1838.[46] Thomson would not have known that other forces were at work that would lead ultimately to the abandonment of Davis's Gothic designs.

In September 1838, when the regents had adopted Davis's designs, they had sought the approval of the governor and of the superintendent of public instruction, and recorded the assent of these two men to the plan on September 17. Sometime thereafter, the superintendent, John Pierce, would reconsider his approval after weighing the probable costs of executing the plan against the financial resources of the university. Although the regents had not as yet embarked on any construction projects, they had not been idle in the promotion of the university's activities. No classes were being held in Ann Arbor, but the regents had very early on begun the establishment of branches in other towns. They saw this as one of the most important duties entrusted to them and began immediately to fulfill the goal. As early as June 1837, a branch was established in Pontiac, which was opened that fall. Branches soon followed in Detroit (using the university's old building on Bates Street), Monroe, Kalamazoo, Niles, and Tecumseh. The operation of the branches, more of which were subsequently to be founded, with the expenses of obtaining facilities and hiring faculty, would prove a heavy financial burden on the young university. It would be these expenses, plus the need for buildings at Ann Arbor, that would lead to the regents' request for a loan of one hundred thousand dollars from the state.

Superintendent Pierce was deeply concerned about the university's finances, and on viewing Davis's designs must have felt that the cost to execute them would be staggering, especially in the use of stone, with large stained-glass windows, and the decorative elaboration. (In July 1838, the regents had passed a resolution, "That the University buildings shall be constructed of brick faced with stone," *RP,* 54.) Perhaps public outcries about the perceived costs, such as that printed in the *Detroit Daily Advertiser,* added to Pierce's decision to veto the plan. Pierce himself subsequently explained his actions:

> One other question of great interest fell to my lot, solitary and alone, to decide of which, for the time being, created much ill-feeling, and brought down upon me a storm of denunciation. Indeed,

46. Envelope consisting of a piece of paper folded and sealed, with seal broken. Addressed to "Mr. Alexander J. Davis, New York, New York University" with return address written along right edge "I. Thompson, Ann Arbor, December 28, 1838." Round postal stamp in upper left-hand corner "Ann Arbor Mich Dec 30," Box 1 Correspondence 1820–80, A. J. Davis Papers, NYPL.

> so intense was the excitement, that an indignation meeting was proposed to be called at Ann Arbor. The occasion was this: The legislature passed an act authorizing the regents to procure a plan for buildings. They employed an architect from New Haven to draft one; that plan, if approved by the governor and superintendent of public instruction, should be adopted. The one prepared was truly a magnificent design, and would, in that day, have involved an expenditure of half a million, if not more. It was accepted by the regents and approved by the governor. It was presented to me. Most respectfully, yet decidedly, I refused it my assent, and gave as a reason that it would absorb so much of the university fund as would cripple it in all time to come; and urged further that a university did not consist in buildings, but in the number and ability of its professors, and in its other appointments, as library, cabinets, and works of art. The result was, the regents receded, and the present plan was adopted, and the university started into being. Twenty years after, or more, at the house of Dr. Denton, one of the medical professors, in company with President Morgan, of Pennsylvania, the doctor, in referring to my course in refusing my assent to their plan for building, and the bitter feeling incited against me at the time, remarked that, while he was unwilling to give me credit for so much sagacity as seemed to be implied by my action, yet he would truly say that it was the best thing that had ever happened in the State. My reply was that I was just as well satisfied then as now that its adoption would have been fatal to the institution.[47]

Pierce, therefore, vetoed Davis's plan "near the end of the year."[48] It may be on this account that Thomson wrote to Davis in the envelope dated December 28, 1838.

This veto notwithstanding, the regents at their next meeting still seemed determined to build at least part of Davis's plan. Perhaps they felt that if they were to reduce the scope of the project and use less costly materials, that they might yet come away with a fine Davis design that would be more palatable to the budget-conscious Pierce. At this meeting, on January 5, 1839, Chief Justice Fletcher proposed three resolutions to address this issue:

> *Resolved,* That instead of proceeding to erect and finish one wing, or the Main Building, and one wing of the buildings for the University according to the plan furnished by A. J. Davis and heretofore adopted by this Board, the Building Committee proceed to erect and finish the main front building according to said plan, and they also proceed to erect and finish the exterior walls and covering of the building designated on said plan for the Chapel and Museum. *Resolved,* That all resolutions and orders heretofore adopted by this Board, inconsistent with the preceding order, be rescinded. *Resolved,* That the resolution heretofore adopted directing that the buildings for the University shall be faced with stone be rescinded and said buildings be built with brick. (*RP,* 60)

47. Ten Brook, *American State Universities,* 135–36, quoting from the *Michigan Teacher*, vol. 4, p. 169. The "architect from New Haven" was Alexander Jackson Davis, who at the time was equally well known for his work in New Haven, with Ithiel Town, as for that in New York City. Pierce could also have confused Davis's home town with Thomson's and Lum's, both of whom were from New Haven and both of whom were in Ann Arbor when Pierce was apparently vetoing the plan. Emil Lorch, writing in 1921, and Burke Hinsdale, in 1906, were also unable to identify the New Haven architect as Davis. This is especially surprising for Lorch, who was so knowledgeable about architecture and architects.

48. Peckham, *Making of University of Michigan*, 20.

The building Fletcher referred to as the chapel and museum is probably the one labeled by Davis as a library and chapel (fig. 36). One could not fail but be inspired by such a dramatic scene with the magnificent chapel, reminiscent of King's College at Cambridge, drenched in rays of light seemingly from heaven. Davis, for his part, might have felt that the decision to build in brick rather than stone might compromise his designs and not be equal to his idea of the high Gothic style, although elsewhere some of his Gothic designs would be executed in stucco over brick. The three resolutions by Fletcher were, however, "laid on the table," and no action was taken at the time.

At that January meeting, Regent Pitcher had submitted to the board the contract executed with the architect. On January 9, 1839, in a show of confidence of the Building Committee members, the regents adopted a resolution, "That the contracts and proceedings of the Building Committee consisting of Edward Mundy, Elon Farnsworth, and Wm. A. Fletcher be hereby ratified and confirmed, and that the said Committee have power and authority to make contracts for materials for the buildings of the University with such other powers as properly appertain to a building committee, until the further order of this Board; and it is further directed, that the said Committee before making contracts for timber or other materials necessary for said buildings, shall give reasonable public notice in two public Newspapers, one in the village of Ann Arbor and the other in Detroit, for proposals for furnishing such materials" (*RP*, 62). One such advertisement appeared in the *Michigan Argus* on January 17, 1839:

> NOTICE TO BUILDERS, &c.—Written proposals will be received by the building committee of the University Buildings, until the first day of February next, for the following materials and labor, to wit:
> 2,500 feet building Stone, suitable for foundation,
> 2,500,000 first quality Bricks,
> 50,000 feet sawed Oak or Pine Lumber,
> 50,000 feet clear Pine Lumber,
> 2000 bushels Lime,
> For excavating 2,400 yards of earth,
> For laying up the entire walls of the University,
> For furnishing the materials for said walls, and laying them up.
> All the materials to be delivered at the site for the University buildings at Ann Arbor, except the pine lumber which is to be delivered to Detroit.
> The proposals to be sealed and directed to Mr. Isaac Thompson the superintendent of the said buildings at Ann Arbor, with whom the plans and specifications are deposited, and from whom any information in the premises may be obtained by any wishing to make proposals.
> January 14, 1839[49]

49. *Michigan Argus*, January 17, 1839, Bentley.

Fig. 36. Library-chapel, University of Michigan, Ann Arbor, 1838. Design by Alexander Jackson Davis. Not executed. Metropolitan Museum of Art, Harris Brisbane Dick Fund, 1924 (24.66.41).

Isaac Thomson was certainly concerned about the state of affairs relevant to the buildings, especially after Superintendent Pierce vetoed Davis's plan. Following the early January regents' meeting, which Thomson apparently attended, he wrote to Davis expressing his concern:

> Ann Arbor. Jany 11, 1839
> Mr. A. J. Davis
> Dear Sir
>
> Agreeable to my predictions the Regents have decided on the erection of the center building. But there are a few that are opposed to having it built of brick, and others that would be willing to have the whole subject postponed indefinitely and what the end will be is more than I can venture a prediction. The committee feel some embarrassment relative to the extent of their powers. A meeting is however to be held in a few days when I suppose their duties & powers will be defined. —But what I am to be doing in the mean time I have yet to learn—and it is certainly dull music to be here with nothing to do and without any books. —I hope however that you will devote what attention you can—to the plans and working drawings and pay particular attention to simplicity and economy—as expence [*sic*] seems to be the great bug bear—that operates on the minds of almost all the gentlemen—I have been trying for several days past to get a payment of Salary but have not succeeded as yet.
>
> Your friend Isaac Thomson[50]

That Thomson wrote this letter to Davis has not been known, nor has the fact that Davis responded. In his office diary Davis noted: "Jan. 1839—Central Building. Wrote to Thompson 22 Jan. enclosing sketches."[51] This was written just below his diary entry of December 1838 in which he had indicated he sent University of Michigan drawings out with Thomson to Ann Arbor. This is an especially notable and intriguing entry. No drawings related to it are known to survive, but the nature of the design might be speculated upon. Isaac Thomson had urged simplicity and economy, wryly noting that expense was the great "bug bear" with the regents. Perhaps this was the time when Davis might have considered providing alternate designs in a classical mode. It is possible Davis would have felt a classical design could be more successfully carried out in a less dear material than stone, which he preferred for these Gothic structures. Although many classical buildings were executed in stone, many others were done in brick and even wood. A common practice was to cover a brick building with stucco and then to score the stucco so that it would resemble blocks of stone. Davis may have had something along this line in mind for the central building. But since no drawings of such a structure survive that are attributed to Michigan, the nature of this design may never be known. It should also be noted that Davis sent drawings for a

50. Letterbook 1821–90, p. 236, A. J. Davis Papers, NYPL. Isaac Thomson was paid on January 11, 1839, or shortly thereafter. The expenditures for the regents reflect a draft that date for Davis and Thomson in the amount of $625, a quarterly installment on their contract.

51. Office Diary 1827–53, p. 195, A. J. Davis Papers, NYPL.

central building only, and not for any "wings" in a classical style, although buildings of this type would subsequently be built (see fig. 56).

At the end of January 1839, there was a flurry of decision making on the part of the regents that would forever change the anticipated face of the university campus. On January 30, the following resolution was presented by Regent Kearsley:

> Whereas, It is believed that the erection of the University buildings, according to the plan heretofore adopted, is premature, therefore, *Resolved,* That no further contracts for materials be made or other measures taken for the erection of the University buildings agreeably to the plan heretofore adopted, and that the order heretofore made directing the University to be built of brick be rescinded. *Resolved,* That the sum of_____ Dollars be and is hereby appropriated for the erection of such buildings as the necessities of the University may at present require, agreeably to such plan as may be submitted by the Building Committee at the next or future meeting of the Board. (*RP,* 69)

This resolution was laid on the table, but taken up again the next day, when the blank was filled in with twenty thousand dollars. No indication was made whether or not the resolution was adopted at this time. But subsequently on that day, January 31, 1839, the regents did adopt a resolution, which for the first time revealed their intention to construct something other than Davis's designs.

> *Resolved,* That the Building Committee be authorized to contract for materials for erecting and furnishing four buildings for the use of the Professors of the University, and to be used until the main buildings of the University be completed for the reception of the Cabinet of Natural History, Library, Philosophical Apparatus, and for other general purposes of the University; and to contract for the erecting and finishing the same; and that the said Committee cause to be prepared plans of the said buildings and submit the same to this Board, with all convenient speed. (*RP,* 70)

The decision thus was made to build four houses for professors until the main building could be built. Although there is no evidence that the regents ever asked Davis to provide designs for professors' houses, and no such drawings exist, it was nevertheless the apparent intent of the regents to still build a main building, which it is assumed referred to a Davis design. However, the regents followed this decision with one of profound effect to Davis. "On motion of Dr. Pitcher, the Building Committee was authorized to annul, modify, or suspend the contract entered into by the Board with Messrs. Davis and Thompson and to enter into a new contract with said Thompson" (*RP,* 70). With these few brief words, the first architect of the University of Michigan was seemingly out of the picture.

It can be assumed that the financial situation was the cause of this action. Having received ample designs from Davis, and having two able builders on site (Thomson and Lum), the regents surely felt they need not continue the expense of Davis's fee. Now that they had decided to build professors' houses to begin with, the regents would have been comfortable in relying on Isaac Thomson's skills to provide them. Thomson was, after all, an experienced architect and builder in his own right. That is not to say that Thomson broke off communication with Davis, which he did not. Thomson, acting on behalf of himself and Davis, agreed on February 14, 1839, to this discharge of their contract, after the receipt of $616, which was determined to be the amount due them under the contract. The contract had specified that the regents could terminate the agreement with three months' notice and payment of salary for that time period. Three months would have been late April or early May, so Thomson and Davis were paid, by warrant drawn February 11, 1839, for the quarter that would have run to mid-June.

The news of the cancellation of the Davis-Thomson contract, and the apparent abandonment of Davis's plans in favor of professors' houses, was not well received by the public. Davis and Thomson were paid a total of $1,841, with the university and the state seemingly to have little to show for it. An item voicing these concerns appeared in the *Michigan Argus:*

> TUESDAY MORNING FEB. 5, 1839
>
> THE UNIVERSITY.—There are strange rumors afloat, with regard to the immediate erection of the University buildings as at first contemplated, and as we see from the Regent's report, determined on, at a sitting of the board a short time since. We know not what may be the cause of this singular move, but we fear all is not right. The matter most seriously concerns our village and county, and we hope that it may be fully enquired into without regard to party; and that too immediately.[52]

The terms of the new contract now entered into with Isaac Thomson are not written into the record at this time, and the contract does not survive. However, later reports by the Building Committee make reference to this contract (*RP,* 125, 191). For a salary of $1,000 per year, to be paid quarterly, Thomson was to act as superintendent of building for the four professors' houses that the regents had just determined to build. Thomson subsequently recommended that Harpin Lum be hired to build the houses. In anticipation of this contract with Lum, the regents had drawn a payment of $1,000 for Lum on February 11, 1839. There is no record of Thomson being paid the first quarterly installment on his new contract, but perhaps because the regents had just paid him $616 for the termination of the Davis-Thomson contract, Thomson did not press for another payment. The agreement entered into between Harpin Lum and the regents specified that Lum would be paid $7,450 each for the first two houses, and $6,000 each for the second two. It was stipulated that the houses would be completed by July 1840. Hereafter, all payments for construction of the houses were made to Lum (none to Thomson) and the agreed-upon fees would have covered materials, laborers, and so forth, in addition to Lum's salary. News of the regents' contract with Lum again ruffled the feathers of local builders, prompting the following item, which appeared in the *State Journal.*

52. *Michigan Argus,* February 7, 1839, Bentley.

> Ann Arbor, Thursday, February 21, 1839
>
> THE UNIVERSITY
>
> Serious complaints are made against the building committee, in relation to the manner of letting the contracts for building the four professors' houses. —We are informed that the contracts were let privately at 7000 dollars for each building, when some of our own mechanics were prepared to furnish better plans and take the contracts at $6000 for each building. It is alleged that the contracts were let in such a way as purposely to exclude the competition of our own mechanics. Our information of the above matters is received through sources that leave no doubt of its correctness.
>
> Without casting censure upon the whole board of regents, we must be permitted to say that the conduct of the body from the beginning, as far as the University is concerned, had been little different from boys' play. Of their management touching the branches we have nothing to remark, for we know little about it.
>
> Their original design of prosecuting the main building next summer, followed up by procuring plans, engaging an architect and superintendent, and then its sudden abandonment, must have cost the fund some 4 or 5000 dollars; this added to the extra cost unnecessarily incurred in the four buildings above mentioned, amounts to a very bad omen of the future prosperity of the institution. This business of letting the contracts looks too much like modern "democratic" justice. No institution can flourish where that miserable spirit of mischief intrudes itself.[53]

Nevertheless, there was finally progress on the building front. When the regents had determined to build the four professors' houses on January 31, 1839, they instructed the Building Committee to have plans for the houses prepared and submitted for the board's approval. A plan was subsequently drawn and presented to the regents at their next meeting, on February 11, 1839, at which time the plan was adopted. This drawing, or plan, does not survive, but can be taken to reflect the design of the houses that were shortly to be built. Who drew the plan for the houses, and whether or not A. J. Davis had a hand in the design, has been one of the greatest mysteries surrounding the birth of the Ann Arbor campus. It seems now, however, that there can be little doubt but that Isaac Thomson drew the plan approved by the regents. Thomson was in Ann Arbor acting as superintendent of building, in addition to which the contract with Davis was annulled before these plans were drawn, and on the same day as the decision was made to build houses.

The more intriguing question is whether or not Thomson had help in developing the design. The houses as built (see fig. 37) were a marked departure from Davis's Gothic designs, but certainly more economically feasible for the university to execute. Thomson, who billed himself as an architect and builder, was doubtless capable of drawing the plans himself. However, his experiences in New Haven, especially with Ithiel Town and A. J. Davis, are likely to have influenced his

53. *State Journal,* February 21, 1839, Bentley.

Fig. 37. Professor's house, northwest unit, front view, University of Michigan, Ann Arbor, photo ca. 1876. Design attributed to Isaac Thomson. One of four identical houses built for professors. Built 1840; enlarged 1879; demolished 1915. Bentley Historical Library, University of Michigan (Sam Sturgis Collection, box 4, no. 675).

design. It is also possible that Davis did provide Thomson with ideas on how he might combine elegance and simplicity, decoration and economy. Although no actual letters or drawings exist that may have passed from Davis to Thomson at this time (early February 1839), there is evidence that they corresponded. An envelope survives of a letter from Thomson to Davis, dated Detroit, February 6, 1839.[54] Thomson, of course, would have written to Davis after January 31 to report the

54. Envelope consisting of a piece of paper folded and sealed, with seal broken. Addressed to "A. J. Davis, Esq., Arch, New York," with return address along right edge "I. Thompson, Detroit." Round postal stamp in upper left-hand corner "Detroit Mich Feb 6," and "1839" written in pencil underneath, Box 1 Correspondence 1820–80, A. J. Davis Papers, NYPL.

Fig. 38. Entry portico, President's House, University of Michigan, Ann Arbor, photo 1996 by J. M. Truettner. Design attributed to Isaac Thomson. House built 1840; enlarged several times; extant.

Fig. 39. Washington Square North town houses, New York City, photo ca. 1940, detail of units with entry porticoes in the Doric order. Design attributed to Martin E. Thompson. Built 1827–33; extant.
Courtesy of New York University Archives.

regents' decision to annul their contract with Thomson and Davis, and to obtain Davis's acquiescence to that annulment. At the same time Thomson may have informed Davis that the regents decided to build four professors' houses, and that they expected a plan for the houses to be presented at their next meeting. Perhaps Thomson asked Davis for advice on how best to develop these designs. Davis, for his part, may have responded to Thomson by referring to houses around New Haven, many of which were designed by Town and Davis, and some of which Thomson probably built. Davis may also have suggested specific design elements that could be used to dress up a less costly structure. But whether there was sufficient time for an exchange of correspondence and ideas between Davis and Thomson is a critical issue, as there were only eleven days between when the house designs were ordered (January 31) and when those designs were presented to the regents (February 11).

The two most notable elements of the professors' houses, the Doric entry portico and the Greek key fret in the parapet, have marked similarities to those used on houses in New Haven and

Fig. 40. Ralph Ingersoll house, New Haven, drawing by William Adams Delano, 1918 (later known as the Earl Trumbull Williams Memorial). Designed by Ithiel Town and Alexander Jackson Davis. Built 1829–31; extant.
Courtesy of Manuscripts and Archives, Yale University Library.

New York designed by Town and Davis, as well as Town's onetime associate Martin Thompson. The Doric entry portico on the professors' houses (fig. 38) is a close copy of that found on the Washington Square North town houses, attributed to Martin Thompson (fig. 39). This evidence indicates that the route taken by this Doric entry from New York to Ann Arbor went via Thompson, Town, and Davis, to Isaac Thomson. The classical entry portico, in numerous variations, was used on many houses designed by Thompson, Town, and Davis. One of the most notable for this discussion is the Ralph Ingersoll house, by Town and Davis, built in 1831 in New Haven (fig. 40). This house sports a Doric entry as well, here with the columns *in antis,* but what also distinguishes it for this discussion is its five-bay form. Davis is known to have primarily designed classical

Fig. 41. Henry Whitney house, New Haven, 1835. Design by Alexander Jackson Davis. Built 1835; demolished 1924.

Metropolitan Museum of Art, Harris Brisbane Dick Fund, 1924 (24.66.1416[33], scrapbook 17, leaf 38).

houses in a three-bay arrangement, therefore casting doubt on his possible relation to the professors' houses in Ann Arbor. But in the Ingersoll house is found a five-bay form remarkably similar to that of the Ann Arbor houses. In addition, the Ingersoll house originally carried a parapet above the roofline with Greek ornamentation that concealed the dormers.[55] Similarly, many of the Wash-

55. Brown, *New Haven: A Guide,* 105.

Fig. 42. Henry Brevoort Jr. house, New York City, photo ca. 1910 by Robert W. Tebbs. Design attributed to Ithiel Town and Alexander Jackson Davis. Built 1834; demolished 1925.
Collection of The New-York Historical Society (neg. 73097).

ington Square North town houses featured parapets above the roofline, in this case with balusters rather than a key fret pattern.

The placement of the key fret in a parapet above the roofline on the professors' houses is also somewhat unusual. The source of this element is not clear. Although use of the fret design on houses was quite common in America, its placement was usually along the frieze, below the roofline or cornice. This device was used numerous times by Davis, such as in his design for the Whitney house (fig. 41), which also reflects his use of the three-bay form, as well as a more monumentally developed classic portico, here in the Corinthian order. An additional piece of evidence provides a tie between Davis and the key fret in the parapet design. This is the Henry Brevoort Jr. house, built in 1834 on Fifth Avenue in New York City, and attributed to Town and Davis (fig. 42).[56]

56. Henry Collins Brown, *Fifth Avenue Old and New, 1824–1924* (New York: Fifth Avenue Association, 1924), 35; Theodore James Jr., *Fifth Avenue* (New York: Walker, 1971), 27; Nathan Silver, *Lost New York* (New York: Houghton Mifflin, 1967), 117; John C. Donoghue, "Alexander Jackson Davis, Romantic Architect, 1803–1892," Ph.D. diss., New York University, 1977, 187; and Hamlin, *Greek Revival Architecture*, 131.

Credited with jump-starting the development of Fifth Avenue as one of the toniest addresses in New York by the construction of this elegant house at Ninth Street, Brevoort was also the grandfather of James Renwick Jr., the architect of St. Patrick's Cathedral. Brevoort's three-bay mansion featured a classic entry portico in the Ionic order, a bay window on the side, and more interestingly, a Greek key fret pattern in the parapet above the roofline.

It would seem apparent that Isaac Thomson derived the details for the houses from his knowledge of the works of Town and Davis. However, there is another source that Thomson could have utilized that would have aided him in developing the designs on his own. These were the builder's handbooks or pattern books that by the 1830s were widely available in the United States.[57] The publication of these sourcebooks was one of the primary reasons for the rapid dissemination of classical orders and details across the country in the early nineteenth century. The handbooks provided not only detailed descriptions based on the antiquities of Greece and Rome, but also measured drawings, which allowed builders to incorporate classic elements in their buildings. This was especially important before the emergence of the professional architect and the widespread practice of the architect's trade. With numerous pattern books readily available, builders could easily dress up simple structures by adding classical elements, including entry porticoes expressed in one of the Greek or Roman orders such as Doric or Ionic.

For accurate information on the classic orders, the writers of the handbooks had relied not on firsthand observations of antiquities but on previously published materials. For Greek orders, Marcus Vitruvius Pollio's *The Ten Books on Architecture* (first century B.C.) was the primary source, and for the Roman orders it was Andrea Palladio's *Four Books of Architecture* (Venice, 1570). Palladio was also a prolific and talented architect whose designs were widely copied and, when combined with the publication of his books in English, touched off "Palladio-mania" in England in the eighteenth century. One of the most important events contributing to the widespread development of pattern books was the publication in London in 1762 of *The Antiquities of Athens and Other Monuments of Greece* by James Stuart and Nicholas Revett. Printed in three folio volumes, it was the first publication to provide complete measured illustrations of Greek antiquities as they existed in situ. In addition, Stuart and Revett provided illustrations of "restored" versions of the antiquities, showing how the structures might have appeared originally, before centuries of degradation. Their illustrations would prove extremely influential and would be widely copied by pattern book writers, as well as architects and builders. As already shown, A. J. Davis was deeply influenced by Stuart and Revett, a copy of whose books Ithiel Town owned. Davis utilized many elements from Stuart and Revett, such as the Choragic Monument on his Indiana capitol (see figs. 12 and 13), the Doric portico or Gate of the Agora for his South Congregational Church (see fig. 16), and the Tower of the Winds at New York University (see figs. 21 and 22).

57. Dell Upton, "Pattern Books and Professionalism: Aspects of the Transformation of Domestic Architecture in America, 1800–1860," *Winterthur Portfolio* 19, nos. 2–3 (1984): 109.

The first original American architectural handbook was written by builder-architect Asher Benjamin. *The Country Builder's Assistant,* first published in Massachusetts in 1797, was followed by several handbooks in many editions, the most popular of which was *The Architect, or Practical House Carpenter* (Boston, 1830). Another author of extremely popular handbooks in America was Minard Lafever. His first book was *The Young Builder's General Instructor* (Newark, 1829), but it was his second book, *The Modern Builder's Guide* (New York, 1833), that was the most popular. As previously discussed, both Asher Benjamin and Minard Lafever were personally known to Ithiel Town and A. J. Davis. In fact, two former Town and Davis employees, James Dakin and James Gallier, had provided illustrations for Lafever's *Modern Builder's Guide* (see fig. 18).

By the 1830s, dozens of pattern books were being published in America and were readily available to builders like Isaac Thomson. Architects such as Davis also utilized these publications as sources for details. We have only to look as far as Asher Benjamin and Minard Lafever to locate sources that Isaac Thomson could have used when designing the professors' houses at Ann Arbor. For example, in his *Young Builder's General Instructor,* Lafever provided a design for a front door in the Doric order (fig. 43), with the columns set *in antis,* as seen on the Brevoort house (see fig. 42). The same Doric entry would be used by architect-builder Charles Lum for the Bank of Michigan, the first structure of dressed stone built in Detroit, which was completed in 1836.[58] Asher Benjamin, in his *Practical House Carpenter,* provided illustrations of key fret patterns, as well as cornices, some featuring a Greek key fret. These are only two examples of the hundreds of details available to builders through the handbooks and pattern books that were widely available in the early nineteenth century.[59] Isaac Thomson could have consulted many—or none—when drawing the plan for the professors' houses.

All this evidence leads to the conclusion that although the plan approved for the professors' houses was probably drawn by Isaac Thomson's hand, the elements that made up the design came to Thomson from his association with A. J. Davis, and Davis's experiences with Ithiel Town and Martin Thompson, as well as from the builder's handbooks available in that day. This design, which had "quiet dignity, good proportion, and excellent detail,"[60] was duly adopted by the regents, who then turned their attention to the placement of the four houses on the large forty-acre campus. This was addressed by the regents at the same meeting where the house plan was approved, February 11, 1839, when Chief Justice Fletcher proposed a resolution, which was adopted.

> That the avenue of one hundred feet in width commencing at the north side of the ground appropriated for a site of the University and running south through the center of the ground be

58. W. Hawkins Ferry, *The Buildings of Detroit* (Detroit: Wayne State University Press, 1968), 33. Charles Lum, noted for several works in Detroit, would later be unsuccessfully recommended for builder for the University of Michigan. The Doric entrance from the Bank of Michigan, built 1836 in Detroit, was acquired by Architecture dean Emil Lorch in 1930 when the bank was demolished. The Doric entry today stands in the courtyard of Lorch Hall, at the University of Michigan in Ann Arbor.

59. For those interested in the subject, additional information is provided in the "Builder's Handbooks and Pattern Books" section of the bibliography.

60. Emil Lorch, "President's House, Michigan University," *Michigan Architect and Engineer,* April 1921, 63.

Fig. 43. Doric entry. Drawn by Minard Lafever for his book *Young Builder's General Instructor* (Newark, 1829), plate 45.
Courtesy of Hatcher Graduate Library, University of Michigan.

> opened, and that the buildings ordered to be erected for the use of Professors and for the general use of the University for the time being, be erected two of them on the south side of the ground, one on each side of the avenue hereby directed to be opened, and two on the north side of the ground, one on each side of the said avenue. (*RP,* 71)

Here then is some evidence that the regents had not entirely abandoned Davis's plans. In fact, at their previous meeting they referred to the main buildings (Davis's Gothic designs) as though they would yet be executed. Both of the campus plans by Davis that survive include a central, or public, avenue of one hundred feet in width (see figs. 29 and 30). The regents must certainly have based their decision to open the avenue on these plans. In addition, their indication to place the houses on either side of the avenue at the north and south ends, corresponds closely to locations marked on one of Davis's plans for "future buildings." It would seem apparent that the regents were still intent on realizing the plans they had paid Davis so handsomely for.

What is not apparent, per the *Regents' Proceedings*, is whether any other plan for the grounds (all forty acres) was drawn at the time the professors' houses were ordered up. Some of the regents may have continued to entertain the hope that one of Davis's designs for a main building might yet be realized. Given Superintendent Pierce's staunch veto, this surely seemed hopeless. Nevertheless, there may have been some feeling that part of Davis's plan for the campus layout could still be executed, even though the actual style of the main building might vary from the Gothic. The one-hundred-foot avenue was certainly taken from Davis's plan, although his idea to place the professors' houses on the rear or east side of campus was not. It probably seemed more logical to place the four houses next to the avenue for convenience and access, until such time as the main building was prosecuted. There may have been a thought that the main building could be placed according to Davis's plan, but not set back so far as indicated. This would certainly work better if there were houses at either end of the avenue.

The creation of the central avenue and the placement of the houses were thus agreed upon in February 1839. It is not recorded, but the decision had apparently also been made to have the four houses face the street, although this may not have required a specific decision, since urban houses invariably did face onto the city streets. In addition, the grounds of the university were more in keeping with a backyard, as the acreage was comprised mostly of pasture. The grounds at that time were better suited for use by the faculty for vegetable gardens and the maintenance of livestock. One regent, however, had a different notion. On March 26, 1839, Dr. Zina Pitcher proposed a resolution that would "cause the four buildings now authorized to be erected on the University grounds, to be constructed facing inwards to the said grounds" (*RP,* 80). The resolution was laid on the table. At the next board meeting on April 2, 1839, the resolution was taken up "for consideration," and again tabled. It is never mentioned again, and the four houses were shortly to be under construction—facing out to the street. With the state of the grounds being what they were, it is no wonder the majority of the regents were opposed to having the houses face the area where the sheep were grazing.

It is probable that Isaac Thomson drew a simple plan of the grounds that showed the central avenue and the recommended sites for the houses. This cannot be confirmed, although it is known that Thomson did provide some plans to the regents. In July 1839, the regents requested that the superintendent (Thomson) provide plans for fencing the grounds and for such out-buildings as may be needed (*RP,* 94). In addition, in their report submitted March 6, 1840 (see appendix), the Building Committee indicated that they had "obtained from Mr. Thompson certain plans and estimates of cost of fences and out-buildings which have heretofore been exhibited to the Board of Regents." At the same meeting, a resolution was adopted, "That the Building Committee be instructed to contract for building fences around the University lands at Ann Arbor, the fence in front of the buildings made after plan No. I, furnished by Mr. Thompson." In addition, it was resolved, "That the same Committee contract for the erection of a wood-house to each of the buildings on the University lands at Ann Arbor, agreeably to the plan furnished by Mr. Thompson" (*RP,* 124–27). Thomson obviously provided more than one plan that included fencing around the campus and the houses, as well as out-buildings such as wood-houses. These wood-houses were by no means shacks, but substantial buildings that carried decorative embellishments in the classical style, to relate them to the houses. These structures, along with the perimeter fencing, may be the first on campus that are clearly attributable to a particular architect. Isaac Thomson did indeed design the wood-houses and fences.

In the *Regents' Proceedings* for July 12, 1839, a reference was made to the "buildings now erecting on the University Grounds in Ann Arbor" (*RP,* 93). This was the first indication that the houses were under construction. The work was begun sometime between mid-April and mid-July on the first two houses. Shortly thereafter the second two would also have been under construction. These houses (see fig. 37) were five bays wide, with a central hall and two rooms on each side of the hall, on both floors. They also had a raised basement, and a low-pitched roof hidden behind a parapet. Built of brick, they were then covered with stucco that was subsequently scored to resemble blocks of stone. The balanced facade featured double-hung windows with six-over-six lights; there were originally no windows on the sides of the houses. Initially shutters were placed only on the first floor front windows. Across the back of the houses was a full-length porch with square columns, supporting an entablature similar to that on the front portico (fig. 44). The parapet above the roofline had a simple Greek key fret design and was most likely made of wood. In the center of the roof was a low square cupola used for ventilation. Of the four houses built, only one survives. This is the southwest unit, which in 1852 became the President's House when Henry Philip Tappan took up residence. There is no known photograph of the President's House before the first of many enlargements was made to it in 1864. The earliest known image of this house is a sketch by Jasper F. Cropsey (fig. 45), drawn in 1855 when he was invited to Ann Arbor by President Tappan to paint a landscape view of the university grounds. Tappan and Cropsey were acquaintances from New York, where Tappan had been on faculty at New York University and Cropsey one of the Hudson River artists, who traveled in the same circles with, among others, A. J. Davis, Ithiel Town, Samuel F. B. Morse, and Thomas Cole. Cropsey's sketch view of the President's House from the back shows the key fret in the parapet, as well as the low cupola on the roof. The cupolas are also clearly visible in Cropsey's view of the campus (see plate 12), and in an 1866 bird's-eye view map (see fig. 75). The front of each house was graced by an entry portico that featured fluted Doric columns carrying a full entablature. Although the columns were correctly placed without a base (per Greek antiquities) many other hallmarks of the Doric style were omitted, as had become the custom in America, including such features as mutules

Fig. 44. Professor's house, northwest unit, rear view, University of Michigan, Ann Arbor, photo ca. 1870. Design attributed to Isaac Thomson. Built 1840; enlarged 1879; demolished 1915. Note wood-house to right and octagon house to left. The octagon stood across the street on the current site of Hill Auditorium.
Bentley Historical Library, University of Michigan (Photo Vertical File, folder D13-267).

with guttae, triglyphs, and metopes (see fig. 7). Surrounding the front door were narrow sidelights and a transom.

With the houses under construction by July 1839, the regents made another decision that would have strong bearing on the execution of the building program. On July 13, 1839, the regents adopted a resolution that "the Building Committee be instructed to give notice to Mr. Thompson that the contract between him as superintendent of the University Buildings and said Committee is annulled by order of the Board of Regents." They further resolved that "the Building Committee be requested to contract with Mr. Lum for completion of the last two buildings mentioned in all respects agreeably to the specifications mentioned in the two first, at the same rate at which he has contracted to finish the said first two buildings" (*RP,* 93). Less than a year since Alexander J. Davis and Isaac Thomson first came to Ann Arbor, and five months after Thomson was made sole superintendent of buildings, Thomson was removed from the scene. The regents certainly must have felt a continued economic pinch, and with the houses designed and under construction, super-

Fig. 45. President's House, rear view, University of Michigan, Ann Arbor, 1855. Sketch by Jasper Francis Cropsey. Design attributed to Isaac Thomson. Built 1840; enlarged several times, extant. Bentley Historical Library, University of Michigan (Jasper Francis Cropsey sketchbook).

vised by an able builder (Lum), they probably felt they could get by without Thomson's continued presence and expenditure of salary.

Thomson was not paid any portion of his contract until August 10, 1839, when he received five hundred dollars. The regents would have determined that this was the amount due him for up to six months' work on his one-thousand-dollar-per-year contract, which had been executed in February 1839. Aside from the money, Thomson must have felt that the termination of his contract cast doubt on his abilities as a builder, for he wrote to the regents to this effect. They responded as follows on August 9, 1839:

> On motion of Mr. Duffield, the following preamble and resolution was adopted: A communication was received from Mr. Thompson expressing some uneasiness and misapprehension in relation to the resolution of the Board dispensing with his services as Superintendent, adopted at their later meeting in Ann Arbor, and after some conversation with the Board, *Resolved,* That the resolution to dispense with his services as Superintendent was induced by a conviction of the necessity of economy on the part of the Board and a belief that having obtained the full benefit of

> his services, it became necessary agreeably to the contract to give him the stipulated notice before the relationship between him and them should cease, and further, that the Board entertain full confidence in his integrity and fidelity and a just sense of the value of his services as their Superintendent. (*RP,* 96–97)

Having his ruffled feathers thus justly smoothed, Thomson then addressed the issue of salary. He was paid in August 1839 for the first six months of his contract. That contract had been terminated in July. The regents indicated that it was written into the contract that it could be canceled after six months and so they paid him for the first six months. However, the contract also stated that three months' notice must be given before it could be terminated. Thomson was given no notice and paid for only one month after the contract ended (so as to fulfill the six-month obligation). Thomson felt he was due the pay for the three-month period he should have been given as notice. Thomson seemed to have a legitimate argument, and it continued to be discussed for some time. Finally, on April 7, 1840, nine months after Thomson had left Ann Arbor, the regents resolved that "the Building Committee be directed to settle with Mr. Thompson and pay him what balance may be due to him, if any, by virtue of his compact with the Board" (*RP,* 127). Shortly thereafter Thomson wrote to A. J. Davis concerning this issue, as Thomson still owed Davis money from when they both were under contract to the regents.

> Mr. Alex. J. Davis
> Dear Sir—
> I have this moment received the first intelligence from Mr. Lum since he left; in December last & am happy to state that after so long a time there appears to be a fair prospect of getting my claim on the Regents until; which it will be utterly out of my powers to pay you any part of your claim against me & when I do receive it it shall be remitted to you without one moments delay. Business is excessively dull here & it is not without difficulty that I get money enough for marketing—
> Your friend
> New Haven Isaac Thomson
> April 22 1840[61]

When they were both under contract, Thomson would receive payment from the regents, as he was in Ann Arbor, and would then send Davis his share. Davis noted in his diary more than once that Thomson was less than punctual in his payments to Davis.[62] But in his letter of April 22, 1840,

61. Letter Isaac Thomson to Alex J. Davis, April 22, 1840, Alexander Jackson Davis Collection II, Folder 31-7, p. 34, Avery.

62. In his office diary for September 1838, when describing their visit to Ann Arbor, Davis indicated their fees would be six hundred dollars, of which two hundred dollars would be Thomson's share. Underneath this entry Davis wrote, "Mr. Thompson received money, but returned me nothing," vol. 1, Diary, p. 61, Alexander Jackson Davis Collection, Met, Harris Brisbane Dick Fund (24.66.1400). A ledger entry in his daybook for September 18, 1839 (a month after Thomson was paid five hundred dollars for six months of his contract) indicates "Received of I. Thompson on acct.—30.00. Due bill for $170.00 payable Dec. 1839. 200 settlement," with no further indication that the balance due was paid. Office Diary 1827–53, p. 201, A. J. Davis Papers, NYPL.

to Davis, it appears Thomson planned to pay Davis if the regents came through. However, Thomson would have to wait a long time for this affair to be concluded. It is not until January 1842, two and a half years after Thomson left Ann Arbor, that the regents finally wrestled with the issue. On January 10, 1842, a resolution was offered that read "*Resolved,* That it is the opinion of this Board that Mr. Thompson has been paid in full for his services as architect and superintendent under his contract with the Board." The resolution was laid on the table, but when taken up again on January 24, 1842, it was adopted (*RP,* 215, 217). One of the most notable things about this resolution is that the regents referred to Thomson as an architect, in addition to superintendent. They would hardly have referred to him as such if he had not acted at least partly in that capacity, which supports the inference that Thomson drew the design that was executed for the professors' houses. In fact, in a report by the Finance Committee on Thomson's claim, dated November 13, 1841, the committee also referred to Thomson as architect (*RP,* 191). At that time, the Finance Committee simply reported the facts and turned the subject back to the full board for decision.

It was July 1839, the houses were under construction, and Isaac Thomson had left the building zone. The regents then entered into a new contract with Harpin Lum to complete the erection of the houses. This was the first time Lum's name appeared in the *Regents' Proceedings,* although he had been acting as builder since February 1839. The terms of the contract between the regents and Lum were not written into the record, and the contract does not survive. However, it was indicated that Lum was to finish the second two houses at the rate he had been contracted for the first two, which was $7,450 each, although the earlier contract had specified $6,000 for each of the last two. In addition, Lum was authorized to finish the houses in stucco and to be paid $250 for each for this work. To execute the stucco work, Lum would hire yet another person from New Haven, George Gill (*RP,* 138–39). Gill (1796–1873) was a highly regarded stucco plasterer in New Haven, and a leading citizen of that town, which named Gill Street in his honor.[63]

Progress on the houses moved rapidly, and by October 1839 they were in "such a state of forwardness as to justify the belief that one of them will be ready to be appropriated" to receive the library and the natural history "cabinet," or specimens (*RP,* 99). No work as yet had begun on the central avenue, when on November 26, 1839, the regents "*Resolved,* That the resolution heretofore adopted, directing an avenue of one hundred feet in width, running north and south through the centre of the University grounds at Ann Arbor, be and the same is hereby rescinded" (*RP,* 102). As a result, the avenue so prominently provided for in A. J. Davis's plans was never realized.

In March 1840 the regents ordered a fence to be built around the entire forty-acre campus, and for wood-houses to be built one at each professor's house, both fence and wood-houses accord-

63. New Haven City Directory 1849, p. 56, listing for George Gill, stucco plasterer; New Haven City Directory 1860, p. 399, listing for Gill and Beach, ornamental plasterers; New Haven Vital Records, p. 1058, marriage of George Gill and Eunice Baldwin, April 1852; Grove Street Cemetery tombstone engravings, "Gill, George, died July 22, 1873, age 77 yrs."; Harpin Lum Papers, New Haven Colony, MSS-82, folder G, receipt from Harpin Lum to George Gill for stuccoing and coloring Hull House, October 1848; and Doris B. Townshend, *The Streets of New Haven: The Origin of Their Names* (New Haven: New Haven Colony Historical Society, 1984), 66.

ing to plans they had obtained the previous year from Isaac Thomson. The wood-houses, as mentioned, were substantial, attractive buildings. They stood close to the houses on their inner sides, or closest to what would have been the central avenue. They appear on all maps of the era. They were one story rectangular "houses" with a hipped roof (see figs. 44 and 82). Built of brick, they were also covered with stucco that was scored to resemble stone. They had doors and windows, and featured a wide frieze board and pilasters—classical elements that married them stylistically to the houses they accompanied. Why such a large structure would be built just to store wood may be questioned. But for the university it was practical to buy large quantities of wood in the off season when the prices were low. Wood to last through the winter would require a large storage facility.

By early spring 1840 the four houses for professors were complete, and the board turned its attention to the issue of the main university building. On April 7 and 8, 1840, the regents would make a decision to prosecute a plan for building that would forever put an end to the possibility that a Davis plan might yet be executed. On April 7, the Building Committee was directed to "procure and report to this Board tomorrow, a plan for a principal building to be erected on the site of the University at Ann Arbor, together with the estimates for erecting and completing the same" (*RP,* 127). The committee was given only one day to prepare this plan, but the feat was accomplished. The next day, April 8, 1840 (*RP,* 128–29):

> Justice Fletcher, from the Building Committee, submitted the following, with plan accompanying the same, which was accepted.
>
> The Building Committee in pursuance of the Resolution of yesterday requiring them to procure and report a plan for a building for the use of the University, together with an estimate of the expenses, hereby report, and submit a plan of such building, with an estimate of the expense of the same.
>
> Ann Arbor, April 8th, 1840.
>
> The accompanying plan is 100 feet long, 42 feet wide, and four stories high, containing 32 studies, 32 wood-rooms, 64 bed-rooms, and 64 closets, which I have made an estimate for the erection and completion, and find that it will not cost more than sixteen thousand dollars.
>
> Harpin Lum

The design presented to the board by Lum survives (fig. 46). It is the oldest extant drawing of a University of Michigan building that was executed, although even in its construction changes were made that caused the actual structure to vary from that adopted by the regents. The drawing is not signed, but there can be no doubt that it was drawn by Lum. In addition, a floor plan related to this design survives (fig. 47), which shows how each floor was divided into four sections accessed by four entrances. This plan is for one of the dormitory floors and shows suites of rooms

Fig. 46. Main Building or North Wing, University of Michigan, Ann Arbor, 1840. Drawn by Harpin Lum. Inscribed at top "Ann Arbor April 8th 1840—This plan for University buildings was this day adopted by the Board of Regents of the University. A. Ten Eyck Sect'y Board of Regents." Anthony Ten Eyck served as secretary to the regents 1839–45. Built 1841; demolished 1950.

Bentley Historical Library, University of Michigan (University of Michigan Architectural Drawings, folder 5).

comprised of a sitting room, two bedrooms with closets, and a wood-closet. Recitation rooms, as well as space for the library and natural history cabinet, were also provided in this building. Although generally accepted as a drawing of the building as executed, Lum's plan was actually altered in execution. The structure when built (fig. 48) featured a central stepped-out portion not seen in Lum's drawing. A floor plan related to this version of the building also survives (fig. 49), and shows the stepped-out central pavilion. On the inside the layout is similar to the other floor plan. The large room on the end is probably a recitation room.

Stylistically, an attempt was made to tie the Main Building to the professors' houses, through the use of the key fret design in the parapet. In addition, this simple building with its clean lines was built of brick, which was covered in stucco and again scored to resemble stone. There is nothing outwardly remarkable about this design, and nothing that would indicate that Lum sought help from anyone in its preparation. Only one day was allowed for the plan to be drawn and presented to the board. Lum may have consulted with some of the regents, and among themselves they may have made reference to other college buildings they were familiar with, such as at Yale, Dartmouth, Columbia, and so on, and offered examples for Lum to draw from. It is possible that in the previous year when the original Gothic designs were being set aside, that A. J. Davis, on the request of Isaac Thomson, could have provided suggestions for a main building in the classical style

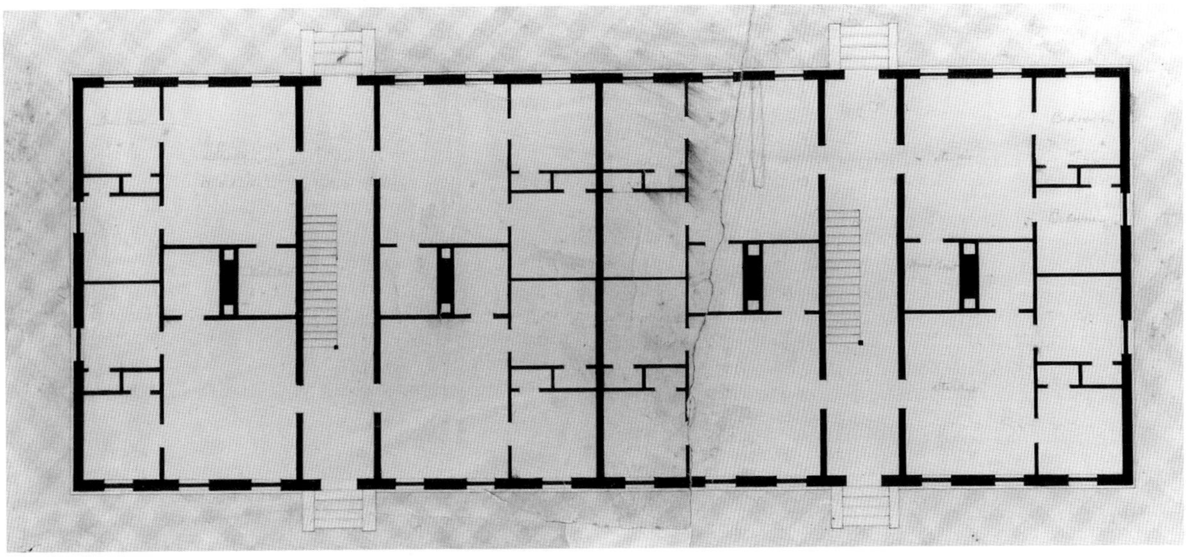

Fig. 47. Floor plan for Main Building or North Wing (flat front), University of Michigan, Ann Arbor, ca. 1840. Probably drawn by Harpin Lum.
Bentley Historical Library, University of Michigan (University of Michigan Architectural Drawings, folder 5).

that would have been an appropriate companion to the professors' houses. However, it is more likely that Lum, an experienced builder who was also familiar with the classical buildings of Yale, had the knowledge and capability to draw this rather simple plan for the Main Building on his own.

The decision to construct a main classroom/dorm building and to adopt the plan drawn by Harpin Lum was not without contention. In fact, when Lum presented his plan to the board, there was some disagreement as to whether it should be accepted. Opposing resolutions were offered that would either adopt the plan or lay the whole decision on the table. Major Jonathan Kearsley stood alone against the rest of the board in staunch opposition to accepting Lum's plan. It is not known if Kearsley was opposed to the plan because he still hoped a Gothic structure would be realized, or because he was simply dissatisfied with Lum's designs, or because he was concerned over finances and felt construction of a main building at that time was precipitous, or for other reasons. At any rate, he was voted down by the rest of the board, who "*Resolved,* That the Building Committee proceed with all convenient speed to erect and finish a building upon the site of the University at Ann Arbor, according to the plan adopted this day." In addition, the committee was "authorized to employ a superintendent to superintend the erection and finishing of said building" (*RP,* 129). The committee wasted no time in proceeding with their task, and quickly advertised for the materials and labor needed:

> PROPOSALS FOR BUILDING MATERIALS AND LABOR—Sealed proposals will be received until the 6th day of May next, for the whole or any part of the following building materials for the use of the University of Michigan, to be delivered upon the University grounds at Ann Arbor, under the direction of the undersigned or their agents, namely:

Fig. 48. North Wing or Mason Hall, University of Michigan, Ann Arbor, photo late 1870. Design attributed to Harpin Lum. Built 1841; demolished 1950. The small wing at the north end of the building (left in photo) was built in 1862 to house a marble copy of Randolph Rogers's *Nydia, the Blind Flower Girl of Pompeii* (now in the university's Museum of Art). The pewter statue of Ben Franklin, seen on the right, was a gift from the Class of 1870; vandalism and the weather caused the statue's demise circa 1900.
Bentley Historical Library, University of Michigan (Photo Vertical File, folder D13-234).

48,000 feet of Oak timber, (sawed.)
85,000 feet of Whitewood boards, plank and fencing stuff.
10,000 feet of Black Walnut, for fence rails, (sawed.)
37,000 feet of Pine boards and plank.
20 m. Pine shingles.
415 m. Brick
6,000 cubic feet stone, (measured in the wall.)
1,500 bushels lime.

All the above materials to be furnished at the times and according to a bill, which may be seen upon application to J. Kearsley, Detroit, or Harpin Lum, Ann Arbor, and to be received subject to the inspection of the said Lum, or any other agent appointed by the undersigned. Satisfactory security to be given for the fulfillment of the several contracts—the names of the sureties to be stated in the proposals.

Payment for the materials furnished to be made at the rate of three-fourths on each delivery,

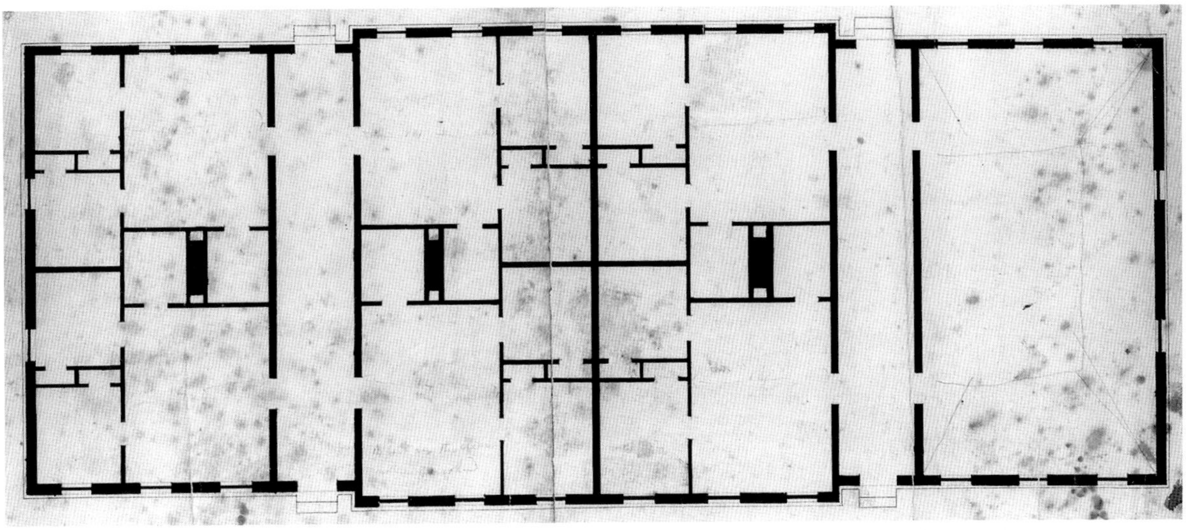

Fig. 49. Floor plan for Main Building or North Wing (stepped-out central part), University of Michigan, Ann Arbor, ca. 1840. Probably drawn by Harpin Lum.
Bentley Historical Library, University of Michigan (University of Michigan Architectural Drawings, folder 5).

until the contract be completed. The right reserved to the undersigned to add to the quantity required at the contract price, upon giving to the contractor fifteen days notice. Any bid to be declined if the undersigned deem it for the interest of the University so to do.

Proposals will also be received until the said 6th day of May, for the labor required in the erection of a brick building on the University grounds at Ann Arbor, as follows, namely:

For laying 400 perches of stone wall, in foundation, (pr perch.)
For laying 390 m brick in walls, (pr m.)
For laying 25 m brick in four cisterns under ground, including the excavations.
For building four wood houses.
For lathing and plastering the main building pr. yard.
For Carpenters and Joiners work of the same, including floors, doors, windows, roof, &c.

For building 350 rods of board fences around the University grounds.

The whole of said work to be done according to plans and specifications in the hands of Harpin Lum in Ann Arbor, and J. Kearsley at Detroit.

J. KEARSLEY,
Wm. A. FLETCHER, } Building
C. C. TROWBRIDGE. } Committee[64]

64. *State Journal,* April 15, 1840, and April 21, 1840, Bentley.

When the regents met on July 7, 1840, the Building Committee reported that they had begun construction of the "Main Building." They also reported that they had retained Harpin Lum as superintendent for the building because his "skill, industry, integrity, have been so fully and satisfactorily exhibited to the Board of Regents in the erection of the Professors' houses" (*RP,* 138). The board also voted an additional 5 percent per annum to Lum to cover the costs of bringing in workers from the east to stucco the building. The hiring of Lum to continue as superintendent again rankled the ire of local builders, who held a meeting of mechanics to protest the regents' action, and subsequently had their minutes widely published.

MECHANICS' MEETING.

At an adjourned meeting of the Mechanics' of the county of Washtenaw, connected with the Art of Building, held at the Washtenaw House, in the village of Ann Arbor on the 29th day of June 1840, Rial B. Chase was chosen Chairman, and C. J. F. Vail appointed Secretary.

The committee appointed at the former meeting to report resolutions upon any of the officers of the University of their Agents, we cannot in justice to ourselves withhold an expression of the keen sense of the disrespect that has been cast upon the Mechanics of this state by the unqualified declaration of certain members of the Board of Regents, and of our disapprobation of the blind and changing policy of the Building Committee as established through their agent Mr. Harpin Lum by which a discretionary power has been vested in him prejudicial to the interest of the Mechanics of this state.

Resolved, That the avowal hitherto made by a member, or members, of the Board of Regents, that "*there were no mechanics in this state who were either sufficiently responsible or capable to superintend the erection of the University Building,*" was a declaration as unjust in its design, so humbling to the mechanics in its expression, and so prejudicial to their credit in its effect, that we are in duty bound to meet it in a spirit of just and manly indignation, and we call upon the inhabitants of the state generally to frown upon every such ungenerous attempt to bring into disrepute any respectable class of citizens.

Resolved, That the building mechanics of this state have just ground for complaint of the business operations of the University for

Reason 1st, That the Building Committee through their Agent Mr. H. Lum, exhibited specifications and plans for work to be done on and around the University Buildings, on which were predicated estimates and proposals for contracts; and after such proposals had been handed in by the different individuals, the plan and manner of the work was *changed,* and let to favored contractors upon a different plan than was exhibited by the specifications.

2d. The Agent of the Building Committee has formed himself an arbitrary rule unknown to the acknowledged customs of building mechanics, and which he did not publish or make known until after the receipt of proposals, and which led to serious disappointment and inconvenience on the part of those who proposed to become contractors.

3d. Mechanics have been invited here from other states to become contractors for the work to the exclusion of those within our own state, who are equally "responsible and capable," and who have been unjustly deprived of the rights of fair and equal competition with the foreign mechanic.

Resolved, That the far-fetched and dear-bo't policy adopted by the Board of Regents by which non-resident mechanics have been specially preferred and favored for the erection of the University buildings, is calculated to injure the credit of the Mechanics of our own state, impair their respectability and usefulness, and to damp their spirit, enterprize and emulation, which alone can enable them to excel in their several occupations, and do credit to themselves and the state.

Resolved, As the opinion of this meeting, that the present Superintendent is incompetent to perform the duties pertaining to his station and hence the necessity for his calling upon under workmen for all his plans and draughts of work: and that the interests of the University as well as a just and respectful policy towards the building mechanics of this state require his removal from the station he now occupies, and the appointment of some competent citizen of our own state to supply his place and perform his duties.

Resolved, That we have entire confidence in the fidelity, in the integrity and mechanical ability of Mr. Charles Lum of Detroit, and cheerfully recommend his appointment to the station of Superintendent and Architect of the University Buildings.

The Committee appointed at the former meeting to drawn up a memorial to the Board of Regents made a report, which was adopted by the meeting.

On motion, Resolved, That a committee of three citizens, not connected with the art of building, be appointed to present the memorial to the Board of Regents.

Messrs. J. Sanders, Peter Slingerland and C. S. Goodrich were appointed said committee.

On motion, Resolved, That we recommend the organization of a permanent society, consisting of the mechanics of the county of Washtenaw connected with the art of building.

Resolved, That a committee of five be appointed to draft a constitution and by-laws for the government of said society, to be submitted to a meeting to be held at the Ypsilanti Exchange, in the village of Ypsilanti, on Saturday the 18th day of July next, at 2 o'clock in the afternoon at which time and place the Mechanics of this community are requested to attend.

On motion, Resolved, That the proceedings of this meeting be signed by the Chairman and Secretary and published in the Democratic Herald and Michigan State Journal.

On motion, adjourned.

R. B. CHASE, Chairman

C. J. F. VAIL, Secretary[65]

65. *State Journal*, July 14, 1840, Bentley.

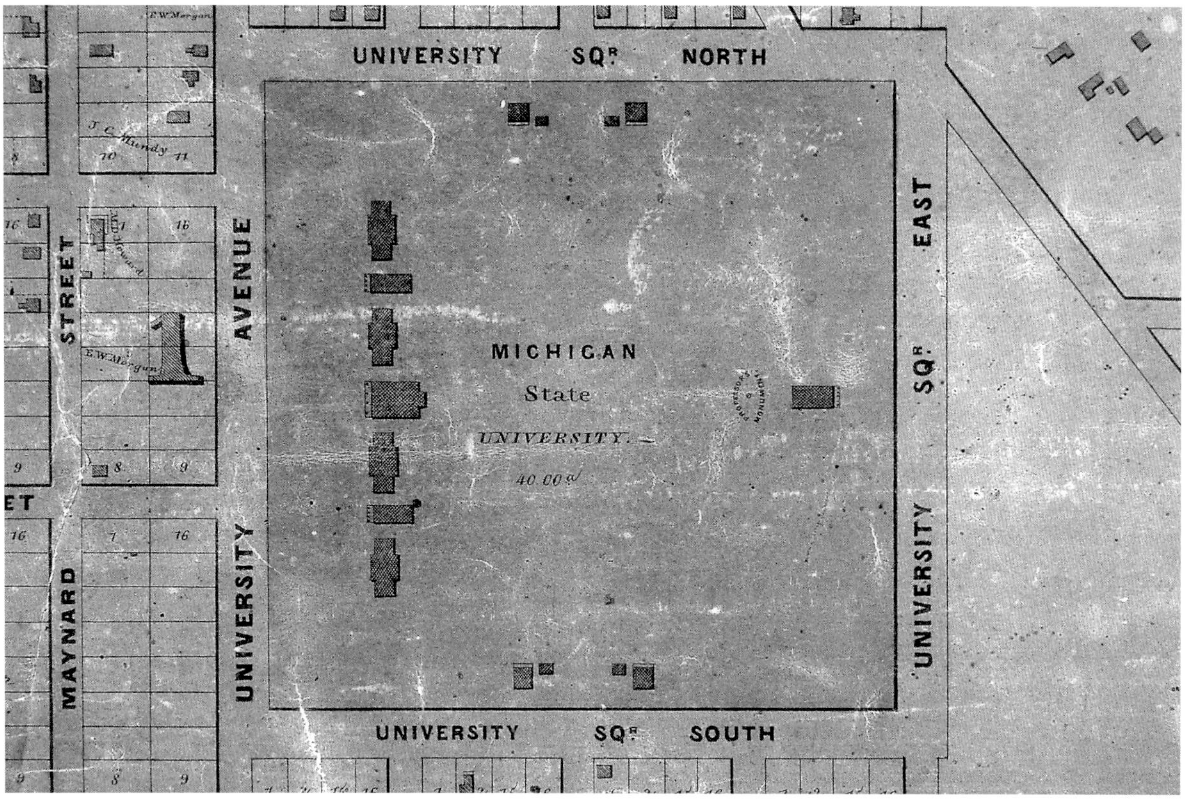

Fig. 50. Map of Ann Arbor, by Henry Hart, 1853, detail of University of Michigan campus area.
Courtesy of Map Library, Hatcher Graduate Library, University of Michigan.

The regents did not record whether the mechanics' "memorial" was presented to them, nor is there any mention of this unhappy situation in their surviving records. The mechanics of the state apparently received no satisfaction on their complaint, as construction on the university building continued apace, with Harpin Lum as superintendent.

As discussed, Lum undoubtedly provided the design for the Main Building that had been presented to the regents. More important than the design of the Main Building, however, was the decision made on where to place it on the forty-acre campus. Nothing was recorded that sheds light on this issue. What is interesting is that although it was consistently referred to as the "Main Building," it was placed not centered north and south, but rather as a wing to a future central building might be placed. How was this decision arrived at, and were any plans drawn that reflected this placement of the first classroom building? A. J. Davis's hand can certainly be seen in the decision to place the building on the west side of campus and facing out toward the street, although even this decision was probably influenced by discussions between the regents and other interested parties before Davis came to Ann Arbor, as indicated by Asa Gray.[66] The Main Building

66. Letters, Asa Gray to Mrs. Torrey, August 12–20, 1838, *Letters of Asa Gray*, 1:75–78, 80–82.

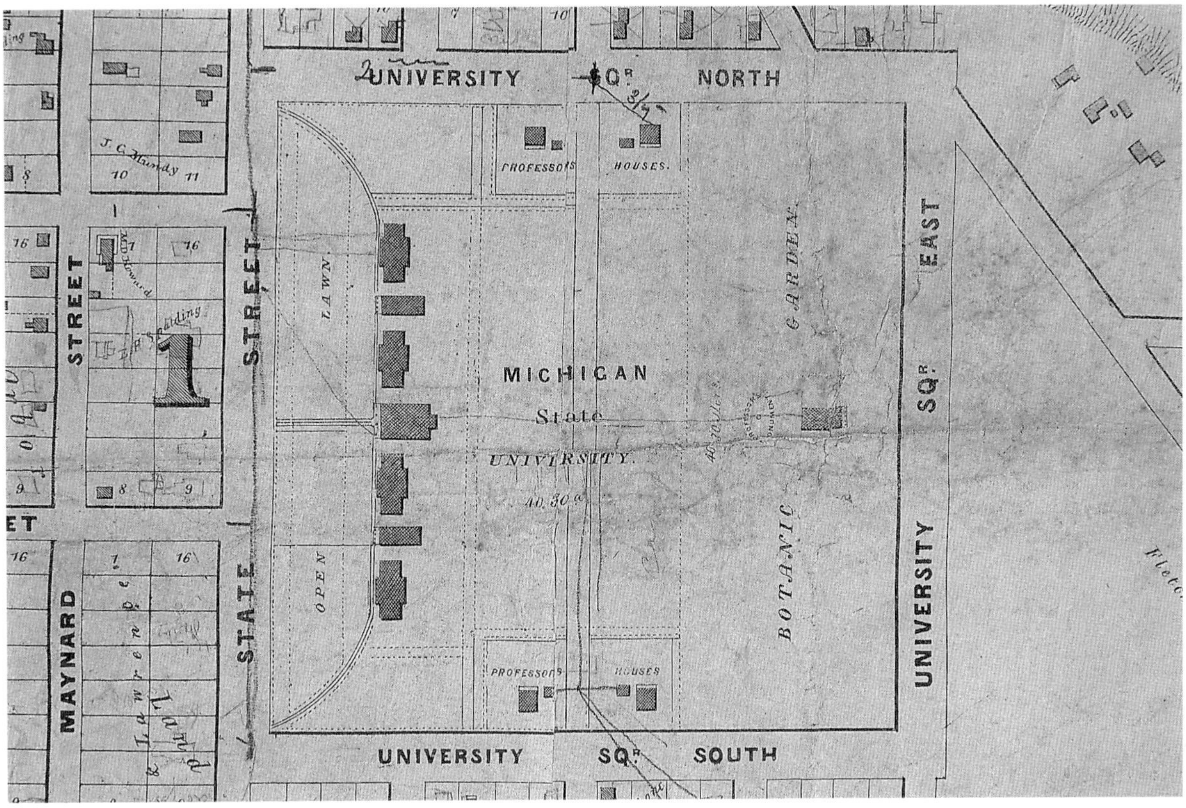

Fig. 51. Map of Ann Arbor, by Darwin A. Pettibone, 1854, detail of University of Michigan campus area. Of the row on the left, only two had actually been built. The Medical Building is on the right and the four professors' houses (accompanied by their wood-houses) are on the top and bottom.
Courtesy of Map Library, Hatcher Graduate Library, University of Michigan.

as placed corresponds roughly to the north wing of the building shown by Davis in his plans (see figs. 29 and 30) and would seem appropriate if the intention was still to build a central structure along the lines of the library-chapel. Once the four houses had been built, it would have seemed more practical to site the Main Building so that it was not set back so far from the street. Even so, a still very generous lawn was provided in front of it.

A plan of the campus exists that, although not clearly dated from the 1840s, enlightens the discussion. This plan was published on at least three maps in the 1850s that purported to accurately represent the layout of Ann Arbor. But each of these maps depicts a campus that never was—at least not in totality (figs. 50, 51).[67] The row of buildings facing State Street were not all in existence at that time (nor subsequently, not in toto). It is interesting to speculate why three different mapmakers would include information on their maps that they knew to be inaccurate. The logical deduction is that they were led to believe—convincingly—that this plan for the campus would in-

67. An 1856 map of Washtenaw County by Gustavus Bechler and E. Wenig shows a campus layout very similar to that shown in the 1853 map by Henry Hart (see fig. 50).

deed be realized in short order. Who could have provided the plan for this row that the mapmakers would have trusted enough that they would have felt assured their maps would reflect an accurate plan? The most reasonable conclusion is that the source was either the architect or the regents. As no architects were employed on campus in the early 1850s, the source for the information would seem to be the university itself. In fact, the answer is as simple as that this plan was prominently displayed on campus and available to the mapmakers to view. As will be shown, plans for the campus were kept in the library-museum on campus, and the author of these plans was apparently Harpin Lum. This authorship cannot be definitively proved since the maps, which are referred to as being on display for some years, are now lost.

The Main Building having been under construction for two months, the regents on October 7, 1840, passed a resolution instructing the Building Committee to "employ the time of Mr. Lum during the coming winter when he is not occupied in superintending the construction of the University Building; in preparing and drawing such plans and profiles, building drafts, etc., as may be necessary for the full execution of the general plan adopted for the University Buildings." The following spring, April 1841, the board "*Resolved,* That the drafts and plans for the College Buildings presented by Mr. Lum and which he has prepared in pursuance of a resolution of the Board to this effect . . . be accepted and that he be and is hereby directed to have the same framed and deposited in the Library" (*RP,* 141, 173). Here then is the source of the "plans in the library" referred to in later regents' correspondence relative to the placement of the second classroom building, or South Wing. The nature of the plans drawn by Lum and placed in the library can only be speculated upon as they apparently do not survive. What the drawings depicted has been unknown for well over one hundred years, but a recently discovered reference to one of the drawings contains the only known written description of the plan and provides the only clue to what Lum developed, and how it echoed row plans, such as those at Yale in his native New Haven (see fig. 55). An article dated March 26, 1870, in the student newspaper of the time, the *Chronicle,* described what can only be one of the Lum plans placed in the library. The author of the article indicated that "two large architectural designs for the University" were on display, and after describing one of them as being a Gothic rendering by Alexander J. Davis, continued with a description of the second drawing.

> The other plan was, it seems, partly carried out. It involved the erection of seven buildings, all in a row, four of which were for dormitories, and were, externally at least, like the present middle and south colleges [North and South Wings]. They were to be 100 feet long and 42 broad. Alternating with them were the library, chapel, and museum. The chapel, standing in the middle probably in the space now left between the literary buildings [again, North and South Wings, which ceased to serve any dormitory function in the 1850s]—was to be a neat church edifice, with a tall spire surmounted by a vane, and provided with a belfry and a clock. It was to be 68 feet by 96, and six Ionic columns were to support the entablature. The museum on the south, and the library on the north, were neat and

> plain one-story buildings, just alike, 85 feet long by 52 broad, and each adorned with six fluted, Corinthian columns in front. One of Pettibone's maps of Ann Arbor, an ancient copy of which hangs in the steward's office, bearing date A.D. 1854, is decorated with a couple of unpretentious lithographs, one claiming to exhibit the "West Front Michigan University," and being a mere modification of the plan just described, in that it contains only the chapel with its tall steeple, and the two dormitories flanking it, ignoring the rest [see figs. 51 & 63]. The dormitories—no longer dormitories, however—stand there now, as some evidence of the original design. Of the chapel, either in this form or any other, no sign as yet appears, though loudly clamored for by alumni and students.[68]

Although the plans drawn by Lum would seem to be the source for the row as shown on the city maps, even this can be debated. Obviously, prior to the direction to Lum to execute these plans, the decision on the placement of the Main Building had been made. A plan of some kind must have been drawn that showed how to place the building relative to the street and the four houses. This plan could have been drawn by Isaac Thomson, since it is known he was asked to provide several plans, including those for the houses and out-buildings. Or Harpin Lum may have provided a site plan when he presented his design for the Main Building.

Whether Thomson or Lum provided the plan siting the Main Building, it was certainly Lum's drawings "in the library" that were utilized by the 1850s mapmakers. In either scenario—Thomson or Lum—the hand of A. J. Davis can again be seen to be moving between them. The campus as shown on the Pettibone map of 1854 (see fig. 51) contains features adopted directly from Davis's earlier plans, including the botanic garden and central north–south avenue. It is tempting to credit Davis with the row idea for Michigan and even with the concepts on the plan drawn by Lum that was adapted for the 1854 map. There is, however, no evidence to support this. Davis was long out of the picture by the time the decision to build the Main Building was made. In fact, when Davis exited the Michigan scene the regents had still seemed intent on executing a main building of his Gothic design. The row plan is also unlike any other plan Davis drew for colleges, and indeed he seemed to have been consciously moving away from the row ideal to something new and unique in his plans. In addition, if the description by the student newspaper was accurate, then a design incorporating two-story buildings alternating with four-story dormitories would never have been developed by so skilled an architect as Davis. This, however, is not the end of the controversy over Davis's part in the early campus planning effort, and it will be picked up later.

One of the characteristics of the campus plan as shown on the 1853, 1854, and 1856 maps that is often remarked upon is the similarity in the alignment of the buildings along State Street to the Old Row at Yale College. There were three buildings extant at Yale at the time John Trumbull drew a plan for the campus in 1792 (see fig. 52). Believed to be the oldest surviving plan for a college in the United States, Trumbull's plan was to prove influential on the development of numerous cam-

68. "Pictures of the University."

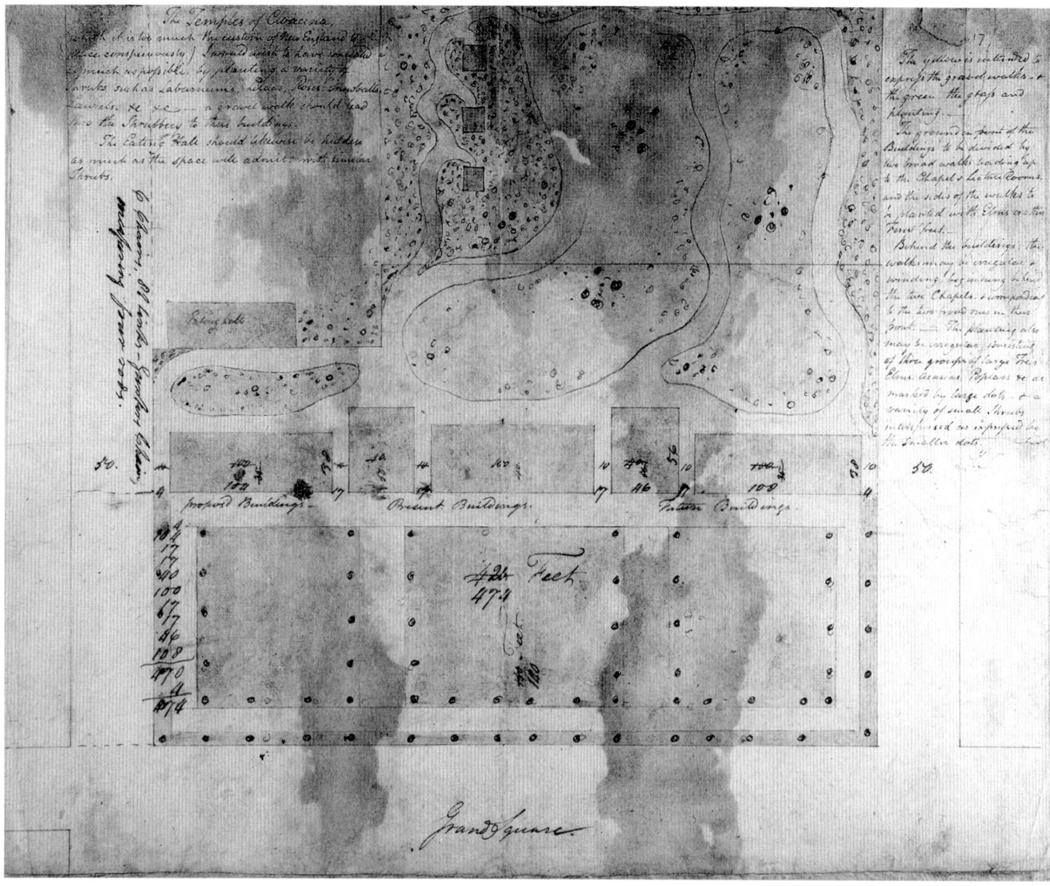

Fig. 52. Plan for Yale College, New Haven, 1792. Drawn by John Trumbull.

Courtesy of Beinecke Rare Book and Manuscript Library, Yale University.

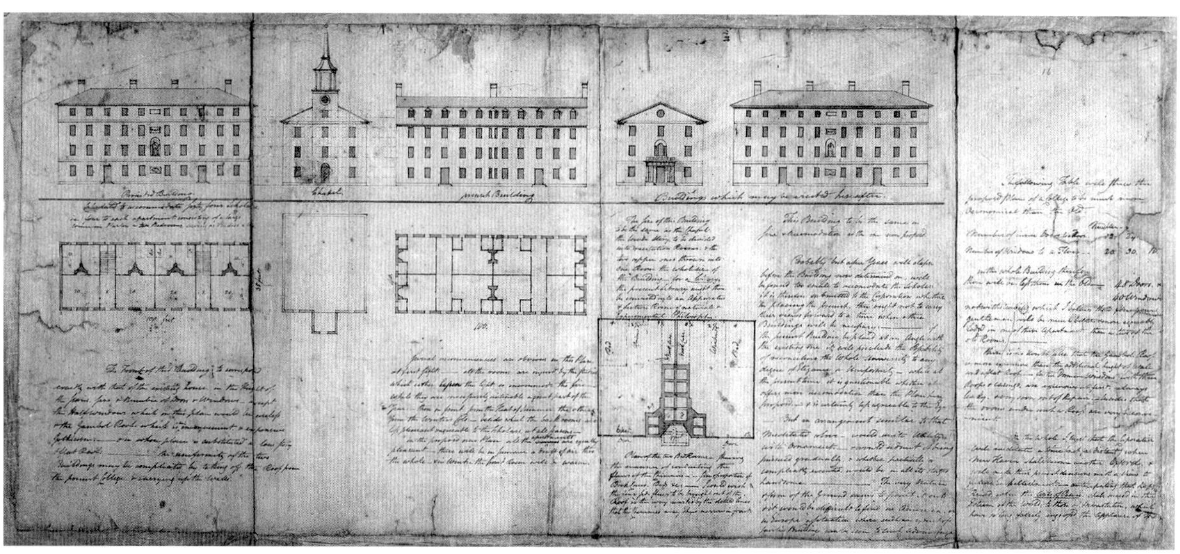

Fig. 53. Plan for Yale College, New Haven, 1792, elevations. Drawn by John Trumbull.

Courtesy of Beinecke Rare Book and Manuscript Library, Yale University.

Fig. 54. View of Dartmouth College, Hanover, 1838. Drawn by Ammi B. Young. From left: Wentworth Hall by Ammi Young (1828), Dartmouth Hall (1791), Thornton Hall by Ammi Young (1829). All extant.
Courtesy of Dartmouth College Library.

puses in America, which would follow the row concept. In addition to the site plan, Trumbull drew a view of the elevations of the main buildings facing the lawn (fig. 53). Two of the buildings shown were extant at the time—old Connecticut Hall in the center, and the chapel to its left. There are several things to be noted in Trumbull's plans, especially in comparison to the 1854 map of the Ann Arbor campus (see fig. 52). The first is that the buildings were placed to alternate long sides with short ones, or gable sides with gable ends. This provides an interesting rhythm and breaks up the monotony of one long row of buildings with facades of similar lengths. This scheme of alternating sides was copied at other colleges including Dartmouth (fig. 54), and the mostly unexecuted 1840s–1850s plan for Michigan. Dartmouth by 1830, as discussed earlier, reflected the designs of Ammi B. Young, who a few years later would be approached about providing designs for the University of Michigan.[69]

Trumbull's plan is also notable for the manner in which the row is well set back from the street to provide a large lawn, although across the street the college already faced the "grand square" or New Haven Green. Ultimately, newer structures were built on the lawn in front of the old row, and most of those earlier buildings were subsequently demolished. The 1854 drawing for Michigan also shows a row set well back from the street, allowing for a large open lawn in front of them. In addition, the botanic garden provided for in the Michigan plan is reminiscent of Trumbull's drawing for Yale with natural areas laid out behind the old row. Figure 55 provides a comparison of the Yale, Dartmouth, and Michigan plans. The botanic garden at Michigan was derived directly from A. J.

69. The Dartmouth Row plan would evolve as buildings were placed forward of the row, in particular Reed Hall, causing the row to become an open U-shape with separate buildings placed around a large open green.

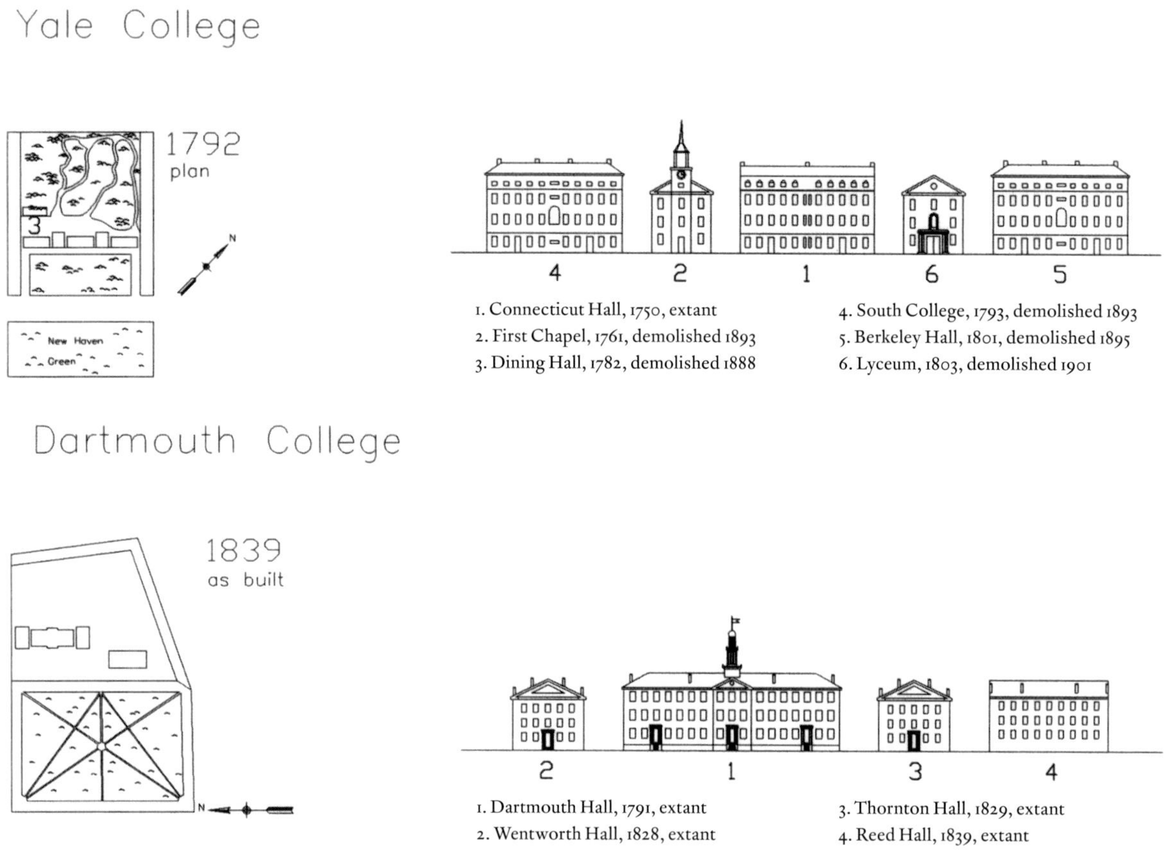

Fig. 55. Comparison of Yale College (from 1792 plan by John Trumbull), Dartmouth College (as built 1839), University of Michigan (from 1854 map by D. A. Pettibone), and University of Michigan (as built 1850 and 1883). Illustration by Yevgeniy Akkerman, University Planner's Office, University of Michigan, 1999.

Davis and his original plans for Michigan of 1838 (see figs. 29 and 30). Can there be a definite link between Trumbull's Yale plan of 1792 and the Michigan plan in the 1850s maps, and can Davis be that link? The answer to both is yes. Davis, as will be recalled, was a close friend and protégé of Trumbull's and would have been familiar with the plans drawn for Yale. Although none of Davis's extant college plans or designs reflect any direct influence of Trumbull's Yale, Davis nevertheless may have considered the row concept as practical for a college grappling with the necessity of executing something less costly than his elaborate Gothic designs. Davis may very well have suggested a Yale row type of plan to Isaac Thomson and Harpin Lum as they were faced with the task of providing plans at Michigan that were economically feasible to produce. It is also possible that Thomson and Lum, both being from New Haven and familiar with Yale, developed the alternate plan on their own. The need for a plan to place the buildings as shown in the 1850s maps does not arise until the main building is authorized. At that time both Davis and Thomson were long removed from Ann Arbor, and Harpin Lum was the person to whom the regents turned for a plan for the building. Since the regents later called on Lum to draw plans for all proposed buildings, it is

University of Michigan

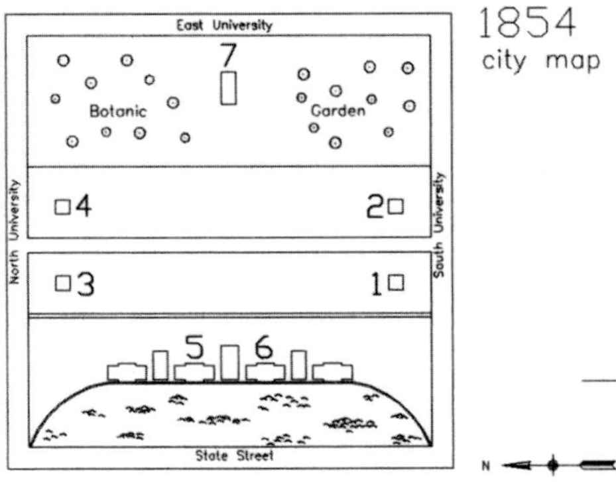

1854
city map

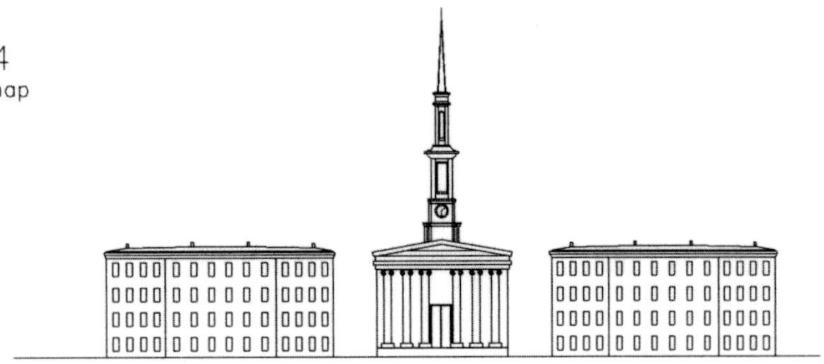

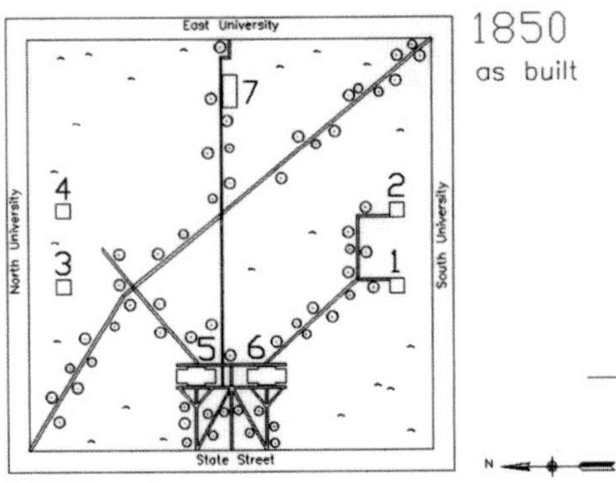

1850
as built

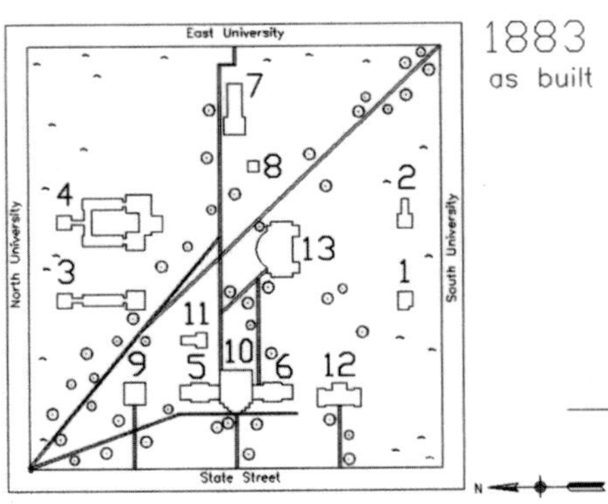

1883
as built

1. Professor's house SW, 1840, became President's House in 1852, extant
2. Professor's house SE, 1840, became Dental School in 1879, demolished 1921
3. Professor's house NW, 1840, became Homeopathic Hospital in 1879, demolished 1915
4. Professor's house NE, 1840, became University Hospital in 1869, demolished 1907
5. North Wing or Mason Hall, 1841, demolished 1950
6. South Wing or South College, 1849, demolished 1950
7. Medical Building, 1850, demolished 1914
8. Chemical Laboratory, 1856, became Economics and Pharmacology in 1908, demolished 1958
9. Law Building, 1863, absorbed by new 1893, burned 1950
10. University Hall, 1872, demolished 1950
11. Heating Plant, 1879, demolished 1923
12. University Museum, 1880, demolished 1958
13. General Library, 1883, demolished 1918

apparent that the plan Lum drew was the basis for that which appears on the Ann Arbor maps. In addition, Lum provided elevations of proposed buildings, per instructions by the regents, and as described in the *Chronicle,* which were of a similar view as Trumbull's for Yale. More evidence of this will be presented here later.

Regardless of who drew the campus plan, the Main Building was begun prior to July 1840 and completed before the fall of 1841. Although the design as executed differed dramatically from Davis's grand Gothic designs, it yet had a simplicity and dignity that was admired at the time, as reflected in this article published in the *State Journal* in August 1841:

> THE STATE UNIVERSITY.
>
> By the circular of the Regents, in this week's paper, it will be seen that the Central Institution goes immediately into operation at this place. Professor Williams ranks high, we are assured, as a classical and mathematical scholar and is in every other respect qualified for the performance of his responsible duties. We doubt not the University will commence with large classes.
>
> We take this occasion to say to the friends of a liberal education abroad that if they wish to send their sons from home for purposes of collegiate instruction, they cannot find a more beautiful and healing place than Ann Arbor, nor an institution that is likely to go beyond this in all the means of a substantial, thorough and useful education. No pains nor expense will be spared to make *education* here what it ought to be—moral, intellectual and physical *discipline.* And parents may safely anticipate such a course of studies that when their sons, at the end of four years, shall be ready to quit the University, they will quit prepared to make good and profitable citizens, whatever may be the duties upon which they shall enter. By a judicious use of our princely fund and the aid of competent professors and tutors, we predict for the University a reputation inferior to that of no other in the Union.
>
> The main building is now completed and ready to be occupied by at least sixty students. It is four stories high, built of brick, and handsomely and durably stuccoed so as to give it very nearly the appearance of Quincy granite. Besides this, four Professors' buildings of the same materials are finished. —More classical models or a more beautiful finish cannot be imagined. They honor the architect while they beautify the village. Professor Houghton will occupy one of them in the fall, and Professor Williams one in the course of three weeks. The others will be occupied and used as circumstances require.
>
> The University grounds form a quadrangular area of 40 acres. They are enclosed by a neat white fence, with appropriate gates on the different sides. When the entire plan of building shall be carried out, and the grounds, romantic even in their natural wildness, covered with trees and shrubbery, they be pronounced by good judges, persons of taste, decidedly superior to those of Harvard, Yale, Dartmouth, Union or any other American college.
>
> The library, selected by Dr. Gray in Europe, contains already nearly four thousand volumes,

> embracing the most valuable books. The cabinet of natural curiosities is quite extensive. The mineralogical specimens, purchase of Baron Lederer, of Austria, are rare and extremely valuable. Dr. Houghton's extensive collections in geology, botany, and zoology are all out here and will be opened and arranged as soon as the Doctor returns from his northern exploratory expedition.
>
> We might say more, but have not room at present. We invite strangers to visit the place and judge for themselves how far the inducements thus held out for them to send their sons here to be educated are in accordance with the facts.[70]

When the Main Building was completed, Harpin Lum left Ann Arbor and returned to his home in New Haven. He received the last payment of his salary in October 1841. Classes were opened for the first time at the Ann Arbor campus of the University of Michigan in the fall of 1841, with faculty and students coming together in the newly finished Main Building. In April 1843, on hearing of the death of former Governor Mason, who had moved to New York when his term as governor expired in January 1840, the regents, "Resolved, That as evidence of the feeling with which this Board cherish the memorial of the late Stevens T. Mason, by whom it was originally organized, the college edifice, now in use at Ann Arbor and known as the 'Main Building,' shall henceforth be called 'Mason Hall.'"[71] Despite the regents' resolution, however, the edifice continued to be called the Main Building, until a few years later when the second university building was built, at which time the original structure became known as North Wing.

In January 1847, the issue of buildings for the university again came to the forefront for the regents, partly as a result of the desire of the newly formed Medical Department for a building to accommodate their needs. Justice Ransom proposed a building to be erected similar in style to the Main Building that would include rooms for a "Laboratory, Lectures, Anatomical Dissections, etc." for the Medical Department. The regents, however, approved an alternate resolution, "That a Building be erected on the University Grounds similar in its dimensions and general plan to the principal building now in use, and that such part thereof as may be necessary be finished for the accommodation of students" (*RP,* 365–66). Silas H. Douglass of the faculty was appointed superintendent of building and was to report to Major Kearsley of the Building Committee. Correspondence relative to the construction of the university's next two buildings (the second dormitory-classroom building called South Wing, and the Medical Building) is preserved among the Douglass family papers at the Bentley Historical Library, in Ann Arbor. On February 11, 1847, Kearsley wrote to Douglass, "It is contemplated that the building shall in all respects be similar in its exterior appearance to that now erected, and be erected upon the ground designated by the plan heretofore adopted by the Board."[72] In April 1847, another regent, Edward C. Walker, wrote to

70. *State Journal,* August 10, 1841, Bentley.

71. RP, 264. In the printed version of the *Regents' Proceedings,* the word "college" before "edifice" is given as "cottage," and was probably the result of a mistranscription by Prof. Demmon.

72. Letter J. Kearsley and Jn. Owen of the Building Committee to Silas Douglass, Superintendent of Buildings, February 11, 1847, Silas H. Douglass Correspondence, January–July 1847, Douglass Family Papers, box 1, Bentley.

Fig. 56. North Wing (or Mason Hall) and South Wing, University of Michigan, Ann Arbor, photo ca. 1860. Design attributed to Harpin Lum. Built 1841 and 1849, respectively; demolished 1950.
Bentley Historical Library, University of Michigan (Buildings and Grounds Department Collection, box 3).

Douglass, "As to place of location the building (South Wing) Dr. Pitcher says that no definitive action was taken by the board, but the common understanding was that it was to be located according to the upright & ground plan of the University in the Library, on the other side of the contemplated chapel from that occupied by the present building, i.e. so that the chapel may hereafter be built between them. If this idea corresponds with the plan, I presume you satisfy yourself of the location."[73] The plan referred to in the library is certainly the one drawn by Harpin Lum. The second building, called South Wing or South College, was begun in the summer of 1847 and completed in 1849. It was indeed a mirror image of the first main building (now called North Wing or Mason Hall) and sat to the south of it (fig. 56). Walker's reference to the chapel that might yet be executed between the two wings implies that a plan existed that the regents yet hoped to bring to fruition. Although execution of A. J. Davis's Gothic chapel (see fig. 36) would seem long forsaken, the concept of filling the space between the wings will draw Davis back into the discussion. This was yet a few years down the line, and as of 1849 there were only the two main buildings on campus, as shown in one of the earliest known depictions of the campus as it appeared in the late 1840s, as drawn from memory by a member of the class of 1849 (fig. 57).

73. Letter E. C. (Edward) Walker to Silas Douglass, April 30, 1847, Silas H. Douglass Correspondence, January–July 1847, Douglass Family Papers, box 1, Bentley.

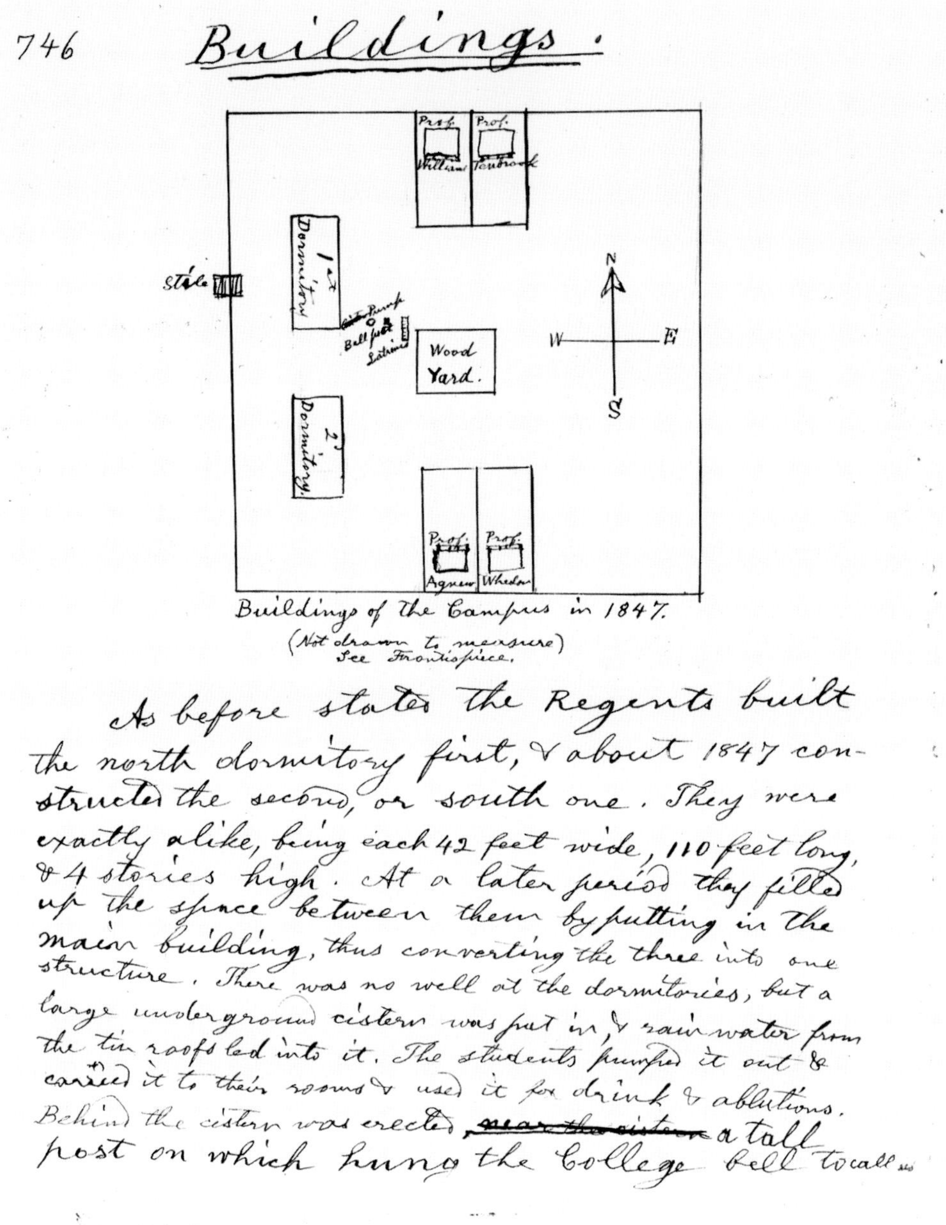

746 Buildings.

Buildings of the Campus in 1847.
(Not drawn to measure)
See Frontispiece.

As before stated the Regents built the north dormitory first, & about 1847 constructed the second, or south one. They were exactly alike, being each 42 feet wide, 110 feet long, & 4 stories high. At a later period they filled up the space between them by putting in the main building, thus converting the three into one structure. There was no well at the dormitories, but a large underground cistern was put in, & rain water from the tin roofs led into it. The students pumped it out & carried it to their rooms & used it for drink & ablutions. Behind the cistern was erected ~~near the cistern~~ a tall post on which hung the College bell to call us

Fig. 57. University of Michigan campus as it appeared in 1847. Drawn by Edmund Andrews, class president, in 1889 for Class of 1849 fortieth anniversary album.

Bentley Historical Library, University of Michigan (Class of 1849 Album, page 746).

Fig. 58. View of New York University, Washington Square, New York. Lithograph from a drawing on stone by Alexander Jackson Davis, ca. 1850. New York University designed by Ithiel Town, Alexander Jackson Davis, James H. Dakin, and David B. Douglass, built 1835–37; demolished 1894. Note Doric column at left edge from Washington Square North town houses.

Metropolitan Museum of Art, The Edward W. C. Arnold Collection of New York Prints, Maps and Pictures; Bequest of Edward W. C. Arnold, 1954 (54.90.907[20]).

The College Designs of Alexander Jackson Davis

The designs produced by the architectural firm of Town and Davis in 1831–32 for the newly created New York University would be the first of a long line of collegiate designs that were executed in part or in total by the hand of Alexander Jackson Davis. Between 1831 and 1870 Davis would provide designs for more than a dozen colleges and become known as the leading collegiate designer of the antebellum era. A precedent set for Davis at NYU would impact some of his later collegiate designs. This was the presentation by the architect, here with his partners Ithiel Town and James Dakin, of alternate designs in both the Greek and Gothic Revival styles. For NYU Davis drew a design in the classical mode (see fig. 21), which was rejected by the client in favor of a Gothic version developed by the partners in toto. Built in New York City facing Washington Square, the castellated university building was the most influential early Collegiate Gothic structure built in America (fig. 58). Constrained by the urban site, the firm did not develop a plan for NYU that would have encompassed more than the main building. However, Davis would soon have ample opportunity for grappling with a larger site.

After dissolving his partnership with Ithiel Town, Davis's first major college commission was for the design of several buildings for the newly founded Bristol College in Pennsylvania. In execution of this project Davis was aided by Russell Warren, with whom he was loosely associated in 1835. Bristol College presented an interesting challenge for Davis because of the large site. In 1833, the Episcopal Education Society of Pennsylvania founded Bristol College as a manual labor school, in which students would be required to spend a significant portion of each day in manual labor tasks, primarily farmwork. The society purchased a farm of four hundred acres on the Delaware River just below Bristol, Pennsylvania. On the land was a large eighteenth-century house called China Hall, which was used when the college opened in 1834. The president of the college, Reverend Chauncey Colton, then commissioned Davis to provide designs for several buildings to be erected on the campus. The designs produced by Davis in four different styles would lead to the assumption that he was offering alternates from which the college would choose one. It would seem unlikely that such a young college would embark on the construction of four significant buildings at once.

However, the four structures as designed were already named by the college, which implies

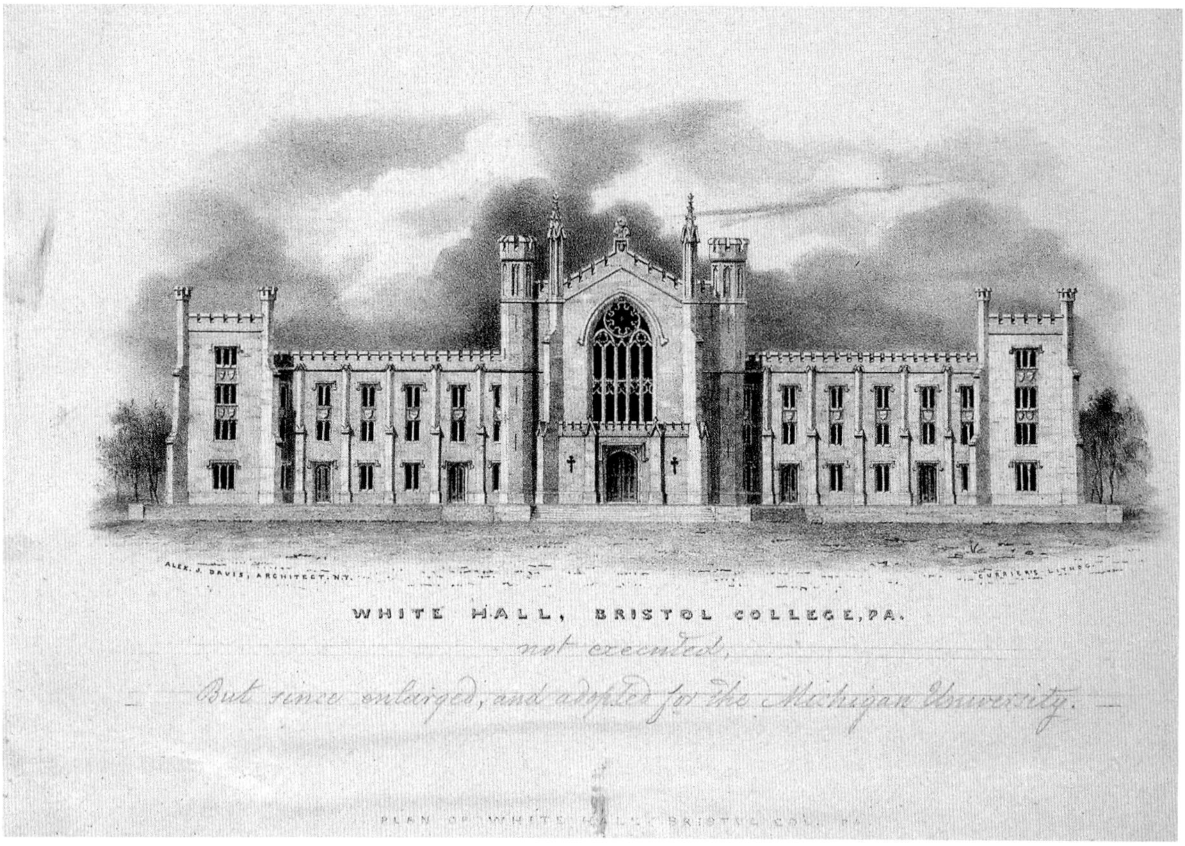

Fig. 59. White Hall, Bristol College, Pa., 1835. Design by Alexander Jackson Davis with Russell Warren. Not executed. With note in Davis's handwriting "not executed, But since enlarged and adopted for the Michigan University." Drawings and Archives, Avery Architectural and Fine Arts Library, Columbia University in the City of New York (collection 2, folder 39-20, page 42a).

they were all to be built in due course. For such a large site, and based on his later designs, it would have seemed more appropriate for Davis to design a large quadrangle or rectangle or to arrange the separate buildings facing an open green space. There is no evidence that Davis provided a campus plan for Bristol, just the individual building designs, but this may have been influenced by the nature of the farmland. However, it is likely that if Davis had produced a campus plan using the buildings as designed, they would not have been set in a row, as all the buildings faced the same, that is, with the long sides forward. If all were to be set on the same campus, it would be more logical for the buildings to be set separately around an open space, forming a detached U-shape or quadrangle, common for American colleges of the time. The designs Davis produced are all in the same form of a central building with wings. Of these designs, one was in the Gothic Revival style, White Hall (fig. 59). The others, in Greek Revival, reflected the three primary orders: Pennsylvania Hall in Ionic, Clifton Hall in Doric (fig. 60), and Milnor Hall in Corinthian.[1] Ultimately the college chose to build only one structure in the Ionic mode, but modified from Davis's design in that the

1. Newton, *Town and Davis,* 236. Newton refers to Milnor Hall as designed in the Corinthian order.

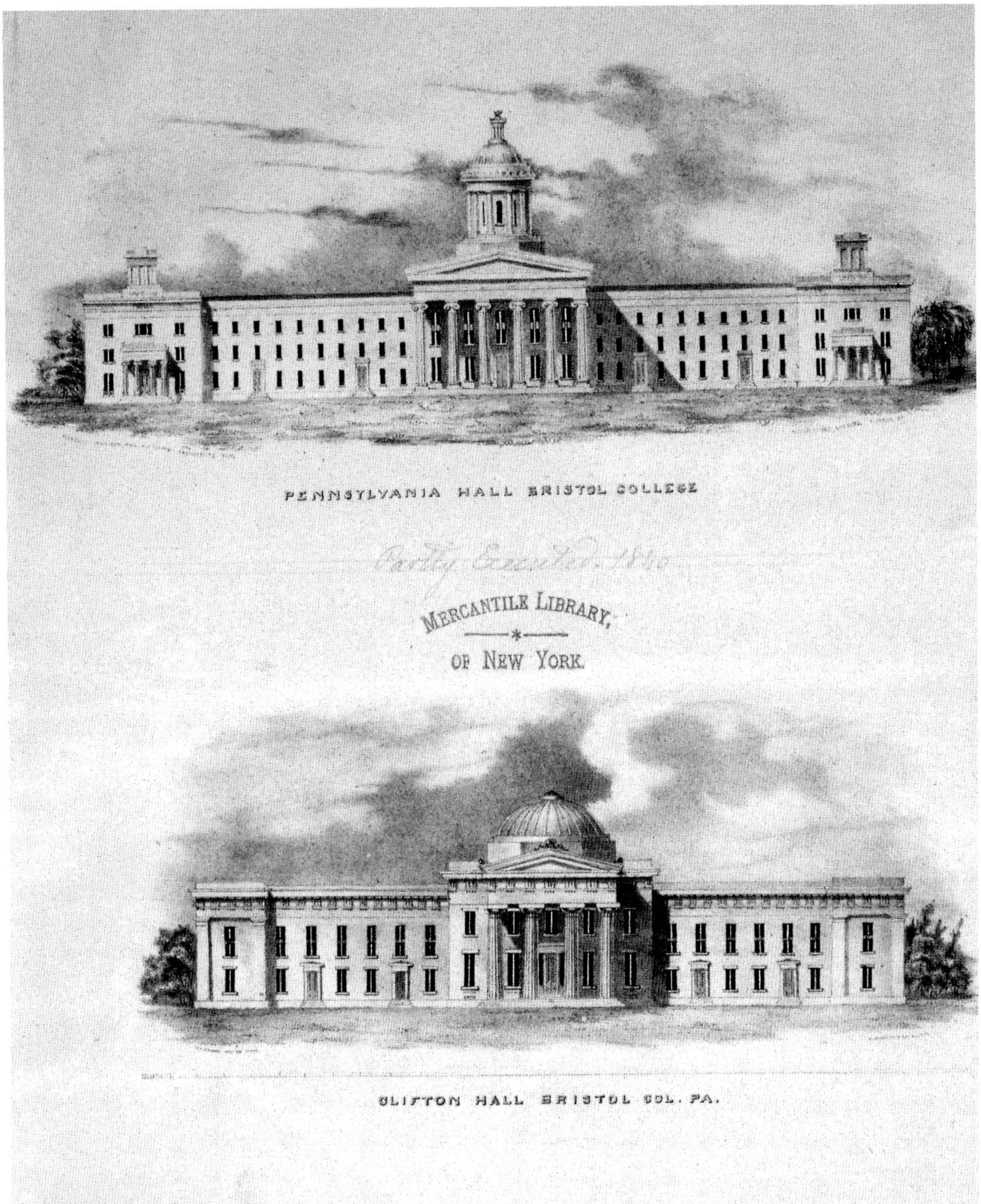

Fig. 60. Pennsylvania Hall and Clifton Hall, Bristol College, Pa., 1835. Design by Alexander Jackson Davis with Russell Warren. Ionic design as in Pennsylvania Hall executed circa 1836, but modified with deletion of end pavilions and tower, and called White Hall; demolished.

Drawings and Archives, Avery Architectural and Fine Arts Library, Columbia University in the City of New York (collection 2, folder 39-20, page 42a).

pavilions on the ends and the tower on top were omitted. The college edifice as built (see fig. 24) was called White Hall rather than Pennsylvania, after a personage of some importance to the Episcopal Church.[2] Built of brick and covered with stucco, White Hall was "two hundred and ninety-six feet long, was quite imposing, the central part being fronted with tall Ionic columns."[3] Bristol College did not flourish and was closed in 1839. The building was thereafter used for numerous purposes.

The form of the Bristol designs by Davis—an accentuated central portion with long wings—would be utilized again in his next collegiate commission, for the University of Michigan. In fact, Davis noted on his Gothic design for White Hall that it was "not executed, But since enlarged and adapted for the Michigan University" (see fig. 59). Davis's design for Michigan (see figs. 1 and 27) shows a natural progression in his Gothic designs and his continually developing artistry and innovativeness. The shape of the structure has also evolved to be a larger, more encompassing U-shape. Here Davis has taken into consideration the large, level site available for the college building, although the decision to place it so far back from the street seems unusual. The large front lawn provided by Davis's plan (see figs. 29 and 30) would appear to reflect other college campuses, such as Harvard, Dartmouth, Princeton, Brown, and so on, where individual buildings—one main building to begin with—faced a large open green space. Yet it is unusual that Davis's Michigan building turns the corners of the U back into the open land of the campus. Davis is here developing something original that nevertheless would pose challenges in the future were a second major building to be contemplated. One presumption is that a mirror image U-shaped structure could be placed on the opposite side of the campus. This indeed was the direction Davis was heading in his college designs. The progression from the Bristol designs to that at Michigan begs, however, an additional question that has continued to surface over the years. As he did for Bristol, might Davis have provided to Michigan an alternate design in the classical mode, such as an adaptation of the unexecuted Clifton Hall? That question will be investigated.

Although occurring after the Michigan commission, Davis utilized both the rectangular form reminiscent of Bristol, along with the U-shaped form, in the design of two buildings for a proposed agricultural college in New York, in 1849–50. In these designs Davis collaborated with landscape architect Andrew Jackson Downing to produce structures suited to a rural setting, although the exact location of the proposed college is unknown. Using the Tuscan Revival style, which both Davis and Downing promoted for country settings, the buildings featured a central structure, one templelike, with wings (see fig. 25). In addition, both contained the Davis invention, the tall, narrow Daviséan windows, to admit plenty of light. These designs were never executed, but reflect Davis's transition from the rectangular shape to the U-shaped collegiate building.

Davis's Gothic U-shaped structure evolved into a more complete quadrangle in his design for

2. S. F. Hotchkin, *The Bristol Pike* (Philadelphia: George W. Jacobs, 1893), 345.

3. James Pyle Wickersham, *A History of Education in Pennsylvania* (Lancaster, Pa.: Inquirer, 1886), 424.

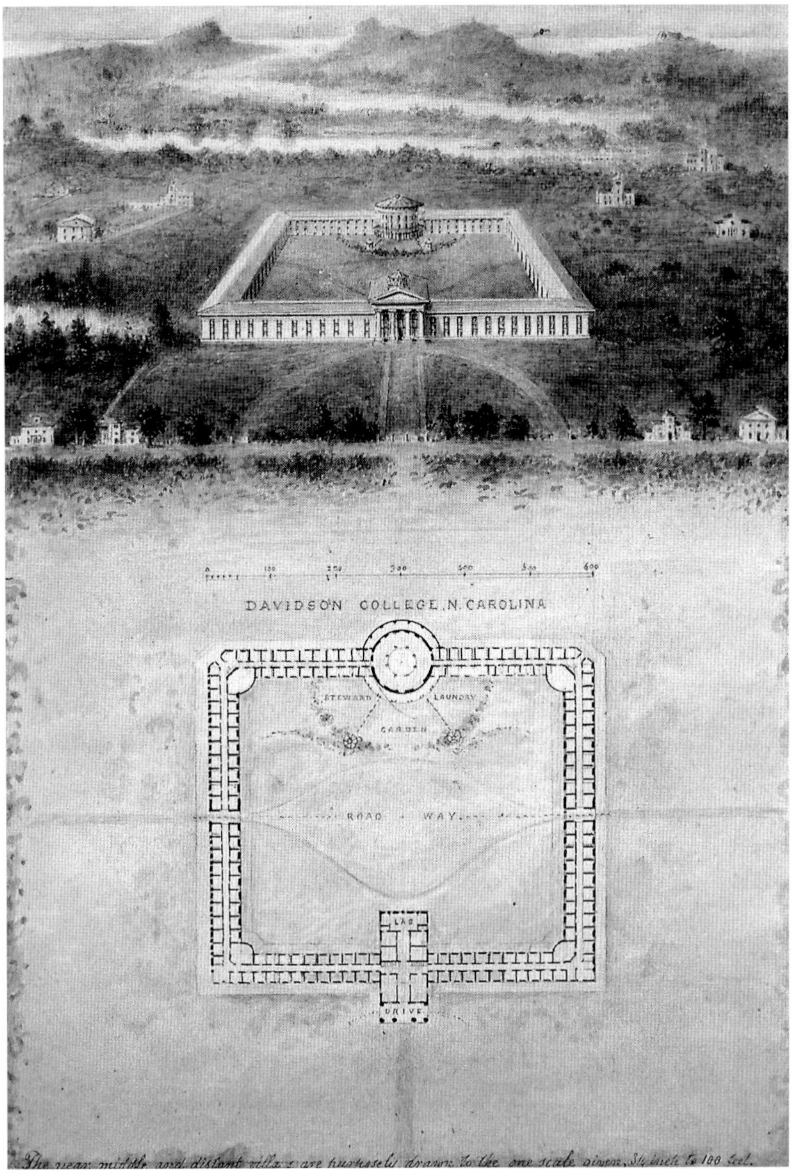

Fig. 61. Davidson College, N.C., 1856. Design by Alexander Jackson Davis. Only the front part of the quad was built in 1859, but shortened, and called Chambers Hall; burned 1924.

Drawings and Archives, Avery Architectural and Fine Arts Library, Columbia University in the City of New York.

the Virginia Military Institute, 1848–61. The main barracks building was executed in a castellated Gothic style similar to the Bristol White Hall design, but formed into a quad. The open space it faced on was a parade ground rather than a botanic garden, and on the large site Davis also provided for professors' houses, officers' quarters, a hospital, and a mess hall. His continued development of the quadrangular form reached its highest expression in his design for Davidson College in North Carolina, 1856–60 (fig. 61). The generous site allowed the quad to be set well back from the road, yet enclose a large open green space. This design also reflected Davis's growing interest in the Tuscan Revival style. But even twenty years earlier Davis was developing this scheme, which was echoed in his widely admired design for the Pauper Lunatic Asylum in New York, an 1834 U-shaped structure, whose long wings were anchored by a central mass, and octagonal structures at the corners. Expressed in a fine example of the Tuscan Revival, the elongated wings of the asylum hinted at the coming evolution of the Davidson quad. As mentioned, the Tuscan mode was again utilized in the designs for an agricultural college. The Davidson College design also featured Daviséan windows.

Spanning forty years and a dozen universities, from major urban sites to wide open spaces, many designs for which were unfortunately never executed, Davis's collegiate plans show a steady progression from individual buildings in Greek or Gothic modes to larger U-shape structures, and the ultimate quadrangle in Tuscan. At both New York University and Bristol, Davis, alone or with his former partners, created designs in alternate styles to better accommodate client wishes. Perhaps Davis did the same thing at Michigan.

Plate 1. Portrait of Alexander Jackson Davis, 1833. Oil painting by George Freeman.

Drawings and Archives, Avery Architectural and Fine Arts Library, Columbia University in the City of New York.

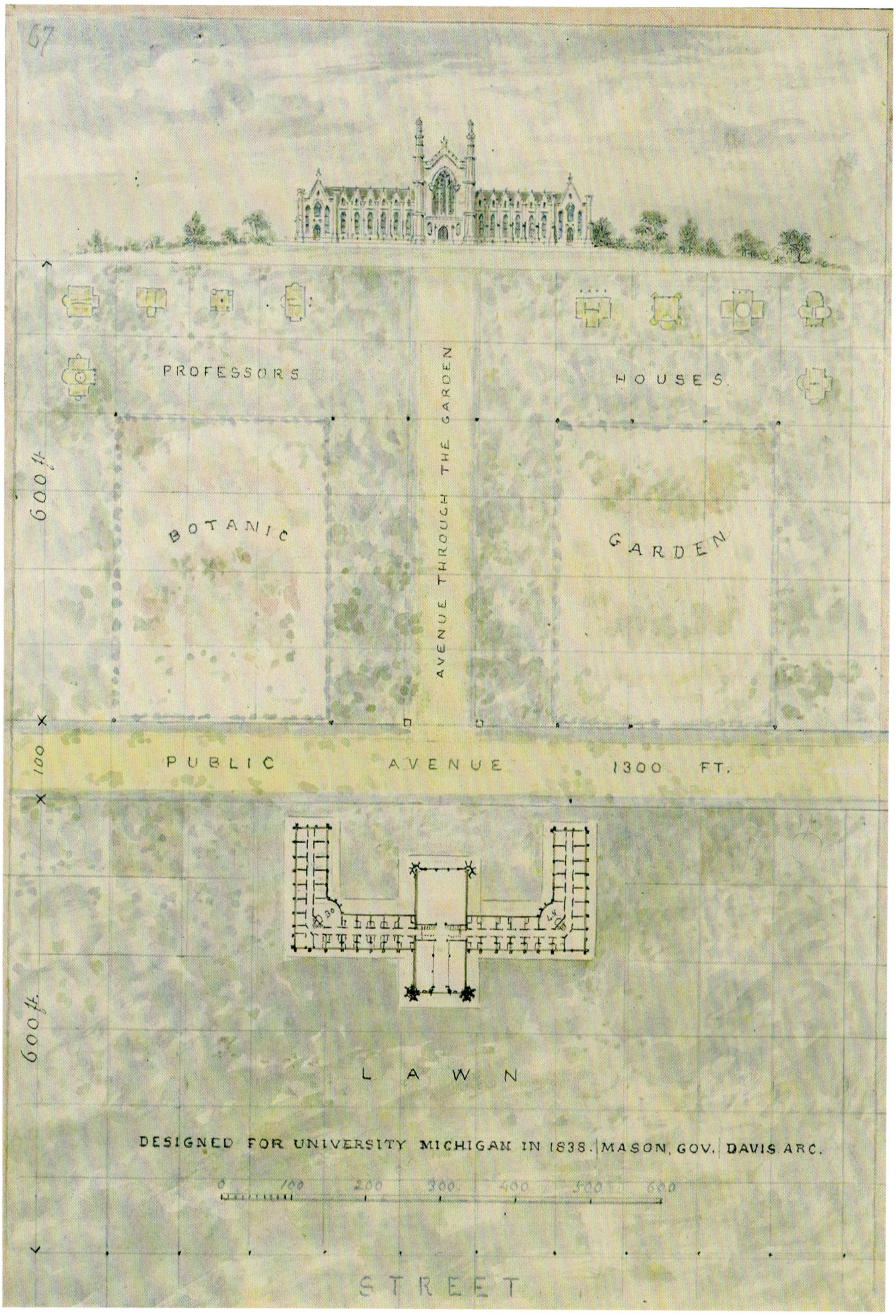

Plate 2. University of Michigan, Ann Arbor, campus plan and elevation, 1838. Design by Alexander Jackson Davis. Not executed. Pen and ink and watercolor on paper, 14 in. x 11⅛ in.

The Metropolitan Museum of Art, Harris Brisbane Dick Fund, 1924 (24.66.1404[81]). (Photograph © 2001 The Metropolitan Museum of Art.)

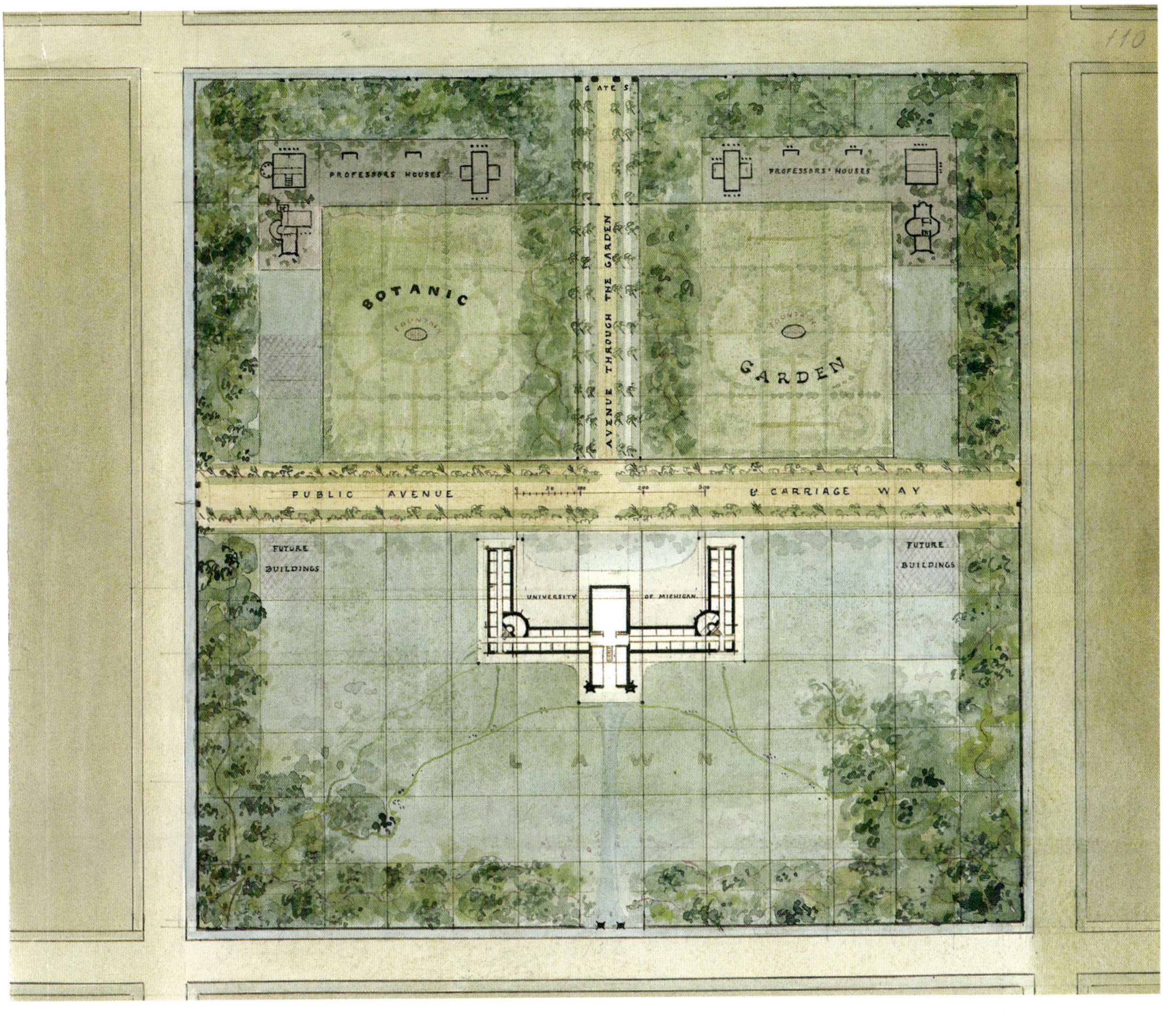

Plate 3. University of Michigan, Ann Arbor, campus plan, 1838–39. Design by Alexander Jackson Davis. Not executed. Watercolor on paper, 13⅜ in. x 16⅛ in.

The Metropolitan Museum of Art, Harris Brisbane Dick Fund, 1924 (24.66.640). (Photograph © 2001 The Metropolitan Museum of Art.)

Plate 4. University of Michigan, Ann Arbor, 1838. Design by Alexander Jackson Davis. Not executed. Watercolor on paper, 15 in. x 10½ in.

The Metropolitan Museum of Art, Harris Brisbane Dick Fund, 1924 (24.66.1405[118]). (Photograph © 2001 The Metropolitan Museum of Art.)

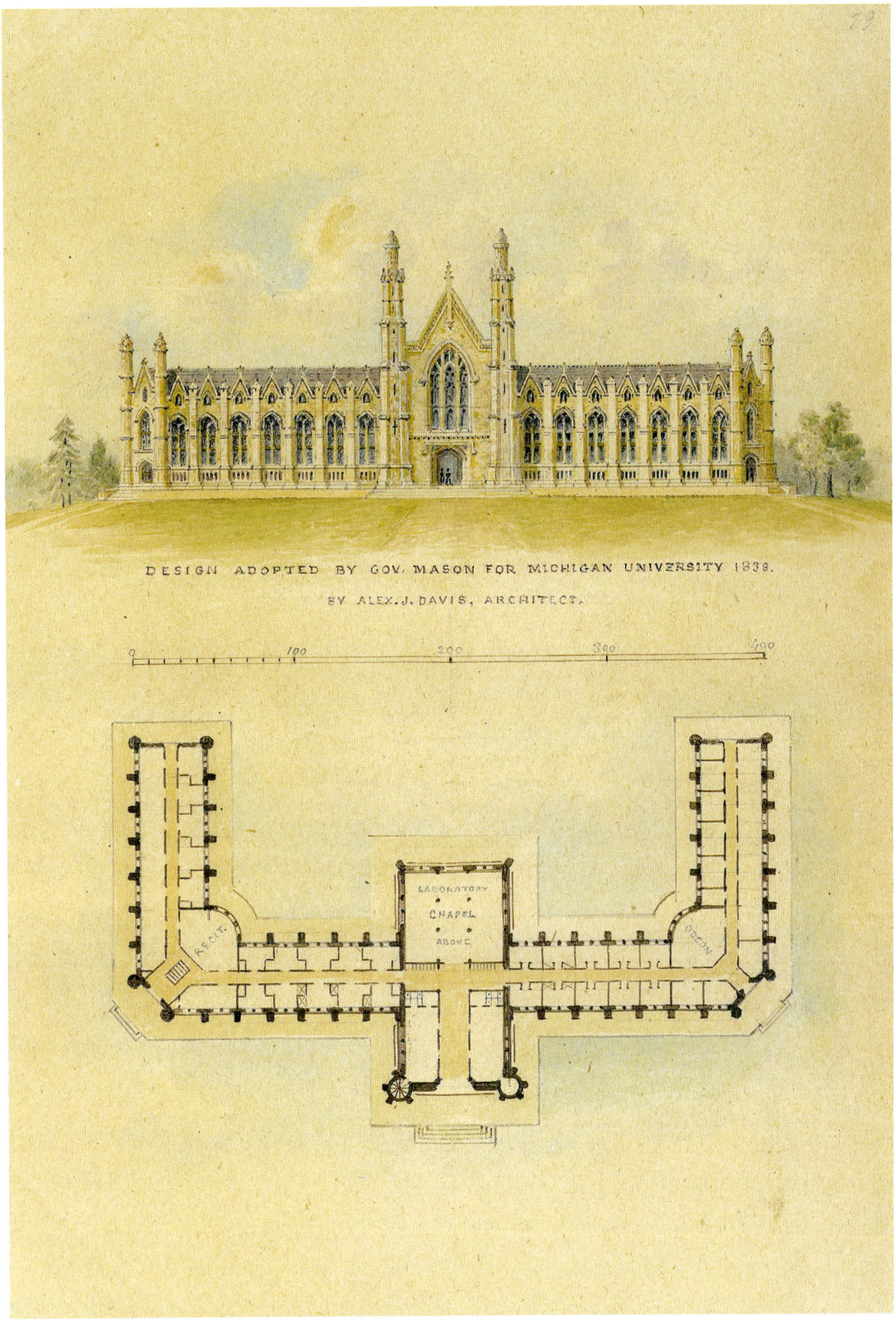

Plate 5. University of Michigan, Ann Arbor, 1838. Design by Alexander Jackson Davis. Not executed. Watercolor on paper, 18 in. x 12½ in.

The Metropolitan Museum of Art, Harris Brisbane Dick Fund, 1924 (24.66.1406[81]). (Photograph © 2001 The Metropolitan Museum of Art.)

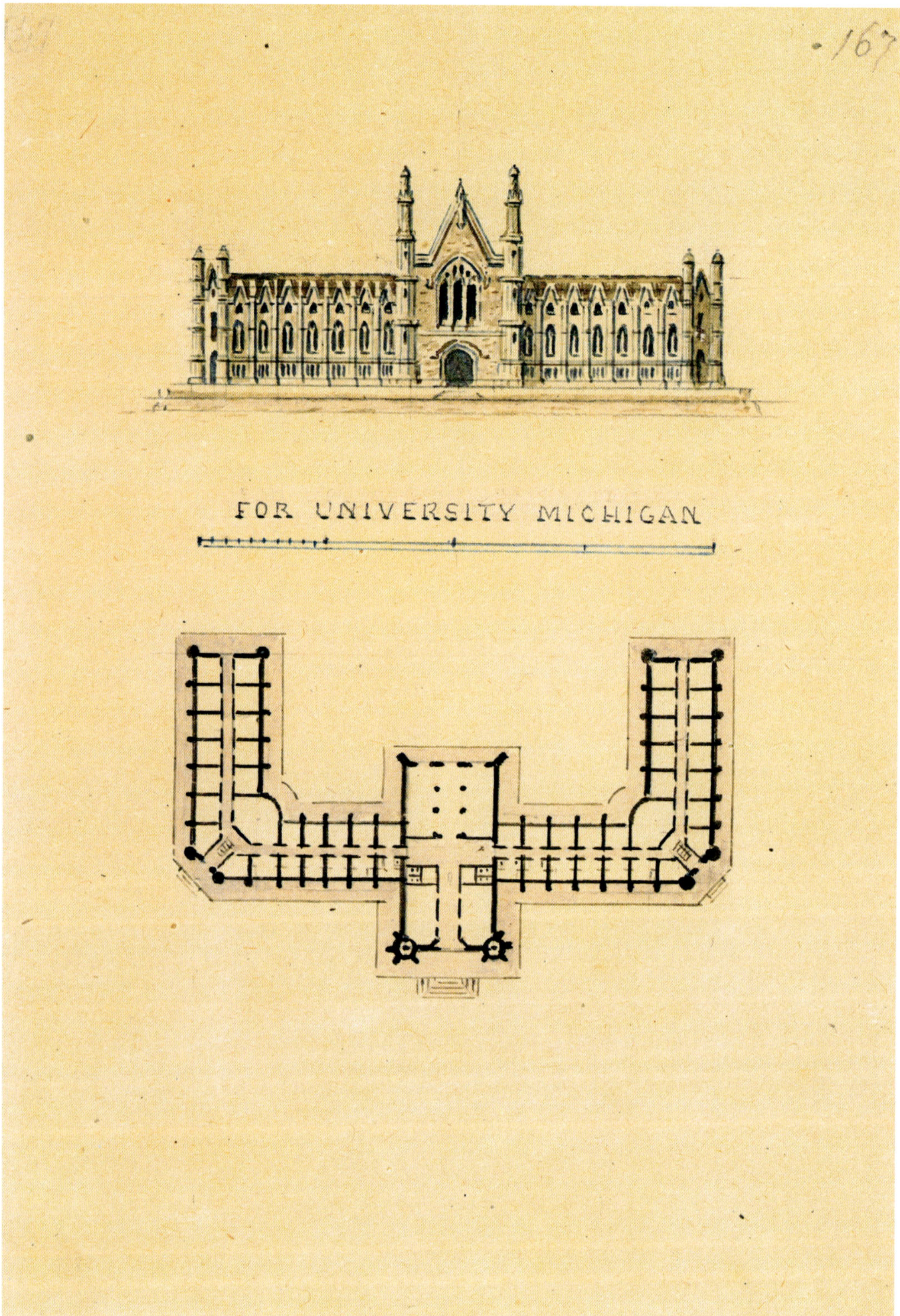

Plate 6. University of Michigan, Ann Arbor, 1838. Design by Alexander Jackson Davis. Not executed. Watercolor on paper, 11½ in. x 9 in.

The Metropolitan Museum of Art, Harris Brisbane Dick Fund, 1924 (24.66.1401[144]). (Photograph © 2001 The Metropolitan Museum of Art.)

Plate 7. University of Michigan, Ann Arbor, library-chapel, 1838–39. Design by Alexander Jackson Davis. Not executed. Watercolor, ink, and graphite on paper, 31⅜ in. x 26⅛ in.

The Metropolitan Museum of Art, Harris Brisbane Dick Fund, 1924 (24.66.41). (Photograph © 1991 The Metropolitan Museum of Art.)

Plate 8. University of Michigan, Ann Arbor, North Wing (west front), 1838–39. Design by Alexander Jackson Davis. Not executed. Watercolor on paper, 18⅞ in. x 26⅞ in.

The Metropolitan Museum of Art, Harris Brisbane Dick Fund, 1924 (24.66.40). (Photograph © 2001 The Metropolitan Museum of Art.)

Plate 9. University of Michigan, Ann Arbor, North Wing (east front), 1838–39. Design by Alexander Jackson Davis. Not executed. Watercolor on paper, 17¾ in. x 25⅞ in.

The Metropolitan Museum of Art, Harris Brisbane Dick Fund, 1924 (24.66.39). (Photograph © 2001 The Metropolitan Museum of Art.)

Plate 10. Gothic entrance on classical wings, probably for University of Michigan, undated. Design by Alexander Jackson Davis. Not executed. Watercolor on paper, 25¾ in. x 17⅝ in.

The Metropolitan Museum of Art, Harris Brisbane Dick Fund, 1924 (24.66.8). (Photograph © 2001 The Metropolitan Museum of Art.)

Plate 11. University of Michigan, Ann Arbor, North Wing, 1840, design as adopted by the Board of Regents. Drawn by Harpin Lum. Built 1841; demolished 1950.

Bentley Historical Library, University of Michigan (University of Michigan Architectural drawings, folder 5).

Plate 12. University of Michigan, Ann Arbor, view from northeast, 1855. Oil painting by Jasper Francis Cropsey. From left: southeast professor's house, President's House, Medical Building, South Wing, North Wing (Mason Hall), northeast professor's house. The Professors' Monument or cenotaph is visible just to the right of the Medical Building.

Bentley Historical Library, University of Michigan.

The Classical Controversy

Roger Hale Newton's 1942 biography of Town and Davis seems to be the earliest source of an oft-repeated supposition that Alexander Jackson Davis provided for the University of Michigan alternate designs in a classical style, in addition to the well-known Gothic ones. Unfortunately, no direct piece of evidence exists to support this contention, such as a drawing of a classical building labeled for Michigan and in Davis's hand. That is not to say that no evidence exists in any form. Substantial, tantalizing circumstantial evidence survives that makes an investigation into this subject worthwhile and fascinating. At the core of the desire to unravel this mystery is the interest in discovering what influence Davis might have had on the classical buildings that were constructed in Ann Arbor between 1840 and 1849. The factual evidence presented earlier had led to the conclusion that the plan for the four professors' houses was drawn by Isaac Thomson, and that for the main buildings by Harpin Lum. This is still likely the case, but it is possible that Davis had more influence on those designs than the facts suggest. Even if this is disproved or simply not provable, it is still of interest to know what the alternate classical designs might have looked like had Davis executed such.

The story begins with an early history of the University of Michigan, written by Elizabeth Farrand and published in 1885. Farrand states simply, "The plan for the professors' houses was drawn by Alexander J. Davis and the buildings were first and for a very short time constructed under the superintendence of Isaac Thompson, and afterward a contract was made with Harpin Lum."[1] This then is the first, and possibly the only, person to flatly state that Davis was the author of the professors' houses. Certainly others since then have noted the marked similarities between features of the houses and some of Davis's known designs in New York and New Haven, but none has made such a straightforward statement as Farrand. There are several reasons for taking Farrand at her word. The first is that she was a well-educated person who had been employed at the University Library for many years and would have been very familiar with its resources.

Elizabeth Farrand was born in Ann Arbor in 1852, to Lucius S. and Frances Shaw Farrand. Her grandfather, Bethunel Farrand, was the first judge of probate of Washtenaw County, and first mail carrier between Ann Arbor and Detroit for the Ann Arbor post office, and had settled his

1. Elizabeth M. Farrand, *History of the University of Michigan* (Ann Arbor: Register Publishing House, 1885), 43. An earlier published history of the University of Michigan was written by Charles Kendall Adams in 1876, in which almost nothing is said about the buildings in Ann Arbor.

family in Ann Arbor in 1825. After graduating from Ann Arbor High School, Elizabeth was employed as first assistant librarian at the University of Michigan Library, where she remained for fourteen years. In 1885, she published her history of the university and then decided to pursue a degree in medicine. Elizabeth received her M.D. from Michigan in 1887, and eventually set up practice in Port Huron. She died in that city in 1900, but was buried in Forest Hills cemetery in her hometown of Ann Arbor.[2] As a longtime librarian and possessing a good education, Elizabeth Farrand would certainly have known the value of adequate research, as well as the dangers of publishing information for which there is no clear source. Farrand did not provide in her book any direct notations on the sources of her information, but it can be assumed that much was at her fingertips in the library, as well as directly from persons at all levels of the university, many of whom had been in Ann Arbor and with the University of Michigan for some years. One source she may have deemed reliable was her own family, whose roots in the city went back to 1825, the year after its founding. Her grandfather Bethunel Farrand certainly witnessed the birth and growth of the university, as her own parents would have. In the preface to her book, Farrand noted: "The attempt has been made to collect from many documents into one volume the story of the University, to put into a convenient and accessible shape what has been already written, and to gather also something from its traditional history, placing upon record what has hitherto remained only in memories which are now fast fading."[3] It is clear that she attempted to access not only all surviving documentation related to the birth and growth of the university, but also to obtain firsthand accounts from persons who had been eyewitnesses to this history. Farrand also noted that she was plagued in her quest by the same problems that haunt the researcher today. One is the wholly inadequate records left by the board of regents, who dutifully recorded many of their resolutions, but virtually nothing of the discussions that led up to them, and many committee reports and other documents were never entered into the record. In addition, the amount of attention given in the newspapers of the time to the activities of the regents and the state university is surprisingly little. As Farrand noted, great events such as President Tappan's dismissal, received some coverage, but "on smaller matters the silence is very profound."[4]

A second reason to believe Elizabeth Farrand's statement that Davis was the author of the professors' houses is that she would have had access to the campus plans that are recorded in various places as being at the library. Certainly these included the plans drawn by Harpin Lum that the regents directed be framed and placed in the library. In addition, some of the plans drawn by Isaac Thomson were probably also on deposit in the library, and it is known that at least one of A. J. Davis's Gothic designs existed for awhile at Michigan. Since none of these plans appear to survive

2. Undated newspaper article from Port Huron, ca. August 18 or 19, 1900, obituary for Elizabeth Farrand who died August 17, 1900, Necrology file, University of Michigan Alumni Records, Bentley; Letter Elizabeth Farrand to C. B. Grant, March 21, 1874, University Library Papers, box 69, folder "Papers concerning removal of Ten Brook 1873–1874," Bentley; *The University of Michigan: An Encyclopedic Survey,* vol. 1, ed. Wilfred B. Shaw (Ann Arbor: University of Michigan Press, 1942), 220; and Chapman and Co., *History of Washtenaw County,* 889, 989–90.

3. Farrand, *History of University of Michigan,* v.

4. Ibid., vi.

today, it seems possible that an additional plan was lost that depicted the professors' houses. It may be as simple as Farrand looking at the drawing and seeing Davis's signature on it. Unless more information concerning the "plans in the library" is unearthed, this cannot be proven.

Another factor working for Farrand is one that has never been taken into account, and that is that at the time Farrand was researching and writing her history, Alexander Jackson Davis was still alive. At the time, Davis would have been in his early eighties, and apparently possessed a good memory, and in fact spent his time sorting through his office diaries, correspondence, and drawings. It is possible that Farrand contacted him directly, and knowing Davis had done the earlier designs, may have asked him if he drew that for the professors' houses. Davis, in turn, may have responded that yes, once the regents determined to build houses, and at the request of his friend Isaac Thomson, he, Davis, sent a sketch out to Thomson for a house that combined the typical five-bay arrangement found across the Midwest with some simple, but elegant classical features. No direct evidence, however, survives to support this.

A second source for the so-called classical controversy was an unintentional one. In 1936, Edna Donnell wrote a monograph on Davis and his part in the Gothic Revival in architecture. Her treatise was based on the large collection of Davis's papers and drawings that had been acquired by the Metropolitan Museum of Art from Davis's son. During her research, Donnell was in correspondence with persons at the University of Michigan, especially Wilfred Shaw, director of alumni relations, and Frank E. Robbins, assistant to the president. Although Donnell was writing about Davis's Gothic designs, she was questioned by Shaw and Robbins as to what part Davis might have played in the design of the classical buildings that were built. Shaw and Robbins, like many others, had noted the similarities between the professors' houses and some designs of Davis's in New England. Donnell informed persons at Michigan that her conclusion was that based on the evidence (primarily the *Regents' Proceedings*) Davis "had no part in the buildings that were executed."[5] But then Donnell used an illustration in her monograph that actually added fuel to the controversy (fig. 62). The drawing was labeled by Donnell "Unexecuted design by Davis for the University of Michigan—A project for Gothicizing a building by adding an entrance in the Gothic style,"[6] although Davis neither labeled nor dated it. Donnell's attribution of the design to Michigan seems to have been based on information she received from Ann Arbor. In 1931, Wilfred Shaw wrote to her about the possible Davis link to the early university buildings.[7] He enclosed some photographs of the old buildings, including one of North and South Wings taken before the space between them was filled up (see fig. 56). Donnell would have recognized at once the similarity between the Ann Arbor buildings and the wings on the drawing by Davis. Her logical conclusion was that Davis's design was made for the University of Michigan.

5. Letter Edna Donnell to Miss Paine, June 26, 1936, Alexander Jackson Davis Collection, M–Z, file folder "University of Michigan," Met.

6. Donnell, "Davis and Gothic Revival," 185.

7. Letter Wilfred Shaw to Edna Donnell, June 16, 1931, Alexander Jackson Davis Collection, M–Z, file folder "University of Michigan," Met.

Fig. 62. Gothic entrance on classical wings, probably for University of Michigan, Ann Arbor, undated. Design by Alexander Jackson Davis. Not executed.

This drawing was published in 1936 and immediately fanned the flames of the controversy simply due to the wings shown on either side of the Gothic entrance. The inference has been that their marked resemblance to the University of Michigan buildings could only mean that Davis had provided the design for those buildings. Although this drawing does not show North and South Wings exactly as executed, since the key fret was ultimately placed in the parapet above the roofline and not in the frieze below it, it nevertheless seems to be definitively associated with the University of Michigan. It would seem logical that Davis provided this design idea to Harpin Lum when the regents chose to go forward with the main building. Lum may then have drawn his own modified version that was presented to the board, with the key fret above the roof, corresponding to the features on the professors' houses. An alternate explanation is that in later years persons in Michigan who may have remained in contact with Davis, asked his advice on how to tie the wings together. Perhaps there was still a hope that a spectacular Davis Gothic design might yet be realized. Davis may have been provided with information on the wings as executed and mistakenly sketched the key fret in the frieze—a more usual location. Harpin Lum could also have been the instigator of the design. When he returned to New Haven after completing construction of North Wing in 1841, Lum may have communicated with Davis and described the main building that he had just built. At the time the regents still seemed inclined to execute part of Davis's plan, and, basing his work on Lum's information, Davis may have created this drawing as a way for the regents to fulfill this goal. Since Davis's drawing is not annotated, it cannot be known why he drew it or when. In the end, the South Wing was placed in such a way that a much larger structure, or freestanding one, would have been needed to fill that gap, on the order of fourteen bays wide rather than the eight shown in Davis's design. Donnell's use of this drawing in her publication, and her label identifying it as being for the University of Michigan, was apparently the source of future references to alternate classical plans by Davis for Michigan. Roger Newton first published such a statement in 1942, and it was picked up from there by others and perpetuated.[8]

One of the most intriguing sources of the controversy appears on the 1854 Pettibone map of Ann Arbor, whose depiction of the campus "row" has already caused so much trouble. On the margin of the map appears an illustration of the main college buildings labeled "West Front Michigan University" (fig. 63). North and South Wings are here fairly accurately depicted, but between them is shown—ostensibly as a factual picture of the university buildings—a building that never was. This drawing has been a never-ending source of problems to persons grappling with the history of the physical development of the campus. What was the source of this image, and why was it included on the map? Did it represent a concrete plan for a building the regents intended at some time to execute? Exploring the answers to these questions once again brings A. J. Davis and his sphere of influence into the story.

The source of the actual drawing of the "West Front Michigan University" was probably the same as for the campus plan as depicted on that map (fig. 64). A discussion of the extant evidence has already led to the conclusion that the author of the plan was Harpin Lum. If so, then he surely drew the image of the churchlike structure also used on the map. It is known that the regents asked Lum to execute drawings of current and planned buildings, including elevations, and to deposit those drawings in the university library (*RP,* 141, 173). Later references from the 1870s confirm the existence, in the museum, of at least one of Lum's drawings, depicting the elevations of a proposed row along State Street.[9] It is likely the mapmaker had access to these drawings and was convinced that the plans would be executed in due course. The drawing of the building itself argues against its having been made by an architect of any training or experience, because of the placement of the

8. Newton, *Town and Davis,* 237.

9. "Pictures of the University."

Fig. 63. West Front Michigan University, detail from D. A. Pettibone map of Ann Arbor, 1854. On left, North Wing or Mason Hall (1841); on right, South Wing (1849); the central church-like structure was never built.
Courtesy of Map Library, Hatcher Graduate Library, University of Michigan.

columns. In classical orders columns are always placed at the outer edges of the pediment and never set in as shown in the drawing. At this time builders' handbooks were plentiful and readily available and depicted the classical orders correctly in great detail. From this drawing it can be inferred that someone with insufficient experience unintentionally placed the columns incorrectly. Perhaps this was Harpin Lum, who was primarily a builder and not an architect. This seems unlikely, however, given Lum's background in building in New England, where countless churches were accurately built in this vocabulary, including in his hometown of New Haven. A more probable explanation for the inaccuracies in the drawing (see fig. 63) is that they were a result of the translation of the drawing by the lithographer or cartographer. In addition to the displaced columns, the building as shown is of a different scale than the two it sits between. A careful study of the illustration reveals that the chapel is a two-story building, while the two main buildings that flank it are four-story. Why the size of the structure should be so exaggerated on the map is unknown. A roofline at four stories would not be in keeping with the classic arrangement of this church-style structure. To avoid being utterly dwarfed by the North and South Wings, a chapel in this design would have been better served if placed elsewhere on campus.

Nevertheless, to include such a chapel in the plans for the Ann Arbor campus was a logical de-

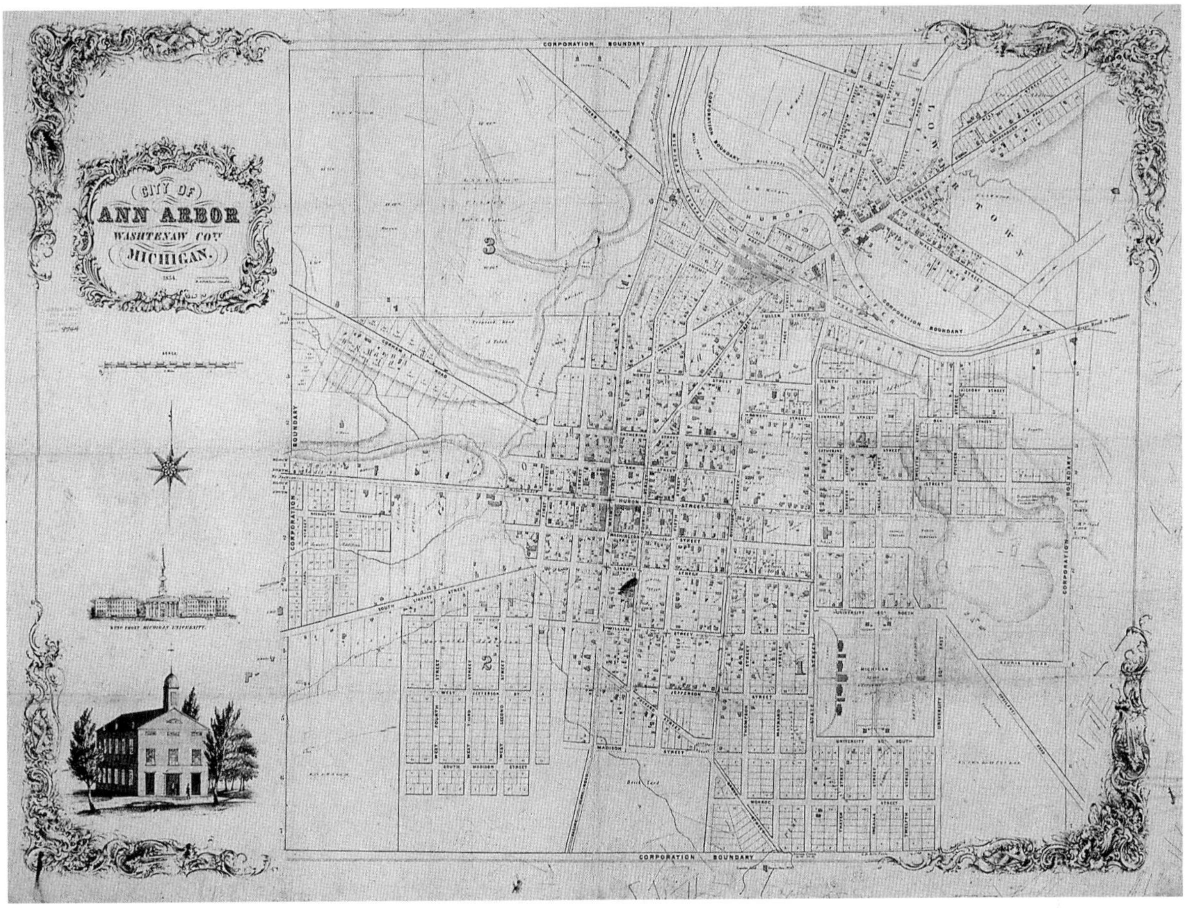

Fig. 64. Map of Ann Arbor by Darwin A. Pettibone, 1854.
Courtesy of Map Library, Hatcher Graduate Library, University of Michigan.

velopment. Since A. J. Davis first provided plans for Michigan, a chapel had been among the anticipated structures, possibly as part of a building also housing the library or museum. Davis drew such a structure for Michigan in the Gothic style (see fig. 36). When the stylistic vocabulary for the campus was changed to the classical mode, it would have been natural for Harpin Lum, and possibly Isaac Thomson, to realize a design for a chapel in this style. That the regents yet intended to build a chapel is verified by Regent E. C. Walker, who wrote in April 1847, "As to place of location the building [South Wing] . . . the common understanding was that it was to be located according to the upright & ground plan of the University in the Library, on the other side of the contemplated chapel from that occupied by the present building, i.e. so that the chapel may hereafter be built between them."[10]

The design sources for this style of church were readily at hand. The motif of adding a steeple or tower to a Greek Revival temple was most influentially executed by British architect James

10. Letter E. C. Walker to Silas Douglass, April 30, 1847, Silas H. Douglass Correspondence, January–July 1847, Douglass Family Papers, box 1, Bentley.

Gibbs, first in his landmark design for St.-Martin-in-the-Fields church, built in Westminster, London, in 1721–27 (fig. 65). So greatly admired was this church that Gibbs was persuaded to publish a book of his designs, which included not only the design for St. Martin as executed, but also alternate designs that Gibbs had made. Gibbs explained his reasoning behind producing this book, which was published in 1728, indicating that "such a Work as this would be of use to such Gentlemen as might be concerned in Building, especially in the remote parts of the Country, where little or no assistance for Designs can be procured. Such may be here furnished with Draughts of useful and convenient Buildings and proper Ornaments; which may be executed by any Workman who understands Lines, either as here Design'd, or with some Alteration, which may be easily made by a person of Judgement," thereby providing guidelines for less experienced or talented builders.[11] In his book Gibbs also provided drawings for numerous variations of some of the building's features, such as steeples or towers. Gibbs's designs, through his book and other venues, became extremely influential on both sides of the Atlantic. By the mid–eighteenth century, churches in the Gibbsian style were cropping up in the United States, such as St. Paul's Chapel in New York City (fig. 66), built 1766 and designed by Thomas McBean, a pupil of Gibbs's. The tower, in the style of St. Martin, was by James C. Lawrence and built in 1796. Pattern book authors also helped to disseminate the style by including designs in this vein in their handbooks, such as that by Minard Lafever, published in his *Young Builder's General Instructor* of 1829 and in *The Modern Builder's Guide* of 1833 (fig. 67). By the early nineteenth century churches in the Gibbsian style could be found in cities and towns across America.

Architects Ithiel Town and A. J. Davis also dabbled in this style. Town's elegant Center Church in New Haven, designed in common with Asher Benjamin, has already been noted (see fig. 8). Another notable example was St. John's Chapel, built 1803–7 in New York City and designed by leading church architects John and Isaac McComb. It took its basic shape and features from Gibbs's designs. An etching of St. John's was made by Davis for his series of views of the city published in the *New York Mirror*. Davis had, at times, been hired by John McComb to create artistic presentation drawings based on McComb's designs, to be used by McComb as marketing tools. Davis would provide the same service for Martin Thompson and other architects.[12] In 1836, Davis, along with Ithiel Town, provided a design for completing the transformation of St. Mark's-in-the-Bouwerie from Georgian to Greek Revival. The body of the church, built 1795–99, had received in 1828 a steeple in the Gibbsian style designed by Town's former associate Martin Thompson (see fig. 10). Town and Davis later sought to give the church a truly classical facade by the addition of a portico in the Ionic order (fig. 68). Here again the influence of Greek antiquities as delineated by Stuart and Revett can be seen, in this case in the decorative details of the Ionic order that were copied from the Erechtheum on the Acropolis. This design for St. Mark's was not executed, but the striking

11. James Gibbs, *A Book of Architecture, Containing Designs of Buildings and Ornaments* (London: By author, 1728), i–iii.

12. Donoghue, "Alexander Jackson Davis," 84.

Fig. 65. St. Martin-in-the-Fields, Westminster, London, west front. Design by James Gibbs in *A Book of Architecture, Containing Designs of Buildings and Ornaments* (London, 1728), plate 3. Built 1721–27; extant.

Courtesy of Rare Book Room, Media Union Library, University of Michigan.

similarities between it and the drawing appearing on the 1854 map of Ann Arbor (see fig. 63) present the question of whether there was a Davis influence. This seems to be a certain possibility, although the path of influence was probably indirect and passed through Isaac Thomson and Harpin Lum. It is possible either of these men could have drawn the chapel as shown based on seeing

Fig. 66. St. Paul's Chapel, New York City, 1827. Engraved by James Eddy from a drawing by Alexander Jackson Davis. Designed by Thomas McBean, built 1766; tower by James C. Lawrence, added 1796; extant. Originally published in the *New York Mirror,* October 20, 1827. From *Early Illustrations and Views of American Architecture* by Edmund V. Gillon Jr. (New York: Dover, 1971).

James Gibbs's book or the innumerable churches built in this style that Thomson, Lum, and other builders would have been familiar with. For Thomson and Lum these included designs by Davis and Town, both of whom they knew from New Haven. The regents themselves, who may have influenced designs made by Thomson and Lum, would have been familiar with this style as well, not simply from their backgrounds in New England, but that in Michigan. In fact, the state capitol in Detroit, where many regents' meetings were held, was itself an adaptation of the Gibbsian form, built in 1828.[13] The mysterious chapel on the "West Front Michigan University" illustration of 1854 is yet another tie between Davis and possible designs for Michigan in the classical mode.

13. The building used as the courthouse and state capitol in Detroit was designed by Obet Wait and built in 1828. It served as the capitol until that function was relocated to Lansing in 1847. The building was later used as a high school and ultimately burned down in 1893.

Fig. 67. Plan and elevation of a church, design in the Grecian Ionic order. Drawn by Minard Lafever for *The Modern Builder's Guide* (New York, 1833), plate 54. Also appeared in Lafever's *Young Builder's General Instructor* (Newark, 1829).

Courtesy of Rare Book Room, Media Union Library, University of Michigan.

One potential source of classical designs for Michigan should be explored even though it is unlikely to have influenced the development of the campus as it occurred. This source concerns the other architect approached by the regents in 1838 to provide designs for the University of Michigan, Ammi Burnham Young. As previously discussed, the relationship between Young and the re-

Fig. 68. St. Mark's Church in the Bowery, New York City, 1836. Design by Ithiel Town and Alexander Jackson Davis for addition of Ionic facade. Lithograph on stone by J. B. Kidd from a drawing by A. J. Davis. Church built 1795–99, architect unknown; tower by Martin E. Thompson, built 1828; Ionic portico by Town and Davis not executed; extant.

Drawings and Archives, Avery Architectural and Fine Arts Library, Columbia University in the City of New York (1940.001.00137).

gents was extremely confused and became more so when A. J. Davis entered the picture. Ultimately Young, who was busy with other commissions at the time, agreed to withdraw from the Michigan project. Young did, however, indicate that he had spent considerable time on designs for

Fig. 69. Thornton Hall, Dartmouth College, Hanover, photo 1884. Designed by Ammi B. Young. Built 1829; extant. Courtesy of Dartmouth College Library.

Michigan and asked to be paid for his work.[14] What those designs may have been is unknown, since no evidence of any such designs appears to have survived. But Young was wedded to the classical style and it seems probable he would have designed something in this vein for Michigan. It is probable such designs would have been similar to those drawn by Young for Dartmouth College, which included Wentworth Hall in 1828, Thornton Hall in 1829 (fig. 69), and Reed Hall in 1839 (fig. 70). Wentworth and Thornton Halls were placed on either side of the main old college building, Dartmouth Hall, and facing a green open space (see fig. 54). The arrangement was not unlike old Yale Row (see fig. 55). It is possible Young anticipated such a grouping for Michigan, but this may never be known. If Young did indeed produce designs for Michigan, they certainly would have been in the classical style. However, given that he removed himself from the picture before (apparently) sending any drawings to Michigan, it can be concluded that Ammi Young had no direct influence on the designs for the buildings that were executed in Ann Arbor in 1839–41. Still, there is the un-

14. *RP,* April 13, 1839, 82–83; and letter Young to Davis, June 20, 1838; see appendix.

Fig. 70. Reed Hall, Dartmouth College, Hanover, photo 1875. Designed by Ammi B. Young. Built 1839; extant.
Courtesy of Dartmouth College Library.

likely possibility that Young gave his Michigan designs to his friend on the board of regents, and that subsequently they were utilized by Lum when drawing the Main Building. The lack of surviving records related to Young's designs for Michigan makes it impossible to prove if they had any part in the development of the Ann Arbor campus, and speculation on what those designs may have been seems fruitless until more evidence is unearthed.

The most tantalizing and intriguing piece of evidence that adds to the controversy of supposed classical designs by Davis for Michigan is written in his own hand. In his later years Davis spent much of his time compiling his drawings and office diaries into albums and scrapbooks. Some of his diaries combined notes about specific jobs with illustrations related to those projects. Four of Davis's nine extant renderings for the University of Michigan can be found inserted in these diaries or albums. (All nine are in the Prints and Drawings Department of the Metropolitan Museum of Art, in New York City.) In volume 7 of Davis's diary, this one cataloged as "scrapbook," appears an interesting entry. This album reflects an attempt by Davis to present some of his designs categorized by styles. The album was never completed, and about half of the drawings referred to in the index had yet to be inserted by Davis. In the front of the album is an "Index to Public Buildings." In this index, under the heading "Greek Temple" is the following entry:[15]

19 Des. University of Mich.

The number 19 was circled by Davis, and the explanation given, on the back of the index for items circled, was "Subjects that are in Vol. I (tho with slight alteration) are inscribed within a circle." Number 19 was the item's number in the index and did not correspond to the page number, as the drawings were being inserted by Davis in alphabetical order. Interestingly, alphabetically under *M* can be found not a "Greek temple" but one of Davis's Gothic designs that is labeled "Design adopted by Gov. Mason for Michigan University 1838" (see fig. 27).[16] Davis's index notation (circled "19") indicated the design was to be found in volume 1. A perusal of this volume did not result in the identification of a drawing that seemed to fit the description, but interestingly, it is here in volume 1 where Davis recorded his trip to Ann Arbor in September 1838.[17] Perhaps, as he often did, Davis had initially attached to this diary entry a sketch he had executed for that client, or perhaps he removed and altered the design for another client.

If it can be taken that Davis had a clear memory and his listing of the University of Michigan as a client for whom he produced a Greek temple design was accurate, then the nature of that design becomes of great interest. Greek temples had been used by Davis in numerous designs, such as for the South Congregational Church (see fig. 16), the Eglisé du Saint Esprit (see fig. 15), and even state capitol designs (see figs. 12 and 14). In 1849, Davis designed Smith Hall for the University of North Carolina as a Greek temple with Corinthian columns (see fig. 74). But it would seem more likely that if Davis designed a Greek building as an alternate to his large Gothic U-shapes for Michigan, it would have been a much larger structure than a simple freestanding temple. The larger building, which needed to accommodate dormitory facilities, as well as recitation rooms and the library, would probably have been on the order of the designs Davis produced for Bristol College immediately before undertaking the Michigan commission. The center structures in both Pennsylvania and Clifton Halls certainly qualify as Greek temples (see fig. 60). In addition, Davis's more fully developed design for Davidson College also includes a Greek temple within the bounds of the quadrangle (see fig. 61). It is also possible that Davis's "Greek Temple" for Michigan may have been for a freestanding chapel or similar structure.

Further adding to this intrigue of the Greek temple design is a rendering that was published in a 1933 *Michigan History* article (fig. 71).[18] This drawing was discovered by Marie Louise Douglas among papers that had belonged to her father, Silas Douglass. With this drawing, Ms. Douglas found others related to the University of Michigan and deduced that they all dated to the 1840s

15. Vol. 7, Scrapbook, Alexander Jackson Davis Collection, Met, Harris Brisbane Dick Fund (24.66.1406).

16. The page number in the scrapbook for this drawing is not clear—the folio is stamped as page 173, but 135 has also been written in pencil.

17. Vol. 1, Diary, p. 61, Alexander Jackson Davis Collection, Met, Harris Brisbane Dick Fund (24.66.81400).

18. Wilfred B. Shaw, "The Early Days of the University of Michigan II," *Michigan History* 17 (winter 1933): 52–107.

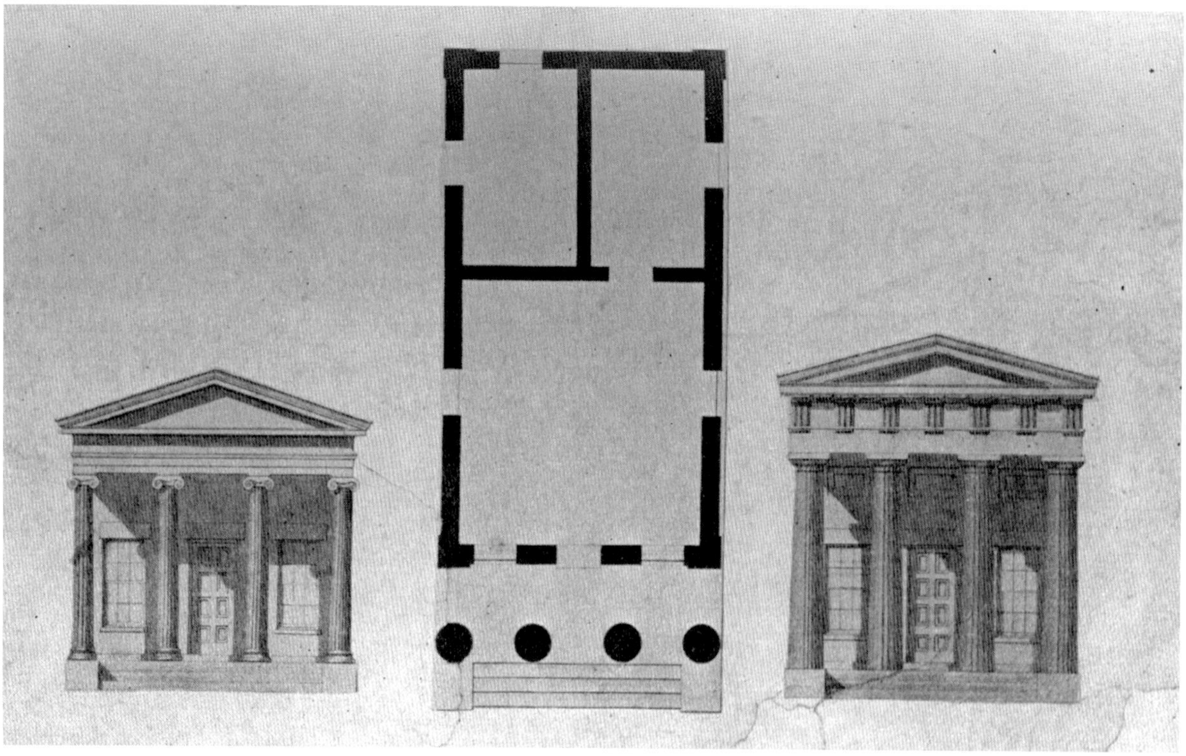

Fig. 71. Temple-front building, probably for University of Michigan, ca. 1850. Design possibly by Alexander Jackson Davis, not executed. As reproduced in "The Early Days of the University of Michigan II," by Wilfred B. Shaw, in *Michigan History* 17 (winter 1933): 77.
Courtesy of Bentley Historical Library, University of Michigan.

and 1850s, when her father was superintendent of buildings at the university. Among the buildings whose construction Douglass supervised were South Wing (1849) and the Medical Building (1850), the latter being in the shape of a Greek temple. Feeling these drawings might have value to the university, Ms. Douglas transmitted them to university president Alexander G. Ruthven on March 23, 1932. "On looking over a drawer which is seldom used," wrote Ms. Douglas, "I found some plans which I am sending you, thinking they may be of historical interest to the University. I suppose my father had them when he was superintendent of buildings and grounds. The large plan you will of course recognize as for the campus, with locations for some of the earlier buildings and space marked off on the North and South sides for the four houses for the Professors. The others are the front elevation and ground plan for the old Medical building, also the front elevation and two floor plans for the combined classrooms and dormitories."[19]

Dr. Ruthven's response reveals his excitement on seeing the drawings. "I was very much pleased to receive the architect's drawings which you sent to me. They caused considerable inter-

19. Letter Marie Louise Douglas to Alexander G. Ruthven, March 23, 1932, Marie Louise Douglas Clippings and Notes, Douglass Family Papers, box 2, Bentley. Marie's father, Silas Douglass, changed the spelling of the family name to *Douglas* around 1875, in order to bring the spelling into conformity with usage in Scotland.

est in my office. We had supposed that these plans had been destroyed. They will now be carefully preserved in our archives and will make a very definite and valuable contribution to our records and the history of the University."[20] Of the drawings that Ms. Douglas mentioned, the "front elevation and two floor plans" survive in the university's archives (see figs. 46, 47, and 49). However, both the campus plan and the front elevation and ground plan for the Medical Building are now lost. Fortunately, soon after they were given to the university, historian Wilfred B. Shaw used them in an article on the early history of the university.[21] As Shaw indicated in his caption, the campus plan (fig. 72) was probably executed around 1850 and depicts the general campus layout of the time, except that the actual footprints of the four professors' houses are not shown, only the outline of the areas set aside for those residences and their gardens. This may, in fact, be a planting plan for the large number of trees that Dr. Douglass recorded that he had planted in 1847, and may also represent an idealized layout for undulating walkways.[22] Most of the trees planted in the university's early years did not survive long, so it is impossible now to know how much, if any, of this planting plan was followed, although sidewalks in this configuration were never laid out. Also, as the decision on placement of the Medical Building was not made until 1848, this planting plan seems to therefore date to sometime after the five hundred trees were planted by Douglass in 1847.

The illustration of two temple-front buildings also used in this article is of great significance (see fig. 71). Although Ms. Douglas indicated the sketches were of the Medical Building, the structures depicted are too small to be the Medical Building as built (see fig. 73) and may have been intended as a chapel or library. The execution of the design shows distinct similarities with many designs by Alexander Jackson Davis and may certainly have been a watercolor rendering comparable in quality to his many works. Shaw, who was able to view and photograph the original before it was lost, indicated in his article that the "beautifully executed" drawing was not annotated in any way, but he also speculated that it was drawn by Davis.[23] Without the original to examine, it remains impossible to know if the design indeed came from Davis's hand, but this remains a distinct possibility. If so, then it would certainly correspond to the "Greek Temple" Davis indicated he drew for Michigan. However, like the chapel in the Gibbsian mode (see fig. 63), this temple-front building is

20. Letter Alexander G. Ruthven to Marie Louise Douglas, March 24, 1932, Alexander Ruthven Papers, box 5, folder 5-6, Bentley.

21. Shaw, "Early Days," 52–107.

22. Letter Silas H. Douglass to Jonathan Kearsley, May 3, 1847, and letter Kearsley to Douglass, May 5, 1847, Silas H. Douglass Correspondence, January–June 1847, Douglass Family Papers, box 1, Bentley. In his May 3 letter, Douglass wrote, "I have just completed the setting of the trees and have paid the men. . . . I have caused each tree to be well manured with chip manure. The trees (400) have been under my own eye & no care has been spared to make them grow." In Kearsley's letter of May 5, he indicated, "I am this day advised that 100 silver leaved maples have been shipped from Buffalo, by order of [Regent] Rev. Geo. Duffield. I presume they will be directed to Ann Arbour and you will have the charge of planting. Will you make enquiry, through your janitor [Patrick Kelly, university janitor and all-around handyman from 1841 to 1847] that they may not be injured before you receive & plant them." If these two letters present an accurate picture, Douglass was responsible for five hundred trees being planted on the forty-acre site in spring 1847.

23. Shaw, "Early Days," 77. Neither Roger Hale Newton nor Edna Donnell, when writing about Davis in 1940 and 1936, respectively, were apparently aware of this temple design, published in 1933, or if they were, they discounted it as not being Davis's work. Surprisingly, both Wilfred Shaw and Frank Robbins did not appear to have discussed this important drawing in their correspondence with Donnell, in which the possibility of Davis designs for Michigan was intently discussed. Neither did Wells Bennett take the drawing into consideration in his 1937 article in which he dissected the evidence related to Davis's designs for Michigan. Certainly he would have known about the drawing, which had caused such a stir in the president's office. Why it is mentioned nowhere beyond Shaw's article is a true mystery, as is its ultimate fate.

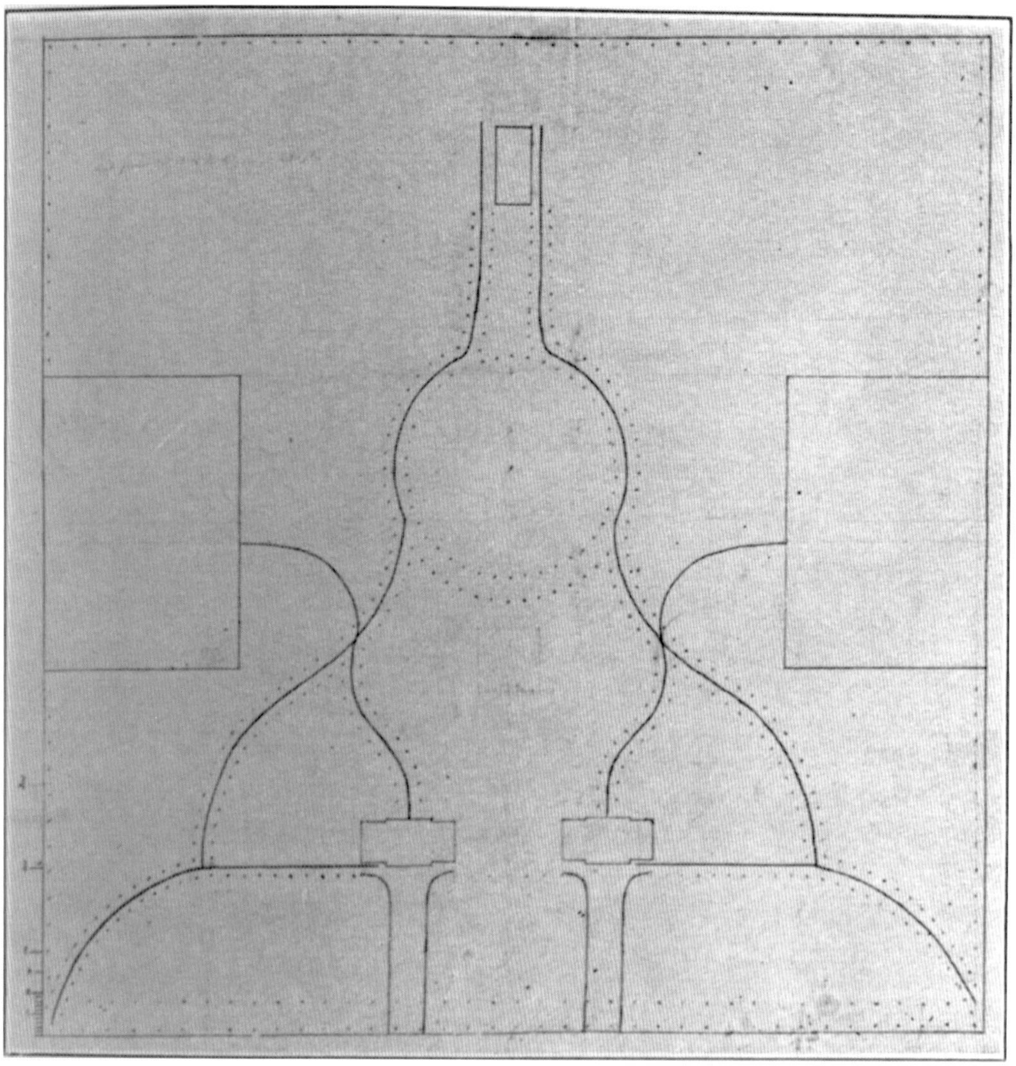

Fig. 72. Campus planting and walkway plan, University of Michigan, ca. 1850. Drawing attributed to Silas H. Douglass; planting plan possibly executed in part. North and South Wings (1841 and 1849 respectively) are shown on the bottom, and the Medical Building (1850) on the top. As reproduced in "The Early Days of the University of Michigan II," by Wilfred B. Shaw, in *Michigan History* 17 (winter 1933): 85. Courtesy of Bentley Historical Library, University of Michigan

too small to have been for a main building, or even for a filler between North and South Wings. Executed in a style artistically similar to much of Davis's work, it does, nevertheless, offer some evidence that Davis may have provided alternate designs in a classical style, this being for a chapel or library-museum, with other designs possibly provided for the main buildings. The temple designs also seem to reflect those drawn by Harpin Lum on his now-missing 1840 plan for the campus, except in that the two buildings on Lum's plan, which were for a museum and a library, had six columns in the Corinthian order, rather than the four columns in Ionic and Doric as shown in the rendering. Therefore, this drawing does not seem to correlate to Lum's work and was in fact probably drawn some years after Lum left Ann Arbor.[24]

Such examples show that Davis did in fact produce Greek temple designs for colleges, and one of them may have been Michigan. These varying sources contribute different elements to the ongoing controversy over whether or not Alexander Jackson Davis produced alternate designs in the classical style for Michigan. Davis himself indicated he did; however, what ties a potential "Greek Temple" can have had to the professors' houses and the Main Building as built in Ann Arbor are still to be clearly revealed. If Davis's temple for Michigan included wings as at Bristol, then the main buildings at Ann Arbor would seem to reflect such a potential scheme, with the central portion, or temple, yet to be realized. Clearly enough evidence survives to make this an honest debate, and in fact Davis's touch can be seen to continue to affect the campus even after South Wing was completed in 1849.

24. "Pictures of the University." The plan by Lum was described in this article as follows: "The other plan was, it seems, partly carried out. It involved the erection of seven buildings, all in a row, four of which were for dormitories, and were, externally at least, like the present middle and south colleges. They were to be 100 feet long and 42 broad. Alternating with them were the library, chapel, and museum. The chapel, standing in the middle probably in the space now left between the literary buildings—was to be a neat church edifice, with a tall spire surmounted by a vane, and provided with a belfry and a clock. It was to be 68 feet by 96, and six Ionic columns were to support the entablature. The museum on the south, and the library on the north, were neat and plain one-story buildings, just alike, 85 feet long by 52 broad, and each adorned with six fluted, Corinthian columns in front."

The Ann Arbor Campus 1850–85

The Ann Arbor campus in 1849 consisted of two classroom-dormitory buildings and four professors' houses. This situation did not remain long unchanged, as the regents were already grappling with the need for another major building, decisions regarding which would have far-reaching implications for the development of the campus plan. As early as 1838, consideration was given by the board of regents to the desire of establishing a medical and surgical college at the University of Michigan. The recommendation was for this college to be located in Detroit and for buildings to be erected there for its use. However, no action was taken in 1838 or in 1842 when the possibility of locating the Medical Department in Detroit again came up for discussion (*RP,* 43, 221). The Medical Department was finally born in Ann Arbor in January 1847, when the need for a building to house the department was also addressed. Although it was recommended that a second building identical to the first (North Wing) be built to accommodate Medical School lectures, laboratories, dissections, etc., the decision was made instead for a new building, called South Wing or South College, to house students and general recitation rooms, as in North Wing (*RP,* 362–66).

Finally, in January 1848, the regents authorized the Building Committee to "procure a plan for a Laboratory to be submitted to the Executive Committee for their approval. That when the same is approved, the Executive Committee select a site for such Laboratory" (*RP,* 389). Hereafter the *Regents' Proceedings* is silent on the issue of the placement of the Laboratory (as the Medical Building was initially called). Other existing documentation reveals the decision made on the placement of the Laboratory or Medical Building. South Wing was under construction at the time planning for the Medical Building was under way. The construction of both was supervised by Dr. Silas H. Douglass of the university faculty. In his capacity as superintendent of building, Douglass regularly communicated with Major Jonathan Kearsley, one of the regents serving on the Building Committee. Once the regents resolved in January 1848 to construct a medical building, plans were immediately begun for the design of the structure and its siting on the campus. No architect is ever referred to in connection with this building, and it is evident from surviving records that Silas Douglass acted as primary designer, aided by Jonathan Kearsley, Dr. Zina Pitcher, and local builder Randall Schuyler.[1] At last, in the Medical Building, a Greek temple form was realized in

1. Letter Jonathan Kearsley to Silas Douglass, February 3, 1848; letter Kearsley to Douglass, February 14, 1848; letter Kearsley to Douglass,

Fig. 73. Medical Building, University of Michigan, Ann Arbor, photo ca. 1880. Design attributed to Silas H. Douglass. Built 1850, enlarged 1864; west half (back) burned 1911, rest demolished 1914.
Bentley Historical Library, University of Michigan (Sam Sturgis Collection, box 3, no. A-407).

Ann Arbor (fig. 73). Why this form was selected for this building is unknown, but sources upon which Silas Douglass and others may have drawn for inspiration were abundant and included builders' handbooks that depicted the classical orders. In addition, Greek temple structures were plentiful across New England and the Midwest, and the designers may have drawn ideas from buildings they were familiar with in their home states (both Douglass and Pitcher were originally from New York), as well as in the Detroit–Ann Arbor area.

The rendering of a smaller temple-front building found among Douglass's papers (see fig. 71) indicates he was in possession of designs in this line, but whether that particular design, which may

February 15, 1848; and letter Douglass to Kearsley, February 16, 1848, Silas H. Douglass Correspondence, January–June 1848, Douglass Family Papers, box 1, Bentley. Randall Schuyler is mentioned in Chapman and Co.'s *History of Washtenaw County,* as trustee in 1840 for Ann Arbor Township, which included the town of Ann Arbor (905); and as township supervisor 1876–79 (909). He is also mentioned in the *Regents' Proceedings* for 1837–64, 395 and 400 (July 1848), in reference to a dispute with the Building Committee.

have been drawn by Alexander Jackson Davis, served as a model for the Medical Building is unknown. Interestingly, the Michigan Medical Building bears a striking resemblance to the Greek temple designed by Davis for the University of North Carolina's Smith Hall, which was built concurrent with the Ann Arbor building, 1849–51 (fig. 74), as well as an unexecuted temple-front design for Annapolis of similar date. In the rectangular North Carolina building, of stucco that was scored, the Corinthian column's capitals took on the shape of corn and wheat. The capitals at Michigan's building also deviated from the traditional Corinthian style and were made of unusually large leaves, with many details of the classical order omitted. More remarkable is that these simplified capitals were made of cast iron and fitted over the tops of the brick columns. The building itself was on a stone foundation, built of brick, covered with stucco and scored to resemble stone. Charles or Francis Letourneau, joiners, drew full-size patterns for the column capitals, from which plaster casts were made by George Sanders, a stonecutter. These were then cast by Letourneau. Both Sanders and Letourneau were from Detroit, where Major Kearsley met with them.[2] A comparison of the Michigan and North Carolina structures (see figs. 73 and 74) reveals a striking difference in the way the classical ideal was carried out, and certainly that at Smith Hall points to the influence of a master designer's hand. The use of marked antae or pilastrades on the sides of Smith Hall, along with tall Daviséan windows, gives the building a strength and elegance not seen in the Michigan Medical Building and makes its appearance more pleasing to the eye. The question of whether or not the Greek temple as expressed in the Medical Building was taken from a previously existing design drawn by A. J. Davis remains unknown. According to his own diaries, Davis did prepare a Greek temple for Michigan, but as noted, no drawing of that description survives that can be attributed directly to the University of Michigan. Perhaps Davis reused that unexecuted design elsewhere, as he did with the Gothic design for Bristol that he adapted for Michigan. In his album Davis did indicate that his temple-front design for Michigan, "tho with slight alteration," was put into another album.[3] Could the Greek temple at the University of North Carolina have evolved from an unexecuted Davis design for Michigan? And could Silas Douglass have made a design for the Medical Building that was drawn from such an unexecuted Davis design or from a published plan for Smith Hall that Douglass may have seen? This cannot be entirely discounted.

The issue of the placement of the Medical Building profoundly affected the development of the campus. If the "plan in the library" was accurately reflected in the 1854 map (see fig. 51), then the

2. Letters Jonathan Kearsley to Silas Douglass, March 27, 1849, and June 13, 1849, Silas H. Douglass Correspondence, 1849, Douglass Family Papers, box 1, Bentley. In his March 27 letter, Kearsley wrote, "As to patterns for the cast iron leaves for the columns, I have consulted Mr. Moffat, Mr. Sanders & Mr. Letorneau. The latter is a competent pattern maker. Moffat will not attempt this job. Sanders will make patterns in plaster & from these, make cast iron patterns. Mr. Letorneu will make them & we all have full confidence in his workmanship." Sanders and Letourneau are regularly listed in Detroit City directories of the time. MacCabe's directory of 1837 lists "Latourno Francis, joiner & builder" (62); Wellings's directory of 1846 lists both "Letourno Francis, joiner shop" and "Letourno Charles, joiner" (114), as well as "Sanders George, stone cutter" (133); and Shove's directory 1852–53 again lists both "Letourneau Francis, carpenter" and "Letourneau Charles, carver" (164), as well as "Sanders Geo. stone yard" (202). It is not clear from Kearsley's letters whether the Letourneau he referred to was Francis or Charles; it may have been either or both, as the joinery was probably a family business. Directories at Bentley.

3. Vol. 7, Scrapbook, Alexander Jackson Davis Collection, Met, Harris Brisbane Dick Fund (24.66.1406).

Fig. 74. Smith Hall or Alumni Hall, University of North Carolina, Chapel Hill, photo 1890. Designed by Alexander Jackson Davis, built 1849–51; extant, a National Historic Landmark (now Playmakers Theater).
Courtesy of North Carolina Collection, University of North Carolina Library at Chapel Hill (neg. 81-916).

logical choice would seem to be to place the new structure in one of the spots designated for buildings in the row facing State Street. Indeed, this was one of the options considered when the regents grappled with the task of siting the building. Three letters from Jonathan Kearsley to Silas Douglass reflect the evolution of the decision, if not the reasoning behind it.

> Please give to me, as soon as convenient, the distance of the West end of the professors' buildings, standing on the East side of the avenue. I mean the brick buildings, not the wood-houses. This distance may determine, in our minds, the location of the Laboratory. (February 15, 1848)

> The location of the Laboratory will claim our careful deliberations. The monument or burying ground need be no impediment, other things being deemed best, to locating the Laboratory East of the Avenue, as the monument &c. can be easily removed. We have not yet had the opportunity to consult Mr. Farnsworth, although we, the Dr. & myself have called at his office, and the Buildg. Com. Even have not compared views, that is, Dr. Pitcher & myself. There are strong reasons on either hand, both for the rear & front locations. (February 18, 1848)

> The Building & Ex. Com. have met to-day and determined, as at present advised, to locate the laboratory in the centre of the grounds north & south, and 150 feet from the fence on the east line, that is on what may be termed the rear or east side of the Un. Grounds. You will please to measure & see how this will affect the one acre designated for the cemetery.[4] (February 19, 1848)

The burying ground referred to was a one-acre section on the east side of the campus that had been designated by the regents as a cemetery for university personnel. No burials were ever made there. Its sole occupant at the time was the Professors' Monument, a limestone and marble cenotaph memorializing four professors who had died early in service to the university, which had been placed on the campus in 1846. The monument would be moved numerous times after this, until today it stands on the southeast side of the Hatcher Graduate Library, where it has resided since 1918.[5] Kearsley's reference, in his letters of February 15 and 18, to the "Avenue" indicates that the Building Committee was still referring to a campus plan that showed the central avenue, although the avenue was never created. The avenue is featured in the plan shown on the 1854 map (see fig. 51) and was derived from Davis's original campus plans (see figs. 29 and 30).

The decision was thus made to place the Medical Building on the opposite side of the campus from the other main buildings. Why it was not placed between North and South Wings or elsewhere along that row is not explained. Perhaps there was a concern for noxious odors that might emanate from anatomical dissections and surgery demonstration rooms. Or possibly there was consideration for the need to surreptitiously bring cadavers into the building at a time when procuring such corpses was illegal—best to keep that activity as far away as possible on campus from the occupied buildings.[6] With the building just under construction, Kearsley reported to Douglass in March 1849, "The Laboratory building will front the East. I have heretofore conversed with Dr. Pitcher and Mr. Farnsworth, who agree that it is to front outward from the University grounds, as do the other buildings."[7] The placement of the building on the east side of the campus, centered north–south and facing to the street, raises the question of whether the thought had been that the building could serve as the center section or anchor of another row that might develop along this side of campus, although the Medical Building was set much closer to the road than the

4. Silas H. Douglass Correspondence, January–June 1848, Douglass Family Papers, box 1, Bentley.

5. For more information on the Professors' Monument, as well as other artifacts, outdoor sculpture, and architectural features on the Ann Arbor campuses of the University of Michigan, visit the university's sculpture website at www.plantext.bf.umich.edu/planner/sculpture.

6. Amusing anecdotes about procuring cadavers for anatomy classes at Michigan can be found in Horace W. Davenport, *Not Just Any Medical School: The Science, Practice, and Teaching of Medicine at the University of Michigan, 1850–1941* (Ann Arbor: University of Michigan Press, 1999), 10; Nicholas Steneck and Joe Borda, "Corpses on Campus," *Ann Arbor Observer,* May 1995, 49–55; and Linda Robinson Walker, "Grave Subjects," *Michigan Today,* fall 1999, 3–5. The law concerning acquisition of cadavers for medical schools did not change in Michigan until 1867, with a comprehensive law adopted in 1881. In 1993, during excavation for an addition to the Randall Physics Laboratory, human remains were uncovered on the Central Campus that, with other medical artifacts, were dated to the turn of the twentieth century. Their location indicated that they were either buried behind the old Medical building, or in its basement, or were deposited behind the Anatomical Laboratory, a structure built in 1889 immediately south of the Medical building. Built as a response to the Michigan Anatomy Act as amended in 1881, the Anatomical Laboratory was demolished in 1902, with no one apparently recollecting where the remains of cadavers of early years had been buried. Better morgue facilities were incorporated into the new West Medical Building, completed in 1904 (now the S. T. Dana Building).

7. Letter Jonathan Kearsley to Silas Douglass, March 27, 1849, Silas H. Douglass Correspondence, 1849, Douglass Family Papers, box 1, Bentley.

buildings on the western side of campus were. Such a plan was never drawn and is not reflected in the manner in which the campus subsequently evolved.

There was an attempt, however, to realize more of the row that faced west on State Street. In 1859, the Law Department began campaigning for a building of its own. Prior to this the only other new building on campus after the Medical was the Chemical Laboratory, a small structure erected in 1856, close to and west of the Medical Building. It was designed by A. J. Jordan of the Detroit firm Jordan and Anderson, who would later design the Law Building. Considered the first building in the country dedicated solely to laboratory instruction in chemistry, the Chemical Lab was enlarged many times over the years. The placement of the Chemical Lab did not follow any plan, but was the result of the logical need to have it located near the Medical Building. The initially small one-story structure read more like an outbuilding than a major structure and therefore did not seem to warrant placement facing East University Avenue.

In October 1859, the Law Committee was authorized to procure a plan for a building and determine a site. It was not until December 1860 that plans were received through competition, and in March 1861 the design by Detroit architects Jordan and Anderson was adopted (*RP,* 860, 921, 956). On December 18, 1861, the regents "Resolved, That said building be placed in the following location on the University Grounds, that is to say, in the space north or south of the present College Buildings as may be designated by the Committee" (*RP,* 973). The Law Building was subsequently built north of North Wing, and completed in March 1863. The campus as it appeared following this construction project is accurately depicted in an 1866 bird's-eye view map of Ann Arbor (fig. 75).

In 1870, University of Michigan president Erastus O. Haven pressed for a new major university building, because of the cramped quarters in North and South Wings, and the need for an auditorium large enough to hold the entire university body. Edward S. Jenison of Chicago, a graduate of the University of Michigan's 1868 engineering class, sought the job of designing the new structure.[8] The building, which he designed in the Second Empire style, was to be sited between and connected to North and South Wings, and the combined building complex was called University Hall (fig. 76). The cornerstone was laid June 28, 1871, and parts of the building were ready for use in October 1872. The style of this building was a far cry from either A. J. Davis's Gothic designs or the Greek temple and Gibbsian-style chapel ideals once contemplated. Davis, who was still alive at the time and who intensely disliked the Second Empire style (calling a public building in the style a "hideous deformity"),[9] must have shuddered to see this development at Ann Arbor. In 1879, the

8. Letter Edward S. Jenison to (Regent) Edward C. Walker, February 22, 1871; and letter E. O. Haven to E. C. Walker, March 3, 1871, Edward Carey Walker Papers, box 1, correspondence 1871, Bentley. In his letter, Jenison describes his abilities as architect and gives examples of his work in Chicago. He implies that he has the support of a number of persons in Ann Arbor for his being appointed architect for the new building (University Hall). Former University of Michigan president Haven (at the time president of Northwestern University) writes to Walker about Jenison's abilities and encourages Walker to hire him.

9. Alexander Jackson Davis, "An Old Architect on Modern Architecture," in the *New York Sun,* October 28, 1878, as quoted by Kowsky, "Simplicity and Dignity," 57.

Fig. 75. Bird's-eye view map of Ann Arbor, 1866, detail of University of Michigan campus area. Printed by Chicago Lithographing Co. Clockwise from left center: South Wing (1849), North Wing (1841), Law Building (1863), professor's house NW (1840) with wood-house, professor's house NE (1840) with wood-house, Medical Building (1850) with large addition to west side 1864, Chemical Laboratory (1856), professor's house SE (1840), with wood-house and barn, and President's House (1840) with third-floor addition of 1864, with wood-house and barn. Note the low cupolas visible on the roofs of the three houses (President's House has a balustrade or captain's walk added with the third floor in 1864). All buildings demolished except President's House, which is extant but much enlarged.

Courtesy of University Planner's Office, University of Michigan.

Fig. 76. University Hall, University of Michigan, Ann Arbor, 1870. Design by Edward S. Jenison. The central section built 1872; North Wing (left) built 1841; South Wing (right) built 1849; all demolished 1950.

Bentley Historical Library, University of Michigan (E. S. Jenison Drawings).

Fig. 77. Bird's-eye view map of Ann Arbor, 1880, detail of University of Michigan campus area. Published by J. J. Stoner, Madison. Clockwise from left: University Museum (1880), University Hall (1872, with South Wing 1849, and North Wing 1841), Heating Plant (1879), Law Building (1863), Homeopathic Hospital (1879), University Hospital (1869), Medical Building (1850), Chemical Laboratory (1856), Dental School (1879), and President's House (1840). All buildings demolished except President's House, which is extant but much enlarged.
Courtesy of University Planner's Office, University of Michigan.

last vestige of the classical style—the balustrade with Greek key fret motif—was removed from North and South Wings.

During the 1870s an additional small building was placed on campus, and the two professors' houses on the north side were substantially enlarged for other uses. A coal-burning steam heating plant, with a tall smokestack, was erected in 1879 just east of University Hall. It was designed by architect Gordon W. Lloyd, a prolific designer of buildings at the university and in the city. A second smaller heating plant was accommodated at the same time in a lean-to addition on the east side of the Chemical Lab and served the buildings in this area of the campus. At about this same time, additions were being made to the two northern professors' houses in such a manner as to defy the logic of any planning effort. In 1869, the northeast house had been adapted for use as the University Hospital; it was the first hospital in the United States to be owned and operated by a university. In 1876, long wood pavilion extensions were added on the back or south side of the house, with an amphitheater added in 1879. (Fig. 77, an 1880 map of campus, shows the buildings discussed here.) The northwest house, adapted for use by the Dental School in 1875, was similarly enlarged in 1879, when it was converted to accommodate the Homeopathic Hospital. Again pavilion extensions were made, also built of wood, in both cases so they could easily be dismantled or burned if necessary to halt any possible spread of contagion. (The Dental School had been moved to the southeast house in 1877.)

Fig. 78. Drawing of west front, University of Michigan, Ann Arbor, as built 1880. From left: Law Building (1863), North Wing or Mason Hall (1841), University Hall (1872), South Wing (1849), University Museum (1880). All demolished. Illustration by Yevgeniy Akkerman, University Planner's Office, University of Michigan, 1999.

The next major building to appear on campus was the creation of William LeBaron Jenney, who had been appointed the first professor of architecture and design at the University of Michigan in March 1876. Although instruction in architecture lasted only two semesters, Jenney remained associated with the university until 1880, more in the capacity of campus architect than professor. A towering talent to have touched Ann Arbor, Jenney would go on to achieve national renown for his designs in the commercial arena, becoming known as the father of the skyscraper. In 1876, Jenney was asked by the regents to draft plans for a new building to house the library and a museum. No action was taken for three years, but in June 1879 the regents again asked Jenney to draw plans for a proposed museum building. On July 24, 1879, the plans for the museum prepared by Jenney were adopted and the Committee on Buildings and Grounds was empowered to make arrangements "as they may deem necessary, in the interests of the University, including the fixing of location of said building."[10] The site chosen for the museum was south of University Hall in the row facing State Street (see fig. 55). Although the row idea now seemed to be developing with the construction of University Hall, the Law Building, and the museum, the variation in the sizes and styles of the buildings deprived the row of the sense of symmetry and cohesion of the row ideal as seen at Yale and other colleges (fig. 78). All thought of further developing the row at Michigan—whether on the west or east sides—seemed to finally be lost when the large new library building was placed in the center of campus in 1883.

This central placement of the library was not arbitrary, but resulted from a discussion concerning where in the row facing State Street the library should be placed. The options were either at the north end next to the Law Building, or the south end next to the newly completed museum. The arguments were heavy against the northern site: a large number of elms would be lost, and, more

10. *RP,* 1876–81, 11, 28, 391, 402–3. Although the designs William LeBaron Jenney was originally asked to provide for the university were for a combined library and museum, the library function was separated from the museum before the final designs were made. Interestingly, Jenney also provided designs for the university's library building, which were not adopted; the regents later accepting designs provided by Ware and Van Brunt. One building designed by Jenney survives in Ann Arbor, the Delta Kappa Epsilon "shant" on East William Street, completed in 1879 as a location for the fraternity to carry out secret ceremonies. It is still in use by the fraternity today.

Fig. 79. General library, University of Michigan, photo 1888. Designed by Ware and Van Brunt. Built 1883; substantially demolished 1918; part of stacks absorbed into new (Hatcher Graduate) library.
Bentley Historical Library, University of Michigan (Photo Vertical File, folder D13-221).

importantly, it would suffer from this placement so near the Homeopathic Hospital. "At that locality," wrote Law dean Thomas M. Cooley to President James B. Angell, "it will be disturbed by all the noises that now disturb the library [at the time located in the law building], & in addition those coming from the hospital immediately under the windows. I understand from the librarian that they are now sometimes disturbed by disagreeable & painful sounds proceeding from the hospital & the liability to this must be greatly increased as the distance is diminished."[11] The decision was subsequently made to place the library in the row to the south of the museum. This did not, however, come to fruition, and the final placement of the library appears to have been influenced mostly by its architect, Henry Van Brunt of Ware and Van Brunt, a Boston firm known at the time for their design of Memorial Hall and others at Harvard. Van Brunt's design for the library (fig. 79), with its large rounded reading room and entrances on the sides, simply could not have been placed

11. Letters Thomas McIntyre Cooley to (President) James B. Angell, May 16, 1881, and May 23, 1881; and letter (Acting President) Henry S. Frieze to Angell, June 23, 1881 (during 1881 Angell was serving as minister to China, and Frieze was acting president at the university); and letter Charles Kendall Adams to Angell, July 6, 1881, James B. Angell Papers, box 2, correspondence, May, June, and July 1881, Bentley.

Fig. 80. Professor's house, southeast unit with addition for Dental School, University of Michigan, Ann Arbor, photo ca. 1885. Note Daviséan style windows in the addition to right. House built 1840, enlarged for Dental School 1879; greatly enlarged 1891 for Engineering College; demolished 1921.

Bentley Historical Library, University of Michigan (Sam Sturgis Collection, box 3, no. A273-11b).

to advantage on the inadequate site south of the museum. Therefore, on Van Brunt's urging, the regents voted to place the library in the central part of campus.[12]

Today, although major buildings still face out to the street, the focal point of the original forty acres has shifted to be inward looking. A large open space, the "Diag," has developed in the center, with the graduate library (built 1920 on the site of the old general library) facing formally onto it. Until the turn of the century, the interior part of the campus continued to be viewed as a backyard or informal courtyard, although tree-lined paths were developed early. It was not until 1898, with an unexecuted campus plan by Henry Ives Cobb, that the idea was first put forth to develop the "Diag" as a formal focal point and to have buildings oriented toward it.[13] This was more fully realized with a campus plan developed in 1907, behind which architecture professor (and later dean) Emil Lorch was the driving force.

12. *RP,* 1881–85, June 28, 1881, 53. Ware and Van Brunt became Van Brunt and Howe during the time the University of Michigan library was in design.

13. At the time, Henry Ives Cobb (1859–1931) was best known for his designs for the University of Chicago (1892–1900), which reflected a mature version of the Gothic quadrangle, or rather a set of quadrangles. Cobb's plan for the University of Michigan called for separate structures instead of a quadrangle, as Cobb was building on the pattern developed during Michigan's first fifty years. Cobb had been hired by the University of Michigan in 1895 to provide designs for an art building, and insisted that to adequately address the design, he needed to draw a plan for the entire campus. Neither of his designs for the art building (watercolor renderings of two alternate designs in the classical mode survive), nor his campus plan (which also survives), was executed. Letter Henry Ives Cobb to James

Fig. 81. President's House, University of Michigan, Ann Arbor, photo ca. 1880, view from front. House built 1840; kitchen wing and third floor added 1864; more additions 1891, 1920, 1933; extant.
Bentley Historical Library, University of Michigan (Photo Vertical File, folder D13-266).

Additions to the two houses on the south side of campus also reflected stylistic features that can be linked, however indirectly, to Alexander Jackson Davis. The southeast professor's house was given over to the Dental School in 1877 and immediately was overcrowded. An addition to the east side was made in 1879 in the form of a long rectangle, approximately twelve narrow bays wide (fig. 80). The most striking feature of the addition was the tall narrow windows separated by pronounced vertical piers. This pattern certainly recalls Davis's invention, the Daviséan window, which can be seen in figures 9, 25, and 61. In 1852, the southwest unit became the President's House when Henry Philip Tappan took up residence. The first president of the University of Michigan (1852–63), Tappan made no substantive changes to the house, except to install gas lighting in 1858. Tappan was, however, responsible for the addition of barns to the two southern houses, which can be seen on the maps of the time (see fig. 75).

The second president, Erastus Otis Haven (1863–69), would make the first substantial changes to the house. In 1864, plans were made for additions to the house, funds appropriated, and construction begun by June 1864.[14] There were two parts to the addition, one of which was a one-story kitchen wing to the west side (fig. 81). Second, the upper attic space was enlarged to form a com-

B. Angell, March 5, 1895; letter Angell to Cobb, May 20, 1895; letter Cobb to Angell, May 21, 1895; letter Francis W. Kelsey to Angell, November 15, 1897; letter Cobb to Angell, June 28, 1899, James B. Angell Papers, boxes 4 and 5; two renderings by Cobb for an art building, University of Michigan Architectural Drawings, folder 2; and campus plan by Cobb, 1898, Bentley.

14. *RP,* 1864–70, 48; and letter E. O. Haven to Regent Edward C. Walker, April 4, 1864, Edward Carey Walker Papers, box 1, folder correspondence 1864, Bentley.

Fig. 82. President's House, University of Michigan, Ann Arbor, photo ca. 1870s, view from back. House built 1840, kitchen wing (right in photo) and third floor added 1864. Note wood-house to left of house, and barn visible on left margin. House, with later additions, extant. Wood-house and barn demolished.

Bentley Historical Library, University of Michigan (Photo Vertical File, folder D13-266).

plete third floor. On the center of the hipped roof was placed a decorative balustrade, sometimes called a captain's walk (fig. 82). Both additions, like their parent house, were covered with stucco and scored to resemble blocks of stone. What is most notable about these additions was the change to a new stylistic vocabulary different from the classical style of the original unit. Paired decorative brackets were placed under the overhanging roof. These features were becoming widespread in the 1860s and became one of the hallmarks of the Italianate style. But prior to this, A. J. Davis was promoting the so-called American bracketed style, of which he was considered the originator. Could the use of these decorative brackets be the direct result of a Davis influence? It is possible, but not likely, although at the time, Davis was still alive and busy in his career. Perhaps someone in Ann Arbor who remembered or knew Davis mentioned the plans to enlarge the house and asked for suggestions on how to dress it up. But by 1864, Davis had long been removed from any Michigan project, and no evidence survives to directly link him to the brackets on the President's House. An indirect influence, however, can be detected. Davis was a leading proponent of

Fig. 83. President's House, University of Michigan, Ann Arbor, photo 1986.
Courtesy of University Planner's Office, University of Michigan.

the bracketed style and picturesque architecture in general. He tried to disseminate these ideals through his well-publicized designs and his own pattern book, published in 1838. More important was Davis's close association with Andrew Jackson Downing, whose books on landscape and rural architecture were widely published. Davis executed many of the drawings in Downing's books, which helped to spread the ideals of picturesque architecture, including many examples of bracketed houses, across the country. Therefore it can be deduced that even if it were indirectly through pattern books, Davis influenced development of buildings at the University of Michigan through the 1870s. The President's House itself is the only one of the early buildings to survive, and although greatly enlarged since the 1860s, it still carries the features that tie it back to Alexander Jackson Davis—the Doric entry portico and the paired brackets under the eaves (fig. 83).

Conclusion

THE EARLY NINETEENTH CENTURY was an extraordinary time for architecture in America. Not only did it see the explosion in publication and availability of builders' handbooks and pattern books, it also saw the emergence of the professional architect in this country. It was at this exhilarating time that the University of Michigan would be created and its Ann Arbor campus born. Those most responsible for its physical development, the first board of regents, found themselves entering the architectural arena at this very exciting time and were naturally drawn to the professional architects whose works were being so widely publicized in the eastern states from which most of the regents came. At this same time, a talented and dynamic man named Alexander Jackson Davis, with an instinctive sense for the artistry of architecture, was coming to the forefront of his profession and gaining widespread notice. Davis was a natural choice for a collegiate commission, and his passion for the Gothic Revival style would result in the creation of breathtaking designs for the new University of Michigan. Some of the Gothic Revival designs executed by A. J. Davis for Michigan, especially one campus plan (see fig. 29), have been publicized over the years and been well known. These designs have been famous not only for their beauty and originality in the collegiate venue in America, but also because they were not executed.

The enduring mystery has revolved not around the Gothic designs, but whether there may have been a link between Davis and the classical buildings that in fact appeared on the Ann Arbor campus in 1840 and 1841. The exploration here of previously unknown documents and the methodical dissection of existing records revealed a scenario in which Davis was only one of several persons who had a hand in developing the physical expression of the newborn University of Michigan. Davis certainly can be seen as the intellect and the talent behind the spark that created the university's earliest buildings, but his vision for Ann Arbor, including the Gothic designs and the campus plans, was formed with healthy doses of inspiration from artists in whose sphere he revolved, especially architects Ithiel Town, Martin Thompson, and James Dakin.

There were, however, other lesser-known persons who figured critically in the birth of the campus. The argument has been presented that the actual designs for the professors' houses of 1840 came from the hand of Isaac Thomson, and the design for the main college building, North Wing in 1841, from Harpin Lum. There can certainly be no doubt but that these men, builders and architects in their own right, played the leading role in developing these designs. Yet it has also been demonstrated that both Thomson and Lum, who were brought into the Michigan endeavor by A. J. Davis, were influenced by earlier designs executed by Davis, often with Ithiel Town, in New Haven and New York. Where the contributions of Davis leave off and those of Thomson and Lum begin will probably never be known. At this juncture, with the evidence so far uncovered, it is still not possible to clearly define Alexander Jackson Davis's role in the design of the President's House at the University of Michigan, the only one of the original buildings to survive. The conclusion that is offered now is that Davis provided the inspiration, by example if not an actual drawing, for the design executed by Isaac Thomson. Davis has also been shown to have provided the spark that led to the development of the campus layout as it progressed over much of the nineteenth century, although Harpin Lum probably drew the actual plan that was reflected in the placement of the earliest classical buildings.

The first board of regents of 1837 proudly embraced and executed their mission of embodying in the built environment the ideals held by the state and its people for their first public institution of higher learning. By seeking designs from two of the most noted architects of public buildings of the time, Ammi Burnham Young and Alexander Jackson Davis, and in obtaining exquisite landmark designs from Davis, the regents succeeded magnificently with their task. Despite Superintendent John Pierce's contention that "a university did not consist in buildings," the physical expression of a college can have a dramatic impact on prospective students and, more importantly, their parents. If the built environment mattered not, then the regents would have been loath to seek a nationally ranked, and therefore costly, architect and cause ill will within the state by hiring talented designers and builders from out of state. From its rebirth in 1837, the regents aspired for excellence in all aspects of the university, from the intellectual atmosphere, to the library and "cabinets," and finally to the buildings that brought together the faculty and students of the state's first public university. Their vision for the physical expression of the institution boldly embodied their ambitions for the high place they felt the University of Michigan would hold among all American colleges. Yet as justly proud as the university should be of its association with such a distinguished and talented person as A. J. Davis, so should it strive to honor and celebrate the contributions of Isaac Thomson and Harpin Lum, by whose hands the face of the newborn campus was surely wrought.

Epilogue

When the Regents of the University of Michigan sought in 1838 to engage a nationally acclaimed architect for their new college, they began a tradition that has continued to influence campus design at the university into the twenty-first century. It was quite extraordinarily ambitious of the board to have attempted to entice a well-known personality such as Alexander Jackson Davis, not to mention Ammi Young, to design a college in the still far-flung frontier of Michigan. The simple force of personality of the members of the board must account for such ambition, and for feeling assured that architects of this caliber would be interested in a newly born college in a small rural town in a state that was hardly out of its infancy. Indeed, both of these leading New England architects seemed eager for the commission, and Davis ultimately provided designs that may seem exceptional for a locale where they would not have been seen by a great number of people. This was quite unlike the college buildings he designed for more populous or well-known cities such as New York and New Haven.

The Regents of the University of Michigan may not have been able to follow through with Davis's elaborate designs, but this did not mean they turned away from the idea of using well-known, even famous, architects for projects at the university. The composition of the board changed over the years, but not their ambitious vision for the university's physical expression. Building on the seeds sown by that first board, which hired Alexander Jackson Davis, future regents sought to employ architects of note on their campus. These included William LeBaron Jenney, Henry Ives Cobb, George Mason, Pond and Pond, and Ware and Van Brunt. Leading architects of Detroit also made their mark on the campus, such as Donaldson and Meier, Spier and Rohns, Malcomson and Higginbotham, Smith Hinchman and Grylls, and among which Albert Kahn not only ranked nationally, but also internationally, due to his landmark designs in the industrial field, especially assembly line production facilities. Kahn began work at the university in 1904 on the West Engineering Building, in association with George Mason. Kahn's influence would be long-lasting. In the 1920s he served as supervising architect to the university during the comprehensive building program that resulted from large state appropriations in 1921 and 1923. Kahn-designed buildings to come out of this building boom of the 1920s included Angell Hall, Clements Library, Randall Laboratory, Ruthven Museums, and the New or East Medical Building (now C. C. Little). Other landmark university buildings by Kahn include Hill Auditorium, Burton Tower, Simpson Memorial Institute, and University Hospital ("Old Main," now demolished), and the firm he founded has continued to be major designers of the university's facilities.[1]

Noted landscape planners were also part of this mix, and included Pitkin and Mott, O. C. Simonds, and the Olmsted brothers. The middle to last half of the twentieth century saw the work of some of the most noted modern architects emerge on the campus, most particularly Gunnar Birkerts, Alden Dow, Harley Ellington, Holabird and Root, Hugh Newell Jacobsen, Charles Moore, Roche and Dinkeloo, Skidmore Owings and Merrill, and Smith Hinchman and Grylls, who continued their long history of designs for Michigan.[2] In addition, both Eliel and Eero Saarinen provided designs for the university, Eliel for unexecuted designs for a carillon tower and school of music in 1925. Following in his father's footsteps, Eero not only provided a plan for the development of the newly acquired eight-hundred-acre North Campus in 1954, he also designed one of the earliest buildings on that site, the School of Music, built 1964.

The waning years of the twentieth century saw a renewed interest in seeking to involve not only nationally ranked architects with university projects, but also those whose reputations are more internationally known. This began with the retaining of Venturi, Scott Brown and Associates in 1997 for the development of a comprehensive campus plan, and has continued with the employment of such firms as Shepley Bulfinch Richardson Abbott, Polshek Partnership, Barton Phelps, and Michael Wilford. Following the lead set by the first board of regents, the university has thus continued to seek designs from some of the leading architects of the time, with the result that noted works by well-known personalities can be found in all corners of the campus. The only drawback from this may be a focus too often on one project at a time, rather than on the architectural unity of the campus. Each new building speaks for itself and often not to its neighbors. Each wishes to be a landmark and not simply a member of a well-outfitted whole. Whether this is leading to a positive or negative overall image for the university depends largely on viewpoint. Never-

1. Some of the most noted works on the Ann Arbor campus by these architects are the following: Henry Ives Cobb, design for an art building and campus plan 1898 (not executed); William LeBaron Jenney, University Museum 1880 (demolished); George Mason and Albert Kahn, West Engineering 1904, Psychopathic Hospital 1906 (demolished); Irving and Allen Pond, West Physics 1889 (demolished), Michigan Union 1919, Michigan League 1929, Student Publications 1932; Ware and Van Brunt, General Library 1883 (demolished); Donaldson and Meier, Dental Building 1908 (demolished), Alumni Memorial Hall 1910; Spier and Rohns, West Medical 1904 (now Dana Building), Law Building 1893/1898 (burned down), Tappan Hall 1893, Newberry Hall 1891; Malcomson and Higginbotham, Mosher-Jordan Dorm 1930, elementary school 1930; Smith Hinchman and Grylls, Chemistry 1909, Central Power Plant 1914, East Engineering 1923, Athletic Administration 1912 (now Hartwig Building), Intramural Sports 1928, Rackham Graduate School 1938, Yost Fieldhouse 1924; and Albert Kahn, Angell Hall 1924, Burton Tower 1936, Clements Library 1923, Graduate Library (Hatcher) 1920, Hill Auditorium 1913, East Medical 1925 (now C. C. Little Building), Natural Sciences (Kraus) 1915, Randall Laboratory 1924, University Museums (Ruthven) 1928, Simpson Memorial Institute 1927, and University Hospital 1925 (demolished).

2. Some of the most noted works by these modern architects on the Ann Arbor campuses include Gunnar Birkerts, Law Library Addition (underground) 1981, Schembechler Hall 1990; Alden Dow, Central Campus Recreation Building 1977, Administration Building (Fleming) 1968, Institute for Social Research 1965, Towsley Center for Continuing Medical Education 1969; Harley Ellington, Administration Building 1948 (now Literature, Science, and the Arts), W. H. Dow Laboratory/Chemistry 1988; Holabird and Root, Kresge Hearing 1963, Kresge Medical Research II 1965, Medical Sciences I and II 1958/1969; Hugh Newell Jacobsen, Alumni Center 1983; Charles Moore, Lurie Tower and Lurie Engineering Center 1996; Roche and Dinkeloo, Power Center for the Performing Arts 1971; Skidmore Owings and Merrill, Kresge Medical Research I/III 1954, Outpatient Building 1953 (now Med Inn); and Smith Hinchman and Grylls, FXB Aerospace 1991, Electrical Engineering and Computer Sciences 1986, Ford Nuclear Reactor 1955, Institute for Science and Technology 1963.

theless, a unique collection of buildings has emerged on the campus that reflects the influence of some of the nation's most distinguished architects and planners, a trend that evolved with the university from the very instant of its rebirth in 1837, and the stimulus provided by the early presence of Alexander Jackson Davis and his ideals in Ann Arbor.

Appendix

Transcription of important extant documents related to the hiring of Alexander Jackson Davis and Ammi Burnham Young.

Note: the documents are transcribed as written, without correction of spelling errors.

Letter from Regent Elon Farnsworth to Alexander J. Davis

Detroit June 1, 1838

Dear Sir,

So long a time elapsed without a reply to either my first or second letter that we came to the conclusion you must have left the city, & the committee, before the recpt of yours had written to Mr. Young of Boston for a plan. I regret exceedingly that you did not receive my letter of Octr. but did not feel myself authorized to incur the expense of an additional plan without the direction of the board. Should the plan of Mr. Young not be satisfactory we probably may address you again on the subject & if so will send you the specifications you require.

Very Resfy
Yr most obt servt
E. Farnsworth
Chief Justice
Michigan

Alex J. Davis Esq)
New York)

Transcription of original handwritten letter, from Letterbook 1821–90, pp. 120, 120a, A. J. Davis Papers, NYPL.

APPENDIX

Letter from Ammi B. Young to Alexander J. Davis

Boston June 20, 1838

A. J. Davis Esqr

Dear Sir

Your favor of the 11th instant was duly recd. In answer I will give you a history of my connection with the business on which you wrote, —I have friends in Michigan who have for some time been quite anxious for me to go to Michigan to reside, supposing it would be much to my advantage in a pecuniary point of view. They have frequently wrote me on the subject, in my answers to them have universally discouraged the idea, unless I could be ensured of good business in my profession, —About a year and a half ago I received a letter from one of my friends there, stating that buildings would be required to be erected for the University of Michigan in a short time, and desired me to hold myself in readiness to engage as an Architect in the erection of them if wanted, as there could be but little doubt I should, as my friend there would make strong interest to have me appointed, —On the receipt of this letter I ~~sat down and~~ immediately answered it, and pointed out the manner in which I should like to engage in it, after I should close my business at Montpelier VT, = I heard nothing more from them, previous to my engaging here, and supposed from the presure of the times they had given up building for the present. The last of April I recd the following letter from the Hon. E. Mundy, Lieut. Gov. of the State of Michigan, and chairman of the Committee for erecting the buildings for the University of Michigan,

"Ann Arbor April 11.1838"

"Dear Sir"

"The regents of the University of Michigan are taking"
"measures prepatory to building —They have not yet adopted"
"a plan nor determined upon the material believing it proper"
"first to consult a suitable architect and give him an opportu-"
"-nity to examine the site and inspect the materials convenient"
"to the place. —The University is well endowed and we"
"wish to put up a building that will combine convenience,"
"durability and magnificence. —You have been mentioned"
"to us by your friend here, in whom we have every reliance"
"and the Committee of building, have instructed me"
"their chairman to invite you to pay us a visit, with a view"
"to your employment as an Architect and superintendent"
"of buildings, —All think that you would find a residence in Michigan"

"pleasant and advantageous, and I do not doubt if you can"
"come, that we can agree upon terms mutually useful and"
"satisfactory. —Be good enough to write me when you get this,"
"whether you can come and when we may expect you."
"Very Respectfully Yours"
"A. B. Young Esq. E. Mundy"

In the same mail came a letter from my friend, stating I must come on to Michigan without fail, that nothing must prevent me, that the opportunity was such as would not in that country occur again, that my compensation would be ample, and my friends all expected me to close with the offer at once, and come out in the course of a day of two, recd another letter from another friend residing at Detroit, who urged me as strongly as the other to come out at once, to let nothing hinder me, = In as much as they had apparently adopted the course I had suggested in order to ensure my services as an Architect & Superintendent, —I felt quite unpleasant at not being able to go out and engage to them, But found I could not and wrote Mr. Mundy to that effect, but stating I should be glad to be of any services to them, I could consistent with my engagement here, = In answer to this Mr. Mundy wrote me May 15 stating that "he was sorry my engagements were such I could not come out to Michigan," that the Committee had concluded to request me to furnish Designs for the buildings consistent with my business here. His sent me a plan of the Village of Ann Arbor with descriptions. [?] from the above you may judge of my surprise at learning from your letter you had previously been applyed to for designs, For my part, do not see why it should be so, as the whole tenor of the letters I have received, do not hint at any thing of the kind in the remotest degree, if they had, should have considered myself released of any obligation to them in consequence of my former letters, and have declined at once to do anything for them as superintending it in any way is altogether out of the question, —If they will but pay me for the trouble and expense I have been at, will willingly relinquish the job of making their designs, = I hardly wish to make designs to be executed by such workmen as they may have there, and would on no account undertake the superintendence of it, unless I could be there nearly all the time, and personaly inspect the work, —By a friend from Detroit now in this City, I learn they want a competent Architect to take the whole charge of the business, to see to the procuring proper stone, and other materials, and do all the business connected with the building, as all the Committee are totally unacquainted with it, —I am satisfied if they do not obtain a proper man to superintend to building, any designs they may obtain, will be spoiled in the execution and consequently have little desire to furnish any for them, [?] I am expecting one of the Regents of the University here in a few days who will have authority to act in business; On learning you have made a set of Designs, he may conclude to take them instead of having me complete those I have begun, —Should that be the case (provided he pays me for my trouble in the thing, as I presume he will) I should be content, as I have as much on my hands as I can well attend to at this time. Am sorry I cannot make it convenient to associate with you in this business and take the superintendence of the buildings. —Had they not applyed to me it would have saved me much anxiety of which I would gladly have been relieved.

Wishing you every success in your Profession
I subscribe myself your friend and obt svt
Ammi B. Young

Transcription of original handwritten letter, from Letterbook 1821–90, pp. 392, 392a, 392b, A. J. Davis Papers, NYPL.

APPENDIX

Contract between Alexander J. Davis and the Regents of the University of Michigan

Articles of Agreement made on the eighteenth day of September eighteen hundred and thirty eight between the regents of the University of Michigan of the one part and Alexander J. Davis, Architect of New York and Isaac Thompson, builder of New Haven of the other part.

First, the said Alexander J. Davis and Isaac Thompson for themselves, their heirs, executors and administrators doth hereby covenant with the said Regents of the University of Michigan and their successors in office, in consideration of the covenant herein after contained, that the said Davis and Thompson shall jointly act and do the duties of Architects and superintendants of the University of Michigan, subject to the control of the Board of Regents or their building committee duly appointed, and to have the plans to be made under another covenant in this instrument by the said Davis and approved by the said Regents or their said committee faithfully carried into execution according to the best interests of the University. And it is further agreed that the said Davis is to furnish specifications, working drawings and details as they may be required for the speedy erection of the various buildings and improvements; and the said Thompson is to reside on or near the site of the said improvements at Ann Arbor, at least six months of each year, at the discretion of the building committee and he is to estimate the costs of the improvements, receive proposals from builders wishing to contract for portions of the work, compare estimates and proposals, ascertain when and in what manner the best materials are to be procured as brick, stone and metal & lumber, paint and other articles necessary for the completion of the improvements, and to lay the same before the Regents of the University or their building committee for their approval. And he is also to procure skilful workmen to work by the day on such portions of the work as he and the said Regents or their building committee may judge to be best for the pecuniary interests of the University and the speedy progress of the work. And the said Thompson is not only to give his personal superintendance to the work during the time specified, when not traveling in the service of the said Regents but he is also to engage and keep employed at his own expense a competent and trusty mechanick to act as working foreman throughout the year and especially during his absence when traveling to procure materials or otherwise.

Second, the said Regents of the University of Michigan covenant for themselves and their successors in office that in case the said Thompson and Davis shall jointly and severally perform the services above specified to be performed by them or either of them, that the said Thompson and Davis shall be paid in full the just sum of Twenty five hundred dollars for each and every year, in current money of the United States, in quarterly instalments (except so much as the said Thompson and Davis may pay to the working foreman above specified, say eight hundred dollars per year which shall be paid monthly.

Third—It is mutually agreed that this contract may be determined any time the said Regents may desire provided they give the said Davis and Thompson three months written notice of their intention to close the same, and pay to them such an amount of this salery as may be due at the expiration of the said period—

In testimony where of the parties to these presents have this eighteenth day of September, eighteen hundred and thirty eight hereunto set their hands and seals—

S.T. Mason, [signed]
Prest. Board of Regents
University of Michigan

Signed and sealed in)
the presence of)

Z. Pitcher [signed]

Alex J. Davis—[signed]
Isaac Thomson [signed]

Transcription of original handwritten contract, A. J. Davis Collection I, file N-6, item 40-9416, Avery.

APPENDIX

Letter from Isaac Thomson to Alexander J. Davis

Ann Arbor. Jany 11, 1839

Mr. A. J. Davis

Dear Sir

Agreeable to my predictions the Regents have decided on the erection of the center building. But there are a few that are opposed to having it built of brick, and others that would be willing to have the whole subject postponed indefinitely and what the end will be is more than I can venture a prediction. The committee feel some embarrassment relative to the extent of their powers. A meeting is however to be held in a few days when I suppose their duties & powers will be defined. —But what I am to be doing in the mean time I have yet to learn—and it is certainly dull music to be here with nothing to do and without any books. —I hope however that you will devote what attention you can —to the plans and working drawings and pay particular attention to simplicity and economy—as expence seems to be the great bug bear—that operates on the minds of almost all the gentlemen —I have been trying for several days past to get a payment of Salary but have not succeeded as yet.

Your friend

Isaac Thomson

Transcription of original handwritten letter, from Letterbook 1821–90, p. 332b, A. J. Davis Papers, NYPL.

Building Committee Report as filed with the *Regents' Proceedings*, April 13, 1839, pp. 82–83

Lieutenant-Governor Mundy submitted the following report and resolution:

The Committee on Building to whom was assigned by a resolution of the Board the duty of procuring a plan for the University Buildings, in relation to that matter report:

That soon after the appointment on the eleventh day of April, 1838, being strongly advised, by several gentlemen of high standing, of the merits and talents as an architect, of Ammi B. Young, of Vermont, they through their Chairman addressed a letter to him inviting him to make a visit to Michigan and proposing to employ him as the Architect of the University. Mr. Young in answer to their letter declined the proposition made to him, having as he informed the Committee, been appointed to superintend the erection of the Custom House in Boston, but proffered to the Committee his professional services in making plan of the buildings.

The Committee, having consulted with other members of the Board, as well as with gentlemen well acquainted with Mr. Young, on the 15th of May last wrote to Mr. Young and giving him particular description of the grounds and map of the village of Ann Arbor, employed him to furnish a design, urging him to give to it his early attention and promising him a proper compensation.

The Committee were told by Mr. Young in answer that he would commence the designs immediately, and devote to them all his spare time. The Chairman of the Committee on the 18th of July last again wrote to Mr. Young from New Jersey sending him the views of the Committee upon some suggestions made by him in his last letter, soon after which the Chairman of the Committee received a letter from Judge Fletcher dated the 19th July, saying that the Board of Regents had the day before determined to proceed with all convenient dispatch with the University Buildings, and that he was requested to write to him desiring him to see Mr. Davis, the Architect from whom the Regents expected a plan, and to urge upon him the necessity of making a visit to Michigan as early as possible to view the site and determine upon the location and arrangement of the buildings and other improvements. Upon receiving this letter the Chairman called upon Mr. Davis, stated to him that Mr. Young had been employed as Architect, informed him of the Judge's communication, and sought from him an explanation of his engagement with the Board of Regents; and learned from him that a correspondence had existed between himself and one of the members of the Board, to whom anterior to the appointment of this Committee had been given authority to procure a plan for the buildings. Mr. Davis, also informed him that Mr. Young in a letter to him had expressed willingness to relinquish to him the production of the plan. From these explanations the Chairman of the Committee was led to suppose that in his absence the Board had resolved to look to Mr. Davis for a design and consequently, according to the instructions in the Judge's letter invited Mr. Davis to visit the Board of Regents. After the Board had agreed upon the plan submitted to them by Mr. Davis and after the return home of the Chairman, having understood that no further correspondence had passed between the Committee and Mr. Young and fearing that Mr. Young might possibly feel himself ill treated by the Committee, although from the length of time since he had been heard from, and the suggestion of Mr. Davis, the probability that he had from his other engagements relinquished in behalf of Mr. Davis this employment seemed strong, the Chairman of the Committee wrote to Mr. Young stating the circumstances under which Mr. Davis had been employed, stating to him what Mr. Davis had said about his relinquishment to him of this employment, and informing him that the Board had adopted a plan furnished by Mr. Davis. In reply to this Mr. Young informed the Committee that he had expended much time and study upon the designs for the University Buildings, that he had completed the most difficult part, the designing, that nothing remained to be done but the mechanical part, and forwarded to them his bill for three hundred dollars, requesting its early payment.

The Committee have thought it due to themselves to make this statement of their proceedings, and although the interests of the University may have warranted all the energy and zeal and dispatch manifested by the Board on it adoption of a plan and preparation for building, yet they cannot but regret that any circumstances should have deprived the Board of the benefit of the study and labour of Mr. Young in whose professional knowledge and fairness of character the Committee have undiminished confidence.

Believing that Mr. Young is entitled to a just compensation for his services, the Committee report the following resolution:

Resolved, That the President of the Board issue a warrant in favor of Ammi B. Young or bearer for . . . . dollars for professional services as architect and that the Building Committee be authorized to place the proceeds of said warrant in the Bank of Michigan to the order of Mr. Young.

Dated Nov. 1838. E. Mundy, Chairman

On motion of Mr. Wilkins, the said report and resolution was laid on the table.

Letter from Regent Edward Mundy to Alexander J. Davis

Detroit Apl 14, 1839.

Sir,

I have been instructed by the Board of Regents to ask of you what correspondence previous to my calling on you in N York last summer had passed between yourself and Mr. Young relative to his relinquishing to you the business of furnishing a plan for the University of Michigan. I understood from you that he had so done, or had expressed a willingness so to do; and it was from your expressions taken in connection with the instruction sent to me while in New Jersey, that I came to the conclusion that Mr. Young had given up the matter in your favor. Mr. Young has sent on his account against the Board for professional services for $300, and this explanation is sought from you to enable the Board rightly to adjust and dispose of this matter.

Very respectfully
Yours—
E. Mundy
(Lt. Gov. of Michigan.)

A. J. Davis Esq—)
Architect)

Direct to me at
Ann Arbor.

E. M.

Transcription of original handwritten letter, from Letterbook 1821–90, p. 236, A. J. Davis Papers, NYPL.

Building Committee Report as filed with the *Regents' Proceedings*, March 6, 1840, pp. 124–27

Chief Justice Fletcher submitted the following report of the Building Committee, which was read; and on motion of Judge Wilkins, the report was accepted.

REPORT.

The undersigned, on behalf of the Building Committee, respectfully submits to the Board of Regents of the University, the following report of their proceedings.

By an order of the Board of Regents of the 11th February, 1839, all further proceedings to erect the University Buildings according to the plan adopted in September, 1838, were suspended and the building Committee by that resolution were directed to give notice to Alexander J. Davis and Isaac Thompson, that the Board of Regents would put an end to the contract made with them on the 18th September, 1838, as Architect and Superintendent; and make a new contract with Mr. Thompson to superintend the building of four houses on the University ground at Ann Arbor, and to proceed to erect those houses according to plans adopted by the Regents. In pursuance to these directions, the Committee notified Mr. Thompson that the contract made with him and Mr. Davis would be determined in pursuance of the provisions of the contract made with them, and Mr. Thompson authorized by Mr. Davis, and acting for Mr. Davis, as well as for himself, on receiving a certificate from the Committee for the amount due them on that contract, did on the 14th February, 1839, discharge the said contract and endorsed his receipt thereon for the sum of six hundred and sixteen dollars, being in full for all claims under that contract. On the same day the Committee also made a new contract with Mr. Thompson to superintend the building of the four houses above mentioned, the compensation to be at the rate of $1,000 per annum; and by the advice of Mr. Thompson, the Committee on the 14th February last, entered into a contract with Haspier [*sic*] Lum, to erect and finish those houses by which they agreed to give him the sum of $7,450 for each of two of the houses to be completely finished, and the sum of $6,000 for each of the other two houses to be finished except as to certain parts of the interior, amounting in all to the sum of $27,500, the houses to be finished by the first of July, 1840; Mr. Lum giving a bond with ample security in the sum of $5,000, as security for any advances made him under the contract. On the 4th of March last, the Committee by the advice of the Superintendent, and being satisfied that it would be an improvement upon the buildings as well in respect to economy as durability, made a further contract with Mr. Lum by which he was to finish the exterior of the buildings in rough cast, or stucco, for which he was to receive the further sum of $250 for each house. And on the 22nd June, the Committee made a further contract with Mr. Lum, by which he was to construct a terrace on each of the houses, for the further sum of $12.50 for each house. On the 13th of July the Board of Regents passed an order directing the Committee to contract with Mr. Lum to finish the interior of all the houses upon the terms and in the manner specified in the original contract, and in pursuance thereof, the Committee entered into such contract. The result of these contracts is that Mr. Lum is to be paid the sum of $7,712.50 for each house, amounting in all to $30,850. Upon these contracts with Mr. Lum, the Committee have given certificates for payments to be made to him amounting in the while to $25,000 and by terms of the original contracts, Mr. Lum was to take 200,000 bricks which had previously been purchased by the Committee, at $1,200, the first cost, so that the whole amount actually paid him is $26,200. On the 13th July last, the Board of Regents put an end to the contracts with Mr. Thompson as Superintendent, of which the Committee gave him notice, and afterwards gave him a certificate for six months' pay, under the contract for $500, up to the 14th August. The Committee have caused the University grounds to be cleared of stumps for which they have paid $346.81, and have caused a well to be dug and stoned and bricked at an expense of $331.70. The Committee at different times remitted small sums to pay for work done in digging the well, and clearing the ground amounting in all to $500, out of which they have paid $346.81 for clearing the ground of stumps, and $119 towards the well, and $2.00 for recording deeds given by the Land Company to the Regents, leaving in the hands of the undersigned the sum of $31.74 unexpended. The Committee have also under the direction of the Board entered into another contract with Michael Horrigan who dug the well, to dig another well upon the same terms as for digging the first, which is now in progress of being completed. The first well is seventy-six feet in depth, and has five and a half feet water. The second well will probably be about the same depth and cost nearly the same, if it shall be finished in the same manner. The Committee by direction of the Board of Regents obtained from Mr. Thompson certain plans and estimates of cost of fences and out-buildings which have heretofore been exhibited to the Board of Regents. Nearly all those matters were submitted verbally to the Board of Regents at their quarterly meeting at Ann Arbor in July last, by Judge Mundy and the undersigned, but for want of time, they were not submitted in writing and since that time Mr. Mundy and Mr. Adam, being a majority of the Committee during the time most of the transactions occurred, have ceased to be Regents,

All of which is respectfully submitted.

Detroit, Feby. 15th, 1840 Wm. A. Fletcher, Com.

Finance Committee Report as filed with the *Regents' Proceedings*, November 13, 1841, p. 191

Mr. Trowbridge from the Committee on Finance, made the following report, the consideration of which was, on his motion, postponed until the next meeting of the Board.

Report of the Committee on Finance on the Claim of Isaac Thompson.

The undersigned, Committee on Finance, to whom was referred the claim of Isaac Thompson, Architect, as Superintendent of the University Buildings at Ann Arbor, have had the same under consideration and have the honor to report, that on the 14th day of February, 1839, the said Thompson entered into a contract with the Building Committee in which he stipulated in consideration of the salary therein agreed upon to render his services as Superintendent of four dwelling houses to be erected at Ann Arbor and to make working drawings for the same.

The said Committee agreed to pay the said Thompson for his services at the rate of $1000 per annum, payable quarterly and the said contract contains the following clause, "It is mutually agreed that this contract may be determined at any time after the expiration of six months by either party giving three months notice of such intention."

The Committee find that on the 13th day of July, 1839, the Regents of the University adopted a resolution declaring the said contract annulled and that on the 10th day of August, 1839, Mr. Thompson received from the Regents the sum of $500 for six months; services up to the 14th August.

Due notice was given to Mr. Thompson of the passage of said resolution about the time of its adoption and on or about the tenth of August Mr. Thompson left the State. Mr. Thompson now claims pay for three months, being the period in said contract specified, "after the expiration of six months."

The Committee with the foregoing statement of facts, beg leave to refer the subject to the decision of the Board.

J. Kearsley,
C.C. Trowbridge,
Z. Pitcher,
Committee on Finance

Bibliography

Archives

Columbia University, Avery Architectural and Fine Arts Library, Drawings and Archives Department, Alexander Jackson Davis Collection. Includes Davis's office diary or daybook dated 1853–69, correspondence, and a large number of drawings.

Metropolitan Museum of Art, New York, Prints and Drawings Department, Alexander Jackson Davis Collection. Includes office journals and diaries, albums, and a large quantity of drawings and renderings.

New Haven Colony Historical Society, Whitney Library. New Haven Colony Historical Society Archives (MSS-1). Arnold Guyot Dana, scrapbooks, "New Haven Old & New," vols. 3 and 102 (MSS-C1). Harpin Lum Papers (MSS-82). Ithiel Town Papers (MSS-105).

New York Public Library, Astor, Lenox and Tilden Foundations, Manuscripts and Archives Division, Alexander Jackson Davis Papers. Includes Davis's office diary or daybook dated 1827–53, one small box of correspondence dated 1820–80, a letterbook with a large quantity of correspondence dated 1821–90, and a collection of drawings.

New-York Historical Society, New York, Alexander Jackson Davis Collection. Includes correspondence, other papers, and drawings.

University of Michigan, Bentley Historical Library. Board of Regents Records. James Burrill Angell Papers. Douglass Family Papers, Silas Douglass Correspondence. Emil Lorch Papers. Frank E. Robbins Papers. Edward Carey Walker Papers. Photo Vertical Files.

References

Alexander, Drury Blakeley. *The Sources of Classicism: Five Centuries of Architecture Books from the Collections of the Humanities Research Center.* Austin: Humanities Research Center, School of Architecture, University Art Museum, University of Texas at Austin, 1978.

Andrews, Wayne. "Alexander Jackson Davis." *Architectural Review* 109 (May 1951): 307–12.

Angell, James Burrill. *University of Michigan. Commemorative Oration. Delivered on Thursday, June 30, 1887, at the Semi-Centennial Celebration of the Organization of the University.* Ann Arbor: University of Michigan, 1888.

Baigell, Matthew. "John Haviland in Philadelphia, 1818–1826." *Journal of the Society of Architectural Historians* 25 (October 1966): 197–208.

BIBLIOGRAPHY

Bartlett, Nancy Ruth. *More Than a Handsome Box: Education in Architecture at the University of Michigan, 1876–1986.* Ann Arbor: University of Michigan College of Architecture and Urban Planning, 1995.

Beakes, Samuel W. *Past and Present of Washtenaw County, Michigan, together with Biographical Sketches of many of its prominent and leading citizens and illustrious dead.* Chicago: S. J. Clarke, 1906.

Benjamin, Asher. *The Architect, or Practical House Carpenter.* Boston: R. P. and C. Williams and Annin and Smith, 1830.

———. *The Country Builder's Assistant: containing a collection of new designs of carpentry and architecture; which will be particularly useful, to country workmen in general.* Greenfield, Mass.: Thomas Dickman, 1797.

Bennett, Wells. "Alexander J. Davis, Architect." *Michigan Alumnus Quarterly Review* 43, no. 11 (1937): 414–20.

———. "Building the University of Michigan." MSS, 1965, Wells Ira Bennett Collection, box 3, Bentley Historical Library, University of Michigan, Ann Arbor.

Bidlack, Russell. "The Board of Regents of the University of Michigan, 1837–1852." Term paper, University of Michigan, summer 1949. Bentley Historical Library, University of Michigan, Ann Arbor.

Bluestone, Daniel. "Civic and Aesthetic Reserve: Ammi Burnham Young's 1850s Federal Customhouse Designs." *Winterthur Portfolio* 25, nos. 2–3 (1990): 131–56.

Brown, Elizabeth Mills. *New Haven: A Guide to Architecture and Urban Design.* New Haven: Yale University Press, 1976.

———. *The United Church on the Green: An Architectural History, New Haven, Connecticut.* New Haven: United Church, 1965.

Brown, Henry Collins. *Fifth Avenue Old and New, 1824–1924.* New York: Fifth Avenue Association, 1924.

Chas. C. Chapman and Co. *History of Washtenaw County, Michigan.* Chicago, 1881.

Clark, Eliot. *History of the National Academy of Design, 1825–1953.* New York: Columbia University Press, 1954.

"College Edifices and Their Relation to Education." *American Literary Magazine,* November 1847, 269–74.

Cooper, Helen A. *John Trumbull: The Hand and Spirit of a Painter.* New Haven: Yale University Art Gallery, 1982.

Cudlip, William B. *The University of Michigan: Its Legal Profile.* Ann Arbor: University of Michigan, 1969.

Cummings, Abbott Lowell. "The Ohio State Capitol Competition." *Journal of the Society of Architectural Historians* 12 (May 1953): 15–18.

Davies, Jane B. "A. J. Davis' Projects for a Patent Office Building, 1832–34." *Journal of the Society of Architectural Historians* 24 (October 1965): 229–51.

———. "Alexander Jackson Davis." In *Macmillan Encyclopedia of Architects,* ed. Adolf K. Placzek, vol. 1, 505–14. New York: Free Press, 1982.

———. Introduction to *Alexander Jackson Davis: American Architect, 1803–1892,* ed. Amelia Peck, 8–21. New York: Rizzoli International, 1992.

———. Introduction to *Rural Residences,* by Alexander Jackson Davis. New York: Da Capo Press, 1980.

———. "Ithiel Town." In *Macmillan Encyclopedia of Architects,* ed. Adolf K. Placzek, vol. 4, 220—23. New York: Free Press, 1982.

———. "Llewellyn Park in West Orange, New Jersey." *Magazine Antiques,* January 1975, 142–58.

———. "Town and Davis." In *Macmillan Encyclopedia of Architects,* ed. Adolf K. Placzek, vol. 4, 223–24. New York: Free Press, 1982.

Davis, Alexander Jackson. *Rural Residences, Consisting of Designs, Original and Selected, for Cottages, Farm-Houses, Villas, and Village Churches: with Brief Explanations, estimates, and a specification of materials, construction, etc.* 1838. Reprint, with an introduction by Jane B. Davies, New York: Da Capo Press, 1980.

Diamonstein, Barbaralee. *The Landmarks of New York III.* New York: Harry N. Abrams, 1998.

Donnell, Edna. "A. J. Davis and the Gothic Revival." *Metropolitan Museum Studies* 5, part 2 (1936): 183–233.

Donnelly, Walter A., ed. *The University of Michigan: An Encyclopedic Survey.* Vol. 4. Ann Arbor: University of Michigan Press, 1958.

Donoghue, John C. "Alexander Jackson Davis, Romantic Architect, 1803–1892." Ph.D. diss., New York University, 1977.

Dunlap, William. *History of the Rise and Progress of the Arts of Design in the United States.* 2 vols. New York: George P. Scott, 1834.

Emery, William M. "Russell Warren." In *Dictionary of American Biography,* ed. Dumas Malone, vol. 9, 610–11. New York: Charles Scribner's Sons, 1936.

Ezequelle, Betty J. "Martin E. Thompson." In *Macmillan Encyclopedia of Architects,* ed. Adolf K. Placzek, vol. 4, 207–8. New York: Free Press, 1982.

Farrand, Elizabeth M. *History of the University of Michigan.* Ann Arbor: Register Publishing House, 1885.

Ferry, W. Hawkins. *The Buildings of Detroit.* Detroit: Wayne State University Press, 1968.

Friedman, Terry. *James Gibbs.* New Haven: Yale University Press, 1984.

Gallagher, Helen M. Pierce. *Robert Mills, Architect of the Washington Monument, 1781–1855.* New York: Columbia University Press, 1935.

Gallier, James. *Autobiography of James Gallier, Architect.* 1864; reprint, with an introduction by Samuel Wilson Jr., and a supplement of illustrations, New York: Da Capo Press, 1973.

Gibbs, James. *A Book of Architecture, Containing Designs of Buildings and Ornaments.* London: By author, 1728.

Gray, Asa. *Letters of Asa Gray.* Ed. Jane Loring Gray. 2 vols. London: Macmillan, 1893.

Hamlin, Talbot. "Alexander Jackson Davis." In *Dictionary of American Biography,* ed. Allen Johnson and Dumas Malone, vol. 3, 103–4. New York: Charles Scribner's Sons, 1958.

———. "Ammi Young." In *Dictionary of American Biography,* ed. Harris E. Starr, vol. 11, supplement 1, 716–17. New York: Charles Scribner's Sons, 1944.

———. *Greek Revival Architecture in America.* 1944; reprint, New York: Dover, 1964.

———. "Ithiel Town." In *Dictionary of American Biography,* ed. Dumas Malone, vol. 9, 610–11. New York: Charles Scribner's Sons, 1936.

———. "Martin E. Thompson." In *Dictionary of American Biography,* ed. Dumas Malone, vol. 9, 467–68. New York: Charles Scribner's Sons, 1936.

———. "The Rise of Eclecticism in New York." *Journal of the Society of Architectural Historians* 11 (May 1952): 3–8.

Heckscher, Morrison H. "The Metropolitan Museum of Art: An Architectural History." *Metropolitan Museum of Art Bulletin* 53, no. 1 (1995): 54–55.

Henderson, Susan. "Llewellyn Park, Suburban Idyll." *Journal of Garden History* 7, no. 3 (1987): 221–43.

Hinsdale, Burke A. *History of the University of Michigan.* Ann Arbor: University of Michigan, 1906.

Hitchcock, Henry-Russell, and William Seale. *Temples of Democracy: The State Capitols of the United States of America.* New York: Harcourt Brace Jovanovich, 1976.

Hotchkin, S. F. *The Bristol Pike.* Philadelphia: George W. Jacobs, 1893.

Huxtable, Ada Louise. *Classic New York: Georgian Gentility to Greek Elegance.* New York: Doubleday, 1964.

James, Theodore, Jr. *Fifth Avenue.* New York: Walker, 1971.

Jones, Theodore Francis, ed. *New York University, 1832:1932.* New York: New York University Press, 1933.

Keister, Kim. "Picture This: American Architect Alexander Jackson Davis Gave Inventive and Abundant Artistic Direction to a Young Nation Searching for Its Cultural Identity." *Historic Preservation,* September–October 1992, 38–45, 89–90.

Kelly, J. Frederick. *Early Connecticut Meetinghouses—Being an Account of the Church Edifices Built before 1830 Based Chiefly upon Town and Parish Records.* New York: Columbia University Press, 1948.

Kimball, LeRoy E. "The Old University Building and the Society's Years in Washington Square." *New-York Historical Society Quarterly* 32, no. 3 (1948): 149–219.

Kirker, Harold. *The Architecture of Charles Bulfinch.* Cambridge: Harvard University Press, 1969.

Klauder, Charles Z., and Herbert C. Wise. *College Architecture in America and Its Part in the Development of the Campus.* New York: Charles Scribner's Sons, 1929.

Kowsky, Francis R. "Simplicity and Dignity: The Public and Institutional Buildings of Alexander Jackson Davis." In *Alexander Jackson Davis: American Architect, 1803–1892,* ed. Amelia Peck, 40–57. New York: Rizzoli International, 1992.

Lafever, Minard. *The Beauties of Modern Architecture.* New York: D. Appleton, 1835.

———. *The Modern Builder's Guide.* New York: Henry C. Sleight, Collins and Hannay, 1833.

———. *The Young Builder's General Instructor; containing the five orders of architecture, selected from the best specimens of the Greek and Roman.* Newark, N.J.: W. Tuttle, 1829.

Laise, C. Stevens. "A. J. Davis and American Classicism." *Magazine Antiques* 136 (1989): 1322–33.

BIBLIOGRAPHY

Lancaster, Clay. "Builders' Guide and Plan Books and American Architecture: From the Revolution to the Civil War." *Magazine of Art,* January 1948, 16–22.

Landy, Jacob. *The Architecture of Minard Lafever.* New York: Columbia University Press, 1970.

Latrobe, Benjamin Henry. *The Architectural Drawings of Benjamin Henry Latrobe.* Ed. Jeffrey A. Cohen and Charles E. Brownell. New Haven: Yale University Press, 1994.

Lee, Antoinette J. *Architects to the Nation: The Rise and Decline of the Supervising Architect's Office.* New York: Oxford University Press, 2000.

Liscombe, R. W. "A 'New Era in My Life': Ithiel Town Abroad." *Journal of the Society of Architectural Historians* 50 (March 1991): 5–17.

[Lorch, Emil?]. "An Earlier Campus Plan." *Michigan Alumnus,* April 19, 1923, 793–95.

Lorch, Emil. "President's House, Michigan University." *Michigan Architect and Engineer* 3, no. 4 (April 1921): 63, plates 23–28.

Mabee, Carleton. *The American Leonardo: A Life of Samuel F. B. Morse.* New York: Alfred A. Knopf, 1943.

Maddex, Diane, ed. *Master Builders: A Guide to Famous American Architects,* National Trust for Historic Preservation. New York: John Wiley and Sons, 1985.

McCadden, Joseph J. *Education in Pennsylvania, 1801–1835, and Its Debt to Roberts Vaux.* Philadelphia: University of Pennsylvania Press, 1937.

Morris, Edwin Bateman. "Ammi B. Young." *AIA Journal* 1, no. 2 (1944): 69–71.

Newton, Roger Hale. *Town and Davis, Architects: Pioneers in American Revivalist Architecture 1812–1870, Including a Glimpse of Their Times and Their Contemporaries.* New York: Columbia University Press, 1942.

Overby, Osmund R. "Ammi B. Young." In *Macmillan Encyclopedia of Architects,* ed. Adolf K. Placzek, vol. 4, 463–64. New York: Free Press, 1982.

———. "Ammi B. Young in the Connecticut Valley." *Journal of the Society of Architectural Historians* 19 (October 1960): 119–23.

Page, Marion. "Historic Restorations: Three Generations of Lyndhurst." *Interiors,* September 1965, 104–11, 218–19.

Parry, Ellwood C. III. *The Art of Thomas Cole: Ambition and Imagination.* Newark: University of Delaware Press, 1988.

———. "Thomas Cole's Imagination in *The Architect's Dream.*" *American Art Journal* 12, no. 1 (1980): 41–59.

Patton, Glenn. "Chapel in the Sky—Origins and Edifices of the University of the City of New York." *Architectural Review* 145 (March 1969): 177–85.

Peck, Amelia, ed. *Alexander Jackson Davis: American Architect, 1803–1892.* New York: Rizzoli International, 1992.

Peckham, Howard H. *The Making of the University of Michigan, 1817–1967.* Ann Arbor: University of Michigan Press, 1967.

Peterson, Charles E., ed. "The Girard College Architectural Competition, 1832." *Journal of the Society of Architectural Historians* 16 (May 1957): 20–27.

"Pictures of the University." *Chronicle* (University of Michigan), March 26, 1870, 194–95.

Pinnell, Patrick L. *The Campus Guide: Yale University.* New York: Princeton Architectural Press, 1999.

Rebora, Carrie. "Alexander Jackson Davis and the Arts of Design." In *Alexander Jackson Davis: American Architect, 1803–1892,* ed. Amelia Peck, 22–39. New York: Rizzoli International, 1992.

Reed, Henry. "Sachem's Wood: The Work of A. J. Davis Destroyed." *Task* 5 (spring 1944): 47–48.

Reynolds, Donald Martin. *The Architecture of New York City: Histories and Views of Important Structures, Sites, and Symbols.* New York: Macmillan, 1984.

Robbins, Frank E. "Historic Home Ready for New Occupant." *Michigan Alumnus,* November 16, 1929, 135–37.

Ryan, Susan E. "Architecture as Educational Symbol: A. J. Davis' Gothic College Designs." Master's thesis, University of Michigan, 1973. Fine Arts Library, University of Michigan, Ann Arbor.

Schuyler, Montgomery. "Architecture of American Colleges." Series of ten articles in *Architectural Record* 26 (October 1909) to 31 (May 1912).

Scully, Arthur, Jr. *James Dakin, Architect: His Career in New York and the South.* Baton Rouge: Louisiana State University Press, 1973.

Shaw, Wilfred B. "The Early Days of the University of Michigan." 2 parts. *Michigan History Magazine* 16 (autumn 1932): 439–63; 17 (winter 1933): 52–107.

———. "Some Early Views of the Campus of the University of Michigan." *Michigan History Magazine* 14 (autumn 1930): 575–78.

———, ed. *The University of Michigan: An Encyclopedic Survey.* Vol. 1. Ann Arbor: University of Michigan Press, 1942.

Sigourney, Lydia H. "Residence of Ithiel Town, Esq." *Ladies' Companion,* January 1839, 123–26.

Silver, Nathan. *Lost New York.* New York: Houghton Mifflin, 1967.

Snadon, Patrick Alexander. "A. J. Davis and the Gothic Revival Castle in America, 1832–1865." Ph.D. diss., Cornell University, 1988.

Stauter, George A. "First Building for 'M' Campus Never Erected." *Ann Arbor Daily News,* August 22, 1936.

Stephenson, O. W. *Ann Arbor: The First Hundred Years.* Ann Arbor: Ann Arbor Chamber of Commerce, 1927.

Stuart, James, and Nicholas Revett. *The Antiquities of Athens and other Monuments of Greece.* 3 vols. London: J. Haberkorn, 1762–87.

Tatum, George Bishop. "Andrew Jackson Downing: Arbiter of American Taste, 1815–1852." Ph.D. diss., Princeton University, 1949.

Ten Brook, Andrew. *American State Universities, Their Origin and Progress, A History of Congressional University Land-Grants, A Particular Account of the Rise and Development of the University of Michigan, and hints toward the future of the American University System.* Cincinnati: Robert Clarke, 1875.

Turner, Paul Venable. *Campus: An American Planning Tradition.* Cambridge, Mass.: MIT Press, 1984.

University of Michigan. *Proceedings of the Regents Meetings.* Ed. Isaac N. Demmon. Vols. 1837–64, 1864–70, 1876–81, 1881–85. Ann Arbor: University of Michigan, 1915.

Upton, Dell. "Pattern Books and Professionalism—Aspects of the Transformation of Domestic Architecture in America, 1800–1860." *Winterthur Portfolio* 19, nos. 2–3 (1984): 108–50.

Vitruvius (Marcus Vitruvius Pollio). *The Ten Books on Architecture.* Trans. Morris Hicky Morgan, with illustrations and original designs prepared under the direction of Herbert Langford Warren. New York: Dover, 1960.

Whitehill, Walter Muir. *Palladio in America.* Milan: Electra Editrice, 1976.

Wickersham, James Pyle. *A History of Education in Pennsylvania.* Lancaster, Pa.: Inquirer, 1886.

Wodehouse, Lawrence. "Ammi Burnham Young, 1798–1874." *Journal of the Society of Architectural Historians* 25 (December 1966): 268–80.

Woodbridge, William C., ed. "Bristol College." *American Annals of Education and Instruction* 4 (April 1834): 193.

———. "Bristol College." *American Annals of Education and Instruction* 4 (September 1834): 435.

———. "Commencement at Bristol College." *American Annals of Education and Instruction* 5 (September 1835): 424.

———. "Manual Labour Schools." *American Annals of Education and Instruction* 1, part 2, no. 1 (January 1831): 37.

Builder's Handbooks and Pattern Books

Builder's handbooks and pattern books were being published in England by the mid–seventeenth century but did not start becoming readily available in America until the late eighteenth century. American publishers began to offer reprints of some of the best-selling English books. The earliest recorded detailed description of the Greek orders was written by Marcus Vitruvius Pollio in the first century B.C. Vitruvius's *The Ten Books on Architecture* became the primary source for information on the classic orders for all writers who followed. The first English translation was made in 1771, but the most popular was an edition published in London in 1826, a translation by Joseph Gwilt that included a series of plates executed by Gwilt to illustrate Vitruvius's text. The most important books to be published about the Roman orders were those written by Andrea Palladio and first published in Venice in 1570. His *Four Books of Architecture* was subsequently published in England in the early eighteenth century and reached America by midcentury. Other important sources of classical details to later handbook writers included Sebastiano Serlio's *Five Books of Architecture* (first English translation 1611) and Giacomo Barozzi da Vignola's *The Five Orders of Architecture* (first published in Rome in 1562). Some of the most popular writers of English handbooks in the late eighteenth century included William Pain, J. C. Loudon, Sir William Chambers, and Peter Nicholson. Chambers's *A Treatise on the Decorative Part of Civil Architecture* (London, 1791) was a source widely used by other writers and contained a description on the sources and progress of building construction and design. Peter Nicholson's books were extremely influential in that they provided detailed information on geometry and carpentry as well as descriptions of classical orders and a discussion of what was different between the Greek and Roman orders. His *New Practical Builder and Work-*

man's Companion (London, 1823) was the most important and popular of his works. Many later pattern book writers credited Nicholson for their understanding of geometry and the dissection of details, from Corinthian columns to stair railings. Recommended works to look for are listed below.

Benjamin, Asher (1773–1845). *The American Builder's Companion; or, a system of Architecture, particularly adapted to the present style of building*. Boston: Etheridge and Bliss, 1806.

———. *The Architect, or Practical House Carpenter*. Boston: R. P. and C. Williams and Annin and Smith, 1830.

———. *The Builder's Guide, illustrated by sixty-six engravings, which exhibit the orders of architecture and other elements of the art*. Boston: Perkins and Marvin, 1839.

———. *The Country Builder's Assistant: containing a collection of new designs of carpentry and architecture; which will be particularly useful, to country workmen in general*. Greenfield, Mass.: Thomas Dickman, 1797.

———. *Elements of Architecture, containing the Tuscan, Doric, Ionic and Corinthian orders, with all their details and embellishments*. Boston: Benjamin B. Mussey, 1843.

———. *The Practice of Architecture: containing the five orders of architecture, and an additional column and entablature, with all their elements and details, explained and illustrated, for the use of carpenters and practical men*. Boston: A. Benjamin and H. Carter, 1833; and New York: Collins, 1833.

———. *The Rudiments of architecture, being a treatise on practical geometry, on Grecian and Roman mouldings; shewing the best method of drawing their curves, with remarks on the effect of both. Also, on the origin of building, on the five orders of architecture, on their general embellishments, with examples for cornice, base and surbase mouldings, architraves and stairs, correctly engraved on thirty-four copperplates*. Boston: Munroe and Francis, 1814.

Biddle, Owen (1774–1806). *Young Carpenter's Assistant; or A System of Architecture Adapted to the Style of Building in the United States*. Philadelphia: B. Warner, 1805.

Chambers, William (1726–96). *A Treatise on the Decorative Part of Civil Architecture*. 1791. Reprint, with illustrations, notes and an examination of Grecian architecture by Joseph Gwilt, London: Priestley and Weale, 1825.

Downing, Andrew Jackson (1815–52). *The Architecture of Country Houses*. New York: D. Appleton, 1850. Downing's books, for which A. J. Davis provided many of the illustrations, were extremely influential in rural "picturesque" architecture and landscape planning.

———. *Landscape Gardening and Rural Architecture*. New York: Wiley and Putnam, 1841.

———. *Victorian Cottage Residences*. New York: Wiley and Putnam, 1842.

Gibbs, James (1682–1754). *A Book of Architecture, Containing Designs of Buildings and Ornaments*. London: By author, 1728. Gibbs's book included the approved and alternate designs for his landmark, and hugely influential, St. Martin-in-the-Fields church, plus numerous variations of design elements such as steeples. The book was widely available in America by the 1760s. The Gibbsian style of church design was picked up, adapted, and published by others such as Asher Benjamin and Minard Lafever.

Haviland, John (1792–1852). *The Builder's Assistant: containing the five orders of architecture, selected from the best specimens of Greek and Roman, with the figured dimensions of their Height, Projection, and Profile* . . . (includes working drawings, with methods of construction and sixty original designs), 3 vols. Philadelphia: John Bioren, 1818–21. Although born in England, Haviland moved to Philadelphia in 1816. His *Builder's Assistant* was the earliest American book to offer Greek as well as Roman orders. For this lengthy handbook, Haviland relied on

Peter Nicholson for his carpentry details and wrote about the origins of the Greek orders based on Vitruvius. He gives detailed descriptions of the orders and compares what is similar and what is different between the Greek and the Roman.

———. *The Practical Builder's Assistant*. Baltimore: F. Lucas Jr., 1830.

Lafever, Minard (1798–1854). *The Architectural Instructor containing a history of architecture from the earliest ages to the present time; illustrated with nearly 250 engravings of ancient, mediaeval, and modern cities, temples, palaces, cathedrals, and monuments; also, the Greek and early Roman classic orders, their principles and beauties*. New York: George P. Putnam, 1856. Lafever derived his practical carpentry and geometry from Peter Nicholson and his Greek orders from Stuart and Revett. Town and Davis's partner James Dakin, as well as employee James Gallier, both provided illustrations, some for original designs, for *The Modern Builder's Guide*.

———. *The Beauties of Modern Architecture*. New York: D. Appleton, 1835.

———. *The Modern Builder's Guide*. New York: Henry C. Sleight, Collins and Hannay, 1833.

———. *The Young Builder's General Instructor; containing the five orders of architecture, selected from the best specimens of the Greek and Roman*. Newark, N.J.: W. Tuttle, 1829.

Loudon, John Claudius (1783–1843). *Encyclopedia of Cottage, Farm, and Villa Architecture and Furniture; containing numerous designs for dwellings*. London, 1833. Loudon was mostly known for his books on landscaping and garden design, including an extensive encyclopedia of plants. A. J. Davis considered Loudon's book a "must read" for clients planning extensive landscaping, such as at Lyndhurst.

Nicholson, Peter (1765–1844). *The Carpenter's New Guide: being a complete book of lines for carpentry and joinery*. 1792. Reprint, Philadelphia: M. Carey and Son, 1818. Nicholson's books were extremely influential and widely used by other pattern book authors, architects, and builders. His *New Practical Builder* was the most important and popular of his works. Nicholson's strength was in mathematics, and he provided very detailed drawings and instructions, including for classical features. His *Encyclopedia* provided comprehensive descriptions of architectural and building terminology, construction methods, materials, tools, etc. Nicholson gives a good history behind the classical orders and describes what is different between the Greek and Roman. His primary references were Vitruvius and Stuart and Revett, although he also used some drawings from Chambers. He included hundreds of detailed diagrams, which he drew himself.

———. *Encyclopedia of architecture. A dictionary of the science and practice of architecture, building, carpentry, etc., from the earliest ages to the present time, forming a comprehensive work of reference for the use of architects, builders, carpenters, masons, engineers, students, professional men and amateurs*. London: 1811–19. Reprint, ed. Edward Lomax and Thomas Gunyon, New York: Martin and Johnson, 1858.

———. *The New Practical Builder and Workman's Companion*. London, 1823.

Pain, William (1730?–90?). *British Palladio* (with James Pain). London, 1786. Reprint, Farnborough: Gregg, 1969.

———. *The Builder's Companion demonstrating all the principal rules of architecture*. 1762. Reprint, New York: R. F. Whitehead, 1931.

———. *The Builder's Pocket Treasure: In which not only the theory, but the practical parts of architecture are carefully explained*. London, 1763. Reprint, Boston: William Norman, 1794.

———. *The Practical Builder, or Workman's general assistant shewing the most approved and easy methods for drawing and working the whole or separate part of any building*. London, 1774. Reprint, Boston: John Norman, 1792.

———. *The Practical House Carpenter; or, Youth's Instructor: containing a great variety of useful designs in carpentry and architecture*. 2d ed. London, 1788. (1st ed. unknown, but circa 1785.) Reprint, Boston: William Norman, 1796.

Palladio, Andrea (1508–80). *The Four Books of Architecture, by Palladio.* Isaac Ware, 1738. Reprint, with an introduction by Adolf K. Placzek, New York: Dover, 1965. Originally published as *Quattro libri dell'architettura,* Venice 1570. Palladio's drawings were purchased by architect Inigo Jones circa 1610 and used extensively in England. First English translation published 1715, reached America mid–eighteenth century. Palladio was greatly influenced by Vitruvius, and his books became the most widely used source for classical designs in, and features of, the Roman vocabulary.

Serlio, Sebastiano (1475–1554). *The Five Books of Architecture*. 1611. Reprint, New York: Dover, 1982. Originally published as *Tutte L'Opere D'Architettura Et Prospetiva,* book 4 (1537), book 3 (1540), books 1 and 2 (1545), book 5 (1547), book 7 (1575). Book 6 was never published, but the manuscript survives. Serlio's were considered the first important books on the subject of architecture intended for the architect, rather than the nobility, since Vitruvius. First English translation published in London in 1611.

Shaw, Edward. *Civil Architecture: or A Complete Theoretical and Practical System of Building*. 4th ed. Boston: Shaw and Stratton, 1830. Shaw's *Civil Architecture* was a widely used source book and contained excerpts and examples from Vitruvius, Stuart and Revett, Chambers, and Nicholson.

———. *Rural Architecture: consisting of classic dwellings, Doric, Ionic, Corinthian and Gothic, and details connected with each of the orders; embracing plans, elevations parallel and perspective, specifications, estimates, framing, etc., for private houses and churches*. Boston: James B. Dow, 1843.

Stuart, James (1713–88), and Nicholas Revett (1720–1804). *The Antiquities of Athens and other Monuments of Greece*. 3 vols. London: J. Haberkorn, 1762–87. Stuart and Revett's book was one of the most influential and popular sources for measured drawings and details on Grecian architecture. The book was widely available after about 1810 in America.

Vignola, Giacomo Barozzi da (1507–73). *The Five Orders of Architecture, the Casting of Shadows and the First Principles of Construction based on the System of Vignola; 76 plates, drawn and arranged by Pierre Esquie*. Boston: Bates and Guild Co., 1890s? This edition adds Greek orders to the Roman ones showcased by Vignola. Vignola's *Five Orders* established him as the universally recognized authority on correct use of Roman forms. William Ware's *American Vignola* (see below) helped launch the American Renaissance in classical architecture in the late nineteenth and early twentieth centuries.

Vitruvius (Marcus Vitruvius Pollio, first century B.C.). *The Ten Books on Architecture*. Reprint, trans. Morris Hicky Morgan, with illustrations and original designs prepared under the direction of Herbert Langford Warren, New York: Dover, 1960. An unaltered replication of the first edition of the English translation by M. H. Morgan was published by Harvard University Press in 1914. Vitruvius is credited with the earliest detailed descriptions of classical structures in books widely referred to that became the basis for most of the pattern books on classical architecture that were to follow. Vitruvius discusses both Greek and Roman architecture but focuses on the Greek as being the true source. The first English translation of Vitruvius was in 1771. The Gwilt edition of 1826 was the mostly widely available and used English version and was important for the drawings added by Gwilt to illustrate Vitruvius's text. There were earlier translations in Latin, Spanish, French, German, and Italian, of which a translation by Fra Giocondo in 1511 is especially notable.

———. *The Architecture of Marcus Vitruvius Pollio, in Ten Books*. Reprint, trans. Joseph Gwilt, with a series of plates by Gwilt, London: Priestley and Weale, 1826.

Ware, William R. *The American Vignola: A Guide to the Marking of Classical Architecture*. 1903. Reprint, New York: Dover, 1994. Ware's book was based on Vignola's *Regola Delli cinque ordini d'architettura,* published in Rome in 1562.

Wotton, Sir Henry (1568–1639). *The Elements of Architecture*. London: John Bill, 1624.

Index